Life
Honestly

Life
Honestly

STRONG OPINIONS
FROM
SMART WOMEN

The Pool

bluebird
books for life

First published 2018 by Bluebird
an imprint of Pan Macmillan
20 New Wharf Road, London N1 9RR
Associated companies throughout the world
www.panmacmillan.com

ISBN 978-1-5098-8719-4

1 3 5 7 9 8 6 4 2

A CIP catalogue record for this book is available from the British Library.

Designed by Andrew Barron @ Thextension

Typeset in 10.5/13.75 pt Whitman Roman by Jouve (UK), Milton Keynes
Printed and bound by CPI Group (UK) Ltd, Croydon, CRO 4YY

Visit **www.panmacmillan.com** to read more about all our books
and to buy them. You will also find features, author interviews and
news of any author events, and you can sign up for e-newsletters
so that you're always first to hear about our new releases.

Contents

Introduction

It's no exaggeration to say that my life was saved by an article I read in a women's magazine.

The article in question ran in an issue of *Cosmopolitan* a very long time ago. Several decades. It was about something called 'charm syndrome', a term coined by Sandra Horley, founder of Refuge, in a then-new book. I'd never heard the phrase but as I read the words everything about it struck a chord. And you would know it now, because charm syndrome was the earliest iteration of what we now know as coercive control. Thanks to that article, decades ago, a lightbulb went on in the head of a terrifyingly young me, giving me the strength to step out of something that was very bad for me indeed, and that went on to have almost lifelong repercussions. Although those repercussions would have been worse and my life might have been a very great deal shorter had I not read that article.

There were other articles, too, that changed the course of my life if not as dramatically. I discovered I wasn't the only one living every single day in fear of being found out, thanks to an article on imposter syndrome. I learnt almost everything I knew about everything aged thirteen from agony aunts Cathy and Claire in *Jackie* magazine. (Thanks to them, among other things, I was relieved to discover you could not in fact get pregnant from loo seats!)

Over the years I have been indebted to the women bold enough to share their stories about everything from cripplingly heavy periods to massive career leaps. Latterly – and less seriously – I have learnt to say 'and' instead of 'but', delete every other 'sorry' from my emails and to say 'yes' unless I really mean 'no'. In which case I just say 'no' and have done with it. When my eggs abruptly and prematurely dried up, it was to other women's stories I turned to get me through.

Women (in the main) who wrote about their personal experiences, who shared their opinions, their sufferings and their successes in the pages of magazines and subsequently on the internet, had such a radical impact on my life, that when Lauren Laverne and I set up *The Pool* we had that very much in mind. We wanted it to be a safe place for women – where they could speak out, swear, howl with laughter, shed tears of sorrow and/or joy. A place free of trolls, abuse and the avalanche of crap that has become part of day-to-day life on the internet. A bullshit-free, truth-telling zone. This is how it is. The anti-Instagram, if you like, where the pain, stress, ridiculousness and joy of everyday life was not airbrushed away.

And we wanted them to tell their own stories in their own way, in their own voices. As the late great Nora Ephron said, 'be the heroine of your own life not the victim', but as she also said 'when you slip on a banana peel, people laugh at you. But when you tell people you slipped on a banana peel, it's your laugh.'

We wanted *The Pool* to be a place where women laughed as much as raged, in the hope that the sharing would help women the world over, would tell them that they were not alone. To use a phrase that has become famous in a very specific sense: Me too. Me too.

Over the years since *The Pool* launched our many and various contributors have done just that. They have put their hearts on their sleeves, shared their most intimate stories of hope, triumph and occasionally outrage. They have raged at bad exes, bad bosses, bad payers. They have written from inside the depths of depression, sexual assault, infertility and grief. They have turned the tables on the first few months of motherhood, partners who don't pull their weight and high street shops that think we all vanish when the clock strikes thirty-five. But by the same token they have shared their successes, given other women a leg up and celebrated their triumphs. When women come together we can move mountains – just look at the Repeal the Eighth movement.

On these pages you will find the tiniest taster of their many millions of words. From bad sex to bad boys, from periods to body positivity to equal pay to the power of female friendship.

Read on, enjoy and maybe, together, we'll move some more mountains.

Sam x

Gender politics & power

LAURA BATES | LILY PESCHARDT | KAT LISTER
ZOË BEATY | CAROLINE O'DONOGHUE
ANON | LYNN ENRIGHT | GABY HINSLIFF
RACHAEL SIGEE | JEAN HANNAH EDELSTEIN
YOMI ADEGOKE

A practical to-do list to make women's lives better

DEEDS *AND* WORDS ARE THE KEY TO FEMINISM'S SUCCESS

BY LAURA BATES

In the fight for equality, members of the women's rights movement have organised mass protests, carried out hunger strikes and even concealed themselves in parliamentary broom cupboards. It's not surprising that 'Deeds Not Words' became such a famous and effective slogan.

Personally, I'm a strong believer in deeds *and* words. Feminism is flourishing and as a new generation takes to social media to speak out about it, they frequently come up against the criticism of shouting into an echo chamber, or being 'armchair activists'. These criticisms miss the point. What starts online can have powerful repercussions offline too, as the success of the No More Page 3 campaign clearly showed. The act of speaking, sharing stories and raising awareness is a vital step in tackling gender inequality, particularly when we live in a society where many people remain unconvinced that the problem even exists.

Rather than focusing on just one or the other, we can combine awareness raising with concrete action for effective change.

So what can you do beyond sharing articles and speaking up about the issues?

SUPPORT EXISTING PROJECTS

There is brilliant grassroots work being done by charities and organisations such as Karma Nirvana (which fights against forced marriage and honour-based violence), Integrate Bristol (which is doing vital work to tackle female genital mutilation) and the End Violence

Against Women Coalition (a group of organisations at the very coalface of the battle for gender equality). These groups can't continue without funding and support – so whether it's volunteering, fundraising or making a donation, get in touch and see how you can help.

START YOUR OWN

In the words of Lily Tomlin: 'I always wondered why somebody didn't do something about that. Then I realised. I am somebody.' Sometimes the most vital resources arise when somebody recognises a gap and steps up to fill it. A brilliant recent example is Pavan Amara's My Body Back Project. Amara realised that there were no specialist services available to provide sexual health screening and cervical smear tests to survivors of sexual assault. Working with her local NHS trust, she set up the first clinic of its kind in the country, and it is already booked up for months ahead.

JOIN A CAMPAIGN

It takes a lot of noise to force people to sit up and take notice, so one of the most effective things you can do is to use your voice to amplify those already shouting for change. Current campaigns in need of support include the Set Her Free campaign to end the detention of refugee women, the It's My Right campaign for statutory sex and relationships education and Plan's Because I am a Girl campaign for girls' rights internationally.

DEMAND CHANGE

Sometimes change means calling on those in positions of authority to wield their power in the service of gender equality. As a constituent you have the right to raise concerns with your MP and you can use that right to urge them to take action on particular issues. This might mean supporting the call for the UK to ratify the Istanbul Convention on Violence Against Women, or writing to your local MP to urge them to take action on domestic violence.

JOIN UP

From the UK's leading charity for promoting gender equality to its newest political party aiming to achieve progress through legislative change, you could sign up today to become a member of a group fighting for women's rights.

SUPPORT WOMEN'S WORK

It's a well-known fact that women are under-represented across a variety of fields – an audit by East London Fawcett found that women make up only 31 per cent of featured artists in London galleries and the latest VIDA count found that just 23 per cent of the authors reviewed in the *London Review of Books* were female. This has inspired numerous campaigns to redress the balance by encouraging individuals to read only female authors for a year, or actively to support female artists.

START YOUR OWN RIPPLE

We live in a society where casual everyday sexism and sexual harassment are pervasive, creating normalised attitudes and behaviours towards women that are difficult to challenge. We can't solve the under-representation of women in politics without also addressing a media that reports on female MPs' shoes instead of their policies. We can't deal with the fact that there are just seven female heads of FTSE 100 companies if we don't also confront workplace gender discrimination. We can't tackle the fact that 85,000 women are raped and 400,000 sexually assaulted in England and Wales every year without also challenging the notion that women's bodies are fair game for comment, harassment and groping in public spaces. This isn't to say that one directly leads to the other; rather that we have to address the full spectrum of the problem if we really want things to change.

And it starts everywhere. The standard we walk past is the standard we accept. Every person who looks out of the window when a woman is harassed on a bus sends the message to the harasser that he can act with impunity. Everyone who sniggers at a sexist workplace joke reminds the victim that it's socially acceptable and she's expected to put up with it. Just a single act of challenging the status quo, whether supporting a victim, talking to a young person about consent or tackling a harasser, can start a ripple that impacts wider attitudes.

A bank refused to close a woman's account – unless she came back with her abuser

LISA CAMERON MP CALLED ON THERESA MAY TO ENSURE UPCOMING LEGISLATION PROTECTS OTHER DOMESTIC VIOLENCE SURVIVORS FROM FACING THE SAME FATE

BY LILY PESCHARDT

A bank refused to close the joint account a woman shared with her violent former husband unless she brought him along to a meeting. Despite informing her bank (unnamed) of the abusive nature of their relationship – her husband subjected her to emotional, mental, sexual, physical and financial abuse for more than two decades – they insisted that he still needed to be present to sign the paperwork.

The case was raised by the woman's local MP, Lisa Cameron, at Prime Minister's Questions when she urged Theresa May to change the laws to ensure that other victims do not have to suffer similar circumstances.

The woman (who did not wish to be named) claimed that she had visited her bank to try and close their joint account, or at least remove her name from it, after fleeing her abusive partner. However, she found that her husband had drained the account, leaving only a small balance in credit, and had then put the account in dispute, meaning both their signatures were required to change the account.

'The bank insisted that we both needed to come down together, even after I told them he was on bail for assaulting me,' she explained. 'This made no difference to them. Even though the account was in credit and I was prepared to forfeit the money they still refused. They then told me it was a civil matter.

'I was distraught and still in shock. I was desperately trying to distance myself from him and struggled with PTSD [post-traumatic stress disorder]. This situation just re-traumatised me. And it dragged on and on. He could have closed the account but then he would not have been able to have control or continue to torment me.'

Even after a woman leaves an abusive relationship, the tendrils of a shared life together can stretch far and wide. They might share children, joint assets, bank accounts – and these things have the potential to force survivors of domestic violence to face their abusers, time and time again.

Everywhere survivors turn, they can be met with roadblocks. From misguided police attitudes – some forces have been found to be entrenched with the belief that domestic violence is a 'lifestyle choice' – to continual cuts in government funding to women's refuges. In family courts, perpetrators of violence continue to be allowed to cross-examine their victims, and known abusers are afforded unsupervised contact with their offspring.

It's this systematic failure by courts and companies to understand the trauma domestic violence survivors endure when leaving abusive relationships that Cameron is calling on May to change.

'My constituent informed me that she had been repeatedly raped and beaten by her ex-partner, requiring an injunction. Much to her horror her bank would not close her joint account unless she attended with the perpetrator,' Cameron stated at Prime Minister's Questions. She continued, 'When banks are left to their own discretion, women's lives are put at risk. Will the prime minister ensure policy to protect survivors is included in the pending domestic violence bill?'

May agreed that it was a 'very distressing case', stressing that she wanted to give 'proper support' to women who have been subjected to domestic violence. She added that (then home secretary) Amber

Rudd would soon be issuing a consultation on proposed domestic violence legislation, which will provide, 'an opportunity for issues such as this to be raised.'

The bank have assured the woman that they now have a 'vulnerable customer team' and if the same thing happened now she 'would be dealt with more sympathetically'. She is calling on the bank to advertise this initiative in all of their branches.

20 years on, Monica Lewinsky has much to teach us about slut-shaming

HAVING ENDURED AN INTERNATIONAL PUBLIC HUMILIATION, LEWINSKY CAN UNDERSTAND THE PERFORMATIVE MISOGYNY OF THE INTERNET BETTER THAN MOST

BY KAT LISTER

If there's one name I was surprised to see trending on social media this morning it was Monica Lewinsky's – a name so synonymous with the 1990s it's filed deep in my brain alongside miscellaneous memories of New Labour, MC Hammer's harem pants, intergalactic Pop-Tarts and my Blockbuster membership card. Why is she back after all this time – and what does she have to tell us today? Post-Weinstein, arguably a great deal.

I was fourteen years old when a stained blue Gap dress became front-page news and nearly toppled a president. Old enough, perhaps, to be acquainted with the dictionary definition of the term 'fellatio', but not quite mature enough to understand the political ramifications of such an act. It would be many more years before I would realise that Monica Lewinsky's story isn't simply her burden, it's a shared narrative that raises profound questions about how we scrutinise gender, politics and power. The Clinton scandal – and the media circus that encompassed it – had something timeless to say about the ways in which we undermine, belittle and bully the women who speak out. Two decades later, it still does. I'm now thirty-four years old – and the sniggers still trail Lewinsky like some kind of prized prey.

In an interview with the *Evening Standard*, the former White House intern has been speaking out about her treatment – nearly twenty years after the Clinton-Lewinsky relationship broke in January 1998 – describing public shaming as 'a blood sport'. Ever since her now-infamous belted shirt-dress was paraded in front of baying reporters and flashing camera lenses, 'shame' has followed Lewinsky wherever she goes, raising powerful questions about who we forgive when power is abused – and who we punish. Perhaps the biggest takeaway from Rosamund Urwin's interview is that Lewinsky's past is very much still her present. And it still hurts.

For those who need reminding, Lewinsky was only twenty-two years old when she met her forty-nine-year-old president (let that sink in: it's a small detail we like to ignore). The young intern stated that between 1995 and 1997 she had nine sexual encounters in the Oval Office. A co-worker persuaded Lewinsky not to dry clean a blue dress stained with the president's semen – and this one item of clothing soon rocked the White House. Under oath, Clinton denied any wrongdoing (who could forget his memorable dismissal, 'I did not have sexual relations with that woman'?) The media-scrum that followed ripped Lewinsky's reputation to shreds and left her with deep scars that, though faded now, are still very much there. Clinton, on the other hand? In a predictable twist, he weathered the storm and eventually reinvented himself through the professional ascendency of his wife, Hillary, as dutiful husband and advisor. We watched him stand on a Democratic convention stage in 2016 and fable both his relationship with his wife – and his past. Two birds, you might say, one stone. 'Bill Clinton's speech made Hillary human again,' Jill Abramson wrote for the *Guardian* in the days that followed. Lewinsky is still fighting for that privilege.

Twenty years after she was weaponised by Washington power

players, Monica Lewinsky is still asking to be heard. This time, she's not alone – and her plea takes on new meaning in the wake of Harvey Weinstein's crimes and the repeated cries of #MeToo. When she speaks of the slut-shaming she's had to endure over the years, I'm reminded of the same slut-shaming that hounded actress Asia Argento into exile. Argento was one of the first women to speak out against Weinstein and was victim-shamed in her native Italy as a result. The bullying hasn't shut her up – nor has it succeeded in shaming Lewinsky into submission despite the taunts and jeers. Like Argento, Lewinsky is a trailblazer, too. The forty-four year old refers to herself as 'patient zero' – a woman who went 'from being a private person to a globally known, publicly humiliated, losing-my-digital-reputation [person]' in a matter of days. In spite of Twitter trolls who still drag her through the mud, she's blueprinted a path for others who now follow her across trip-wired terrain.

Lewinsky's 1990s fat-shamers (she recalls how in 1999, in one of her first interviews, a reporter wrote 'Lewinsky lumbers into the room like an elephant') may pre-date our current social media age, but her experience of abuse has much to tell us about the ways in which trolls target women today. Social media has become, according to Lewinsky, the digital equivalent of the Roman coliseum. 'When we wrap fear around difference, that's what creates the chasm between [people],' she told the *Evening Standard*. 'We're living at a time when we see the best of people and the worst of people.'

Monica Lewinsky might be back, but in some ways, she never really went away. It's just that we're finally listening. Which is why Lewinsky has bravely stepped back into the ring in order to tackle bullying in all its varying forms, both online and off. Her focus, the interview reveals, is on victims ('because that's what I feel most con-nected to') and a 'digital reslience' that she'd like us all to build up like a muscle. 'It's almost like wearing a seatbelt,' she told the *Evening Standard*. 'It's not because you know you'll get into an accident now, but because there's a high likelihood you could one day. More and more people will find themselves publicly shamed.'

As the US writer Sady Doyle wrote on Twitter, 'In a perfect world, we'd have been talking about how scummy Bill Clinton was to

Monica Lewinsky forever.' In the real world, we're only just approaching that conversation now – tentatively but with increasing urgency as Hollywood unravels. Type 'Bill Clinton' into Google search and the headlines finally flip the narrative. 'What about Bill?' the *New York Times* asks the world.

Nearly twenty years after Monica Lewinsky was shamed in the most public of ways, her story is finally being told – in her own time, on her own terms. In her own words.

Why didn't I take this sexual offence more seriously?

WHEN WE'RE TOLD REPEATED STREET HARASSMENT IS 'JUST A JOKE' WE BECOME CONDITIONED TO PLAY IT DOWN. OR SO ZOË BEATY FOUND OUT LAST NIGHT

BY ZOË BEATY

Late last night, as I made my way home from a friend's party, I noticed a male figure appear alongside me. The man was shorter than me; around five foot nine or ten inches to my six foot, and almost chasing to keep up with my stride. I glanced towards him without turning my head. He was trying to speak to me. I thought he might be asking for change, or for help with something. I removed my headphones, to address him. 'Are you OK?' I asked. 'You have pretty feet,' he said, without missing a beat.

I said a rushed, uncomfortable 'thank you' in a bid to appease him and encourage him to leave me alone, rolled my eyes and quickened my pace to the bus stop just up the road. But, in my peripheral vision, a short figure began approaching me as I waited to get home. I knew it was him immediately but I stared straight ahead. I was trying to ignore his presence, but as he edged towards me, it started to feel like a threat of some kind. He was persisting, not satisfied with making lewd comments to me, and I started feeling increasingly combative.

He moved until he was about a metre away from me. I couldn't ignore him any longer. I looked to my right, to see him staring down at my feet, masturbating.

What would you do? What should you do? I didn't know. I shouted at him, and he told me that he was 'just day-dreaming' like it was the most natural thing in the world. As soon as I ran behind the bus stop, away from him, he started scuttling in the opposite direction. I didn't know whether I should have accosted him, whether I should ring the police emergency number or write a report online. I realised, despite writing about cat-calling and harassment and sexual abuse and domestic abuse and assaults on women, for quite a few years, I had no fucking clue what to do.

I didn't know what number to ring. Instinctively I thought that using a 999 call to report some creep wanking over my sandals in the street would be more of a nuisance than anything – the prevalence of cat-calling and this type of sexual behaviour is so commonplace that I didn't consider it urgent. I went over to a woman at the same stop, and explained what had happened. She wasn't shocked – she tutted, said she was sorry, and rolled her eyes like, 'men!' – and she also didn't know what to do. I considered going to Lewisham police station, around the corner from where I stood, but felt worried that I'd be considered to be wasting their time too. I settled on dialling 101, and spent thirty minutes on hold, waiting to speak to someone.

But why did I think it was in any way unimportant? Why didn't I think that I could class a man, intimidating me, behaving in a sexually threatening manner, on a street where I stood alone at night, as something to be taken seriously?

Perhaps, I thought, because we're told over and over that it is nothing serious. Cat-calling and street harassment over our lifetimes are a million sexualised and internalised moments, absorbed and expertly ignored and buried by women. Don't make a fuss. Don't whinge. There are far worse things that happen, aren't there? Don't ever seem too highly strung, or emotional or 'crazy'. Don't appear like you 'can't take a laugh'. The way women are publicly treated – shamed and embarrassed by uncaring, self-righteous, self-centred men – is diminished as 'just a joke'. And so when something happens, we – at least, I did last night – diminish its gravitas too.

And because we're told that there are certain ways we should and shouldn't act, we suddenly believe we can be part of the problem. A thread on Reddit about how it feels to be cat-called revealed the same thing: women are given a myriad of mixed messages of the 'right' way to deal with harassment, and the 'right' way to be a victim, and nothing ever works. Women are told that they should completely ignore harassers, only to be followed for being 'rude'. We're told to fight back, only to be threatened and 'putting themselves at risk'. 'It's scary,' one user on Reddit said. 'You're met with limited options. You can smile/laugh, which encourages it more. You can tell them to fuck off, which could turn ugly really quickly. Or you can ignore it, in which case they normally get more aggressive. It makes me feel really small, like I'm not a whole person but rather walking real estate, and it fucking sucks.'

I wasn't upset at all last night, but I did feel some murky embarrassment. It knocked me a bit. There was something humiliating and exposing about the whole thing, and I think some of it was feeling a little unsure and a little more powerless, and some of it was about my own response. Why did I even acknowledge him? What if I'd told him 'fuck you' when he cat-called, not 'thank you'; did appeasing him actually encourage it? No. Of course not.

He would have done it anyway. Strangers will snatch at ownership of our bodies, thinking they have the right. Cat-calling and flashing and wanking over a woman's feet in chilly Lewisham on a Sunday evening are not about 'compliments' but power. It's men who think they have a god-given right to determine a woman's fuckability; to undermine, sexualise, degrade and abuse women to soothe their own inferiority complex and attempt to bolster their delicate egos.

Thankfully, the police did take it seriously, and were incredibly helpful. They said that, actually, I should have dialled 999. If I'd have done that, and told them where I was, they would have picked me up in a police car and gone for a drive round to see if I could spot him. There would have been a chance to catch him and stop him from doing it to another girl.

I'm surprised at myself that I missed that chance. It shocked me that – even after writing about this subject many, many times, and arguing about it many, many times, even after simply being a woman – I didn't know what to do. And I didn't immediately take it seriously enough; I unwittingly internalised messages about women, and the (lack of) seriousness of sexual crimes against women that I've been decrying for years.

Not anymore. I've stopped analysing my response because, of course, I didn't fucking ask for it. And it is serious. Next time – should there be a next time – I will dial 999. And, yes, thanks, I will make a fuss.

On the sad inevitability of the grown man and the teenage girl

ACTING SURPRISED BY THE CRIMES OF ADAM JOHNSON FEELS DISINGENUOUS BECAUSE TEENAGERS ARE SEDUCED BY GROWN MEN EVERY SINGLE DAY

BY CAROLINE O'DONOGHUE

It's Sunday evening and we're two pints deep, and the day's football is done and dusted, and talk has finally – blissfully – moved on to other things. Gavin and Harry are talking about Adam Johnson, the player who has pleaded guilty to grooming and sexual activity with a fifteen-year-old.

'He tried to make out like he didn't know how old she was. But he did. He CLEARLY did. It wasn't one of those "he found out she was underage after the fact" situations. He knew she was in school. He added her on Facebook. He gave her signed shirts.'

The operative nouns here – school, Facebook, shirts – are said in italics. Emphasis, in their minds, of the proof of Johnson's wrongdoing. Of the mistakes he knew he was making but made anyway: risking his record and his career and his ability to look his mum in the face again.

They look to me, as if waiting for my outrage. Waiting for me to weigh in, expecting that despite my general ignorance of football I will definitely have an opinion on this man's indiscretion. The truth is that I don't have one, and the reason I don't have one is because it's the lack of originality or surprise here that makes it hard to react to. It's hard to sound surprised about what happens every day. It's hard to talk now about what me and my female friends talk about all the time: the teenagers we were, the men we met, the connection we thought we felt that turned out be a simple yet evidently one-sided transaction.

I grew up in a university town. A city where it was an easy bus ride to a pub that closed at 2am and played good, loud music you could dance to. The pubs were largely concerned with whether you had ID, and far less concerned with whether it was you in the photograph. At sixteen, we shared cigarettes with men in their mid or late twenties – down from a different county, and eagerly finishing their masters – and we didn't feel like we needed to lie about how old we were. It was rare that anyone would go home with one of them. They got a certain excitement out of talking to us – 'You're HOW old?' – and we got a similar buzz from them. The older the guy, the more sophisticated a shadow it seemed to cast on us. And that was enough. That was mostly enough.

At seventeen, I met a man who stopped me during my walk home to tell me he loved my eyes. He was in his late twenties, doing an MA in computer science, and would dutifully wait until my lunch break so I could text back. 'We're doing *Jane Eyre*,' I said, with a frowny face. He would reply quickly: 'Do you know that the Brontës were origin-ally called Prunty?'

When attempting to be the teenage lover of an older man, being taught things is a big part of the job. The school uniform is actually a very small fraction of the attraction, I think. It's your eagerness to be the smaller person that singles you out. You are there to be dictated to, to be taught things, to be made into a protégée. The thing the media has clutched onto about the Adam Johnson story is his talent and fame, his beautiful girlfriend and the 'Why would a man like this have to do a thing like that?' aspect of the story. But even then, he's not that remarkable. What about Priscilla Presley, who went to live with Elvis in her teens? What about Julia Holcomb, who claims that Aerosmith frontman Steven Tyler forced her to abort his child at sixteen? What about the hundreds, thousands, of young women who have seen their youth chewed up and spat out by the older men they were seduced by? Are we really acting like any of this is a surprise anymore? Do we need to pretend to be shocked every time?

The man who seduced me as a teenager wasn't talented or intelligent, or even a capable adult. He had dropped out of several degree programmes, lost several girlfriends and had alienated various batches of friends before he met me. A grown man doesn't usually have a teenage girlfriend unless he needs to feel good about himself, unless he is fresh out of people to be impressed by him. He had no TV, so the first time I visited his house he showed me a box of photographs from his travels in Asia. No woman his own age would have tolerated such a poor excuse for a date, which is the exact reason no woman was. I was there instead, thinking: God. Someone who has been to Asia also fancies ME.

I need to state here that my experience was not at all similar to the girl who became Adam Johnson's victim. Reading her testimony, it is clear that I was complicit in a way that she was not. That she was damaged in a way that I was not, and that her hero-worship of a football player was turned against her. I'm making the parallel for one reason: that you do not have to be a famous football player, or even a famous anything, to pursue a young girl. You could be anyone.

I ended things quickly, after realising that his interest wasn't based on who I was, but rather, who I wasn't. I wasn't sophisticated, I wasn't knowledgeable. I didn't expect things, and I didn't know what to expect. What I was, was eager, and lonely. I was in recent possession of a sexuality that felt like a party trick, one that could draw a very specific crowd if used correctly. I don't know how many months were between Adam Johnson's teenage girlfriend and me, during my time with an older man. I don't know anything about her, and I definitely don't presume to think that my time with a college burnout was remotely similar to hers with a Premier League footballer. But I think this is how all teenage girls feel, at the heart of themselves. The desperation for love and glamour, of knowing things and being known, consumes you for a short time. Usually, you move on. Usually, you look back on that phase of your life with a sad curiosity, sharing it with a future partner as he squints and tries to imagine that very vulnerable version of you. Maybe she will too: I hope she does.

But more than that: I want us to stop acting surprised. I want us to stop assuming that these girls – these girls like Priscilla Presley, or Julia Holcomb, or Adam Johnson's teenage Sunderland fan – are the odd sexual curiosities of sick men. I want us to own up to the fact that society creates teenage girls who are eternally receiving mixed messages about their own sexuality. I want there never to be a picture of a child star captioned by how she's 'all grown up'. I want us to be frank about the fact that we parade and place very young girls atop very high altars, at the centre of huge fashion or media campaigns, and then are surprised when they are treated as sexual objects. I want us to acknowledge the brokenness that leads to these stories, and see them as the result of a sickness, and not the entire sickness. In the specific case of Adam Johnson, maybe this represents a sea-change: he has, after all, lost his job and his sponsorship deal, and he will likely face jail time. I am reminded by my football-loving friends that this is huge, and that football players rarely get fired for their sexual misconduct.

I received an email from him, the man who is now in his late thirties, about six months ago. He is now a teacher in Korea, and says he was reminded of me when he saw my initials on a menu somewhere. He asks how I am, and then signs off with a comment about my boobs. I feel sick for a minute, furious at this man for entering my orbit again after all these years, for leaving a slimy mark on my Gmail. And then I realise that while I am stuck with the memory of him, he is stuck with himself. He is stuck with himself, and always will be.

On 24 March 2016, ex-England footballer Adam Johnson was jailed for six years for sexual activity with a fifteen-year-old girl.

A rape victim can be the worst victim-blamer. I should know. I have been both

AFTER A SEXUAL ASSAULT, IT CAN TAKE YEARS FOR A VICTIM TO COME TO TERMS WITH WHAT HAPPENED. ONE WOMAN TELLS HER STORY

BY ANON

When I saw the newspapers and realised he had been accused of sexual misconduct, I felt almost sorry for him. Only almost, because he had raped me, a few years earlier. Back then, I had said to my best friend: 'One day, that man will be charged with rape and he will not understand why.' At that time, and for many years afterwards, I actually had sympathy for him.

I met him at a party when I was twenty-two and found him vaguely sexy in a smarmy way. He asked me out, I said yes, we went for dinner then back to his house, where I willingly kissed him, stripped to my pants (I always kept my pants on as a message and barrier, until I was ready to not need messages and barriers) and got into his bed. Then he started tugging at my underwear, I was wriggling away, saying, 'No, no, really, no,' but trying to keep it light and nice and not make a big drama or anything, and he wasn't listening. Then he was lying on top of me, so wriggling away wasn't an option any more, but I kept on pushing at his chest and saying, 'No, come on, no,' more urgently now, but definitely not screaming or shouting or clawing at him, the way a woman would if she were about to be raped, right? Then he was in me and I froze while I worked out what to do, which, it turns out, was nothing. The voice in my head said, 'Oh, shit, oh, shit.' Then it said, 'OK, well you probably would have had sex with him on date three or four, so this is no big deal, stop

17

being a dick.' So, I did stop being a dick and we had sex. No screaming and clawing, like a woman would do if she was being raped, right? So, it wasn't rape.

What I believed then and for years to come was as follows: I was a grown woman responsible for her choices. If you go home with a strange man, get into bed with him (nearly) naked and aren't prepared to get extreme in your efforts to stop him having sex with you, then you can't claim it's rape. I actually said: 'If you are not prepared to call a man a rapist to his face, in the moment, then you can't call him one in hindsight.' I even came up with an alternative name for what he did: Pressure Sex. Consensual sex comes in shades of grey, I told myself, but only rape is jet black. I said he was a creep, but it wasn't fair to call him a rapist.

In my defence, I wasn't just a moron. I adamantly believed that the encounter with him was my experience, so I got to decide how to label it. I was no kind of victim. I was a grown woman. I was responsible. This narrative felt like I was protecting myself. Being strong. Taking control. I was dealing with it in the best way for me, so everyone else could fuck off.

I stuck with that story for years. But here are some things I began to notice: I hate being touched unexpectedly – hugs, kisses, even arm squeezes can make my flesh crawl. I have always told my husband this was a hangover from every creep in every nightclub who ever groped me as I walked past, but honestly I don't know if that ever even happened. Really, truthfully, it only started after that man forced himself on me. I also want my husband to stroke my back (it feels nice, it feels safe) for fifteen minutes before foreplay goes any further, just to let my body get used to the idea that something more intimate is coming. Spontaneous sex is out.

So, not really coping after all. And certainly not protecting other women, as I turned into a victim-blamer. Whenever I spoke about my experience with that man, I included extra details, as if they were relevant: I had only had three previous lovers so, you know, I wasn't slutty (in actual fact, the number was higher, but did that make me look culpable?); I never fucked on a first date (true, but again not relevant); I had only had one glass of wine that night. I chose to believe women should be responsible for their own safety and, if we are drunk, naked or giving mixed messages, we need to be realistic about the consequences. Not that we deserved them, but we needed to accept them.

Then, a few years ago I heard the phrase: 'Let's stop teaching women how not to get raped, and start teaching men not to rape.' It made my stomach hurt. Even with all my advantages (my education, my career, a platform), it was an idea that had never occurred to me – that the responsibility for men's sexual behaviour lies with men. For the first time, a little voice said that maybe this man was a rapist. I silenced it.

But more voices followed. The brave, extraordinary victims who spoke out about every entitled bastard who thinks that consensual sex is sex they can get away with. And the millions of women – and men – who stood in solidarity with those survivors. I heard the words: 'There is no such thing as non-consensual sex; there is sex and there is rape.' I remembered my clever Pressure Sex phrase and I felt weak, ashamed and, for the first time, like a rape victim.

But being a victim also makes me a survivor of rape. I have cried a lot these past months, but owning it means dealing with it. Finally, fifteen years into our relationship, I told my husband what had happened. I explained that until now I hadn't considered it rape, just a shameful sex story. Part of me always will. It's only when I picture another woman in my place in that man's bed, feeling and reacting exactly as I did, that I feel justified in calling him a rapist.

My shame stays with me, but it has taken a different shape – this time around my victim-blaming. I'm going to lay that on him, too – he didn't just screw my body, he screwed my mind, so fuck him. When I hear allegations about high-profile men I don't feel sympathy for them, of course. I don't feel relief. I just feel horrified that, despite all the conversations and headlines of the past years, defining over and over again what is harassment, what is assault, what is rape, so many men have learnt absolutely nothing. That, more than anything, breaks my heart.

The writer remains anonymous for legal reasons

#HomeToVote – and what it means to watch Irish women boarding planes to Repeal the 8th

FOR DECADES, TENS OF THOUSANDS OF IRISH WOMEN HAVE BEEN FORCED TO TRAVEL TO ACCESS SAFE AND LEGAL ABORTIONS. NOW THEY ARE BEING REMEMBERED

BY LYNN ENRIGHT

Clattering around London with a wheelie suitcase, even a small one, is a faff – when it gets caught on the kerb or when you have to man-oeuvre it up the stairs at the train station. Yesterday, I spent the day dragging my case around – from home onto the bus, to a hospital appointment, onto the bus again and into work. Then, after that, onto a train, and then another, to the airport, where I got a plane home to Ireland.

Thousands and thousands of us have come home – either to vote or, if we are no longer eligible to vote because we have lived away for too long, to support the vote. Today, Ireland goes to the polls and decides whether or not to remove – or repeal – the Eighth Amendment from its constitution. The Eighth Amendment was introduced in 1983 after a bitter and divisive referendum – and it is this piece of the constitution that gives an embryo or a foetus an 'equal right to life' to a pregnant girl or woman. Abortion is illegal in Ireland – it has been since the mid-1800s – but, more than that, a pregnant girl or woman's life is deemed to be worth as much, and no more, as the 'unborn'.

Since the introduction of the Eighth, there have been numerous heinous cases, in which the restrictive abortion legislation has made difficult situations much, much worse. A suicidal teenage asylum seeker who had been raped was refused an abortion and later forced to give birth by caesarean section. A brain-dead woman was kept on life support, against the wishes of her family, because she was pregnant and medics were worried that by turning off the machines they would be breaching the law. Savita Halappanavar, a thirty-one-year-old dentist originally from India but living in Galway, died after being denied a termination that would probably have saved her life.

Alongside those shameful and nightmarish cases have been tens and tens of thousands of other, less conspicuous, stories: those of girls and women who needed abortions, not necessarily because their lives were in danger but because they couldn't or didn't want to go through with a pregnancy. Because the baby they were carrying would not survive after birth or because they couldn't afford another child or because their relationship was in bad shape. They had their reasons. At least 150,000 women have travelled from Ireland to seek abortions in the UK or in other parts of Europe since the Eighth Amendment was introduced.

That's 150,000 air and ferry fares. That's 150,000 women wandering around unfamiliar neighbourhoods. That's 150,000 suitcases clattering up and down train-station steps.

And that's why the #HomeToVote initiative, the great swell of people crossing the Irish sea or the Atlantic, or coming all the way from Australia or China or South Africa, feels so momentous. For decades, Irish women have been travelling to access healthcare that should have been available in their own country. They've told fibs when they were booking days off work or arranging childcare. They've shelled out hundreds of euros for last-minute flights. They've crouched uncomfortably in tiny airplane loos, their morning sickness made worse by the travel. They've acted as though they were going on a holiday when actually they were on their way to an abortion clinic in a faraway suburb.

That's what a wheelie suitcase usually signifies: a holiday. Yesterday, as I walked around with my little case, I kept being asked, by the nice nurse at the hospital and by the friendly woman in the coffee shop and by all the other well-meaning strangers, 'Where are you off to? Anywhere nice?' And each time I answered, my voice croaked, my heart beat faster, my eyes filled with tears. I was nervous, tired, worried, hopeful.

All day, my Irish friends and I sent each other messages of support as we travelled, tweeting little hearts and texting pictures of our tear-stained cheeks as we sat in the airport Wetherspoons. And it did help, the solidarity and the sense that we were all in this together. Because while there was a small number of young people travelling home to vote No, they were outnumbered. Ireland's diaspora is desperate to repeal the Eighth. And we've been helping each other out: hundreds of Irish people who are no longer eligible to vote paid for flights for younger people who are eligible but struggled to afford the airfare. I bought an Irish student a flight from Finland to Dublin and, as I was entering my debit-card details, I thought of all the students who have been forced to gather hundreds and thousands of euros at the last minute, when they've faced a crisis pregnancy. Other women I know sponsored students and people on low incomes in Hanoi and in New York and in Berlin.

It felt a little like Christmas Eve last night, the thousands of young people flocking into the airports, the families reunited for a brief time, the hope and promise of the next morning.

Yesterday, we travelled because we wanted to. Today, we vote for the women who travelled because they were forced to.

On 25 May 2018, the Irish people voted to repeal the Eighth Amendment in a two-to-one landslide. It is estimated that 35,000 people returned home to vote that Friday. Their votes were important – as were the stories that women told during the campaign. In one poll, 66 per cent of voters said that hearing personal testimony was the single biggest factor in deciding how they would vote. Women who told their personal abortion stories changed Ireland. Women who travelled home to vote changed Ireland.

Hate is hate – except if you're targeted for being a woman

THE IDEA OF CLASSING MISOGYNY AS A HATE CRIME REMAINS INTENSELY CONTROVERSIAL – BUT IT MUST BE TACKLED

BY GABY HINSLIFF

Hate is hate is hate. No matter how you vent it – screaming at someone on the street, scrawling swastikas on their front door or abusing them on Twitter – it's unacceptable and the law will punish those overstepping the line.

So said Alison Saunders, the director of public prosecutions, outlining plans to treat online abuse motivated by the victim's race, religion, disability, sexuality or transgender status not just as the criminal offence it already can be but as a hate crime, meaning it could attract stiffer sentences. She argues it's not just about deterring trolls, but tackling potential root causes of real-life violence like that seen in Charlottesville, where a far-right rally against a statue being removed ended in the death of counter-protester Heather Heyer. Hate whipped up online doesn't always stay online. Words have power.

But, welcome as they are, these measures aren't going to stop the tide of abuse against women in the public eye, or indeed in private life. None of this makes any difference to knuckle-draggers enraged by the very existence of the academic Mary Beard or the MP Jess Phillips, or men who can't stand sexual rejection and harass any woman who turns them down, because weirdly the one thing hate crime legislation doesn't cover is offences motivated by misogyny. Hate is hate, except if you're targeted specifically for being a woman, when it's – well, not worth a stiffer sentence, apparently. But now a group of determined women MPs on the all-party group against domestic violence, including Phillips and the former Tory minister Maria Miller, are trying to get that loophole closed.

It's surprising misogyny isn't already covered, given how entwined we know crimes like domestic violence are with deep-seated attitudes to women. Yet the idea of including it remains intensely controversial. When Nottinghamshire Police announced last year that they would record misogyny-driven offences as hate crimes, chief constable Sue Fish was accused of trying to outlaw wolf whistles and stop men chatting women up in bars. Critics said police would be swamped with silly, trivial complaints, while men lived in fear of accidentally causing offence.

Well, relax, everyone – nobody's arguing that misogyny in itself should become illegal. For something to be classed as a hate crime under the current law, you have to do more than just hate; it's defined as the committing of a criminal offence – like assault or vandalism or harassment – which is specifically motivated by hatred of something about the victim's identity, like their skin colour or the fact they're gay. Hating or resenting women, if that's how you really want to spend your life, would still be allowed. You just wouldn't get to grope someone, or punch her, or throw a brick through her window or make threats to her in a public space specifically because of that hatred without attracting a potentially tougher sentence.

All of which means that haters who manage not to also break the law should have no more to fear from this legislation than drunks who always get a taxi home from the pub fear from drink-driving crackdowns. Obviously, the safest option would be to cut down on the booze or the hating, since both cloud your judgement and can lead to publicly embarrassing situations. But men who treasure the right to resent women that much – who genuinely would choose that hill to die on – would still be free do so. They'd just have to avoid breaking the law as a result.

And, yes, the police might have to deal with some complaints about behaviour that's horrible but not criminal, just as they do within the existing law. But the evidence from Nottinghamshire is that it's not only provided a way of officially responding to intimidating or distressing incidents that fall into a legal grey area – it's also led to serious offences, including sexual assault and kidnapping, being reported. The force's willingness to record sexual offences as hate crimes, too, where appropriate seems to convince women that they'll be taken seriously.

So women MPs, including Phillips, Miller, the Green MP Caroline Lucas and Labour's Melanie Onn, have written to their local police forces, asking them to follow Nottinghamshire's example, to establish how widespread hate-fuelled crime against women is and how it's best tackled. This may not be the most pressing issue in Theresa May's Brexit-laden in-tray. But in a week where she found time to comment on Big Ben not ringing, it would be nice to think she's listening.

Our desire to rehabilitate men is classic 'himpathy'

WHEN WE TRY TO REDEEM AND EXONERATE BADLY BEHAVED MEN, WE ARE GETTING DISTRACTED FROM THE REAL PROBLEM

BY RACHAEL SIGEE

A few days after the story broke, in October, about his decades of sexual abuse, Harvey Weinstein took a private jet to an exclusive rehab clinic. On his way, he told reporters: 'Guys, I'm not doing OK but I'm trying. I gotta get help. I'm hanging in, I'm trying my best.' He had released a statement, pleading 'allow me to resurrect myself with a second chance'. It wasn't the first time a man has turned to 'treatment' in the hope of salvaging his reputation following a sexual-assault scandal.

We are living in remarkable times. Times when women's voices are finally being listened to and some men appear to be facing real consequences for their actions. One man even apologised properly and in a way that his victim accepted.

But, as we collectively navigate this new state of affairs, there is an uncomfortable pattern emerging. The concern and sympathy that should be directed towards women who have survived assault and harassment is being siphoned off and, instead, directed at the men who have inflicted that behaviour on them – the men hoping to be 'cured'. If men are going to topple, it seems we want to at least give them a soft landing.

Coined by philosopher Kate Manne, in her book *Down Girl: The Logic of Misogyny*, 'himpathy' is 'the excessive or inappropriate sympathy extended to a male agent or wrongdoer over his female victim'. The counterpoint to this, Manne says, is 'the aggressive impulse that we show to a woman who testifies against a man with whom we sympathise is really predictable'.

It may be a newly coined concept, but it is, sadly, a pervasive one – especially post-#MeToo – and, unfortunately, there are many examples to help convey what it means today.

The example Manne uses in her book is Brock Turner, the Stanford student convicted of sexual assault in 2016, and the way his supporters focused on the narrative of an all-American young man cut down in his prime. The media was criticised for repeatedly describing him as the 'Stanford swimmer'; concentrating on the damage to his promising future, rather than the damage done to his victim. Another example would be Harvey Weinstein checking into a rehab centre (the same one as Kevin Spacey, incidentally, when many were asking why he wasn't being arrested for his alleged abuses).

This is what we mean when we talk about 'himpathy'. It's a desperate scramble to rationalise men's behaviour, without having to accept that it might result from ingrained systemic misogyny. Or having to acknowledge our own complicity in a society that has allowed men's behaviour to go unchecked: he has struggled with mental-health problems. He has a sex addiction. He's 'seeking treatment'.

It applies to courtrooms and police investigations where a victim's lifestyle, looks and relationships might be used against her – like the judge who told an assault victim she should be flattered by the attention as she was 'a little overweight' in his opinion. And it is relevant to the ongoing debate over whether those accused of sexual crimes should be granted anonymity in the same way their victims are. It is why the term 'witch hunt' is being bandied around by men who are quaking in their privilege.

People are tripping over themselves trying to answer the question of how we can possibly rehabilitate these men and their reputations, before they have fully considered the very behaviour that has landed them in trouble. They are far more interested in resolving that issue than resolving the culture that led to abuse in the first place. It is not dissimilar to when people are more upset at being called racist than at racism itself.

And tied up in our desire to exonerate men is the whole inconvenience of having to change our minds about people we like – our problematic faves. Consider how quickly the conversation around Aziz Ansari turned on disparaging 'Grace', the woman who told the story.

We pull out statistics about false accusations and denigrate women in an attempt to absolve ourselves of the responsibility to think about difficult things. But these excuses, these paths to exoneration, are an insult to victims. To invoke sex addiction is to imply that sexual assault is to do with sex and not power. And if we are looking to psychology for the solution to women systematically being abused in myriad ways, we are looking in the wrong place.

They are a distraction from the very necessary work of interrogating the power structures and culture that has led to the systemic abuse of women.

In Weinstein, we had a watershed moment, but we also have an extreme baddie – a baddie whose behaviour other men's conduct is now being compared against and rated. And, as long as we all agree that Weinstein is the worst, there is hope for other men who aren't him. It's the spectrum of sexual assault that Matt Damon infamously cited as a method for determining how far men should be punished.

Of course, the notion of 'himpathy' becomes a great deal more complicated when you consider intersectional elements: the majority of the men who are benefitting from it are white, straight, cis and economically stable. And, if they have lost their jobs, they will, in all likelihood, be OK in the long run. They are news anchors, actors, movie producers, politicians, comedians and journalists – and, while there are certainly a lot of them, they are undoubtedly outnumbered by countless more men who are still in their jobs and continuing to exhibit the same behaviour, or worse.

For every man who has lost something – a job, a booking, an invitation – because of an allegation of sexual aggression towards a woman, there are thousands of women who have lost a great deal more for being on the receiving end of that aggression. It is they who deserve real redemption.

The trouble with compliments in a post-#MeToo world

SUDDENLY, WOMEN ARE PUTTING THEIR HANDS UP TO SAY, 'I DON'T WANT YOU TO TELL ME THAT I LOOK HOT.' IT'S BEEN A LONG TIME COMING

BY JEAN HANNAH EDELSTEIN

THE CASE OF MORGAN FREEMAN

A distinguished man in Hollywood doesn't trend on Twitter these days unless he's died or been accused of sexual harassment, and the actor Morgan Freeman was very much alive when his name rose to the top of the clamour. Eight women had come forward to accuse him of sexual harassment. Among the most common complaints: that Freeman habitually commented on women's bodies, clothing and his perception of how attractive they were in professional settings, causing them great discomfort.

Two cases have surfaced in old footage from the syndicated American television show Entertainment Tonight. In one, when journalist Ashley Crossan thanks him for the interview by saying, 'Pleasure to meet you,' Freeman responds, 'Mine. Look at yourself.' In another,

Freeman goes into a brief soliloquy about the journalist Janet Mock's skirt: 'I don't know how you all manage to do that all the time. You got a dress halfway between your knee and your hips, and you sit down right across from me and cross your legs.'

Mock was unequivocal in her objection to this behaviour, saying: 'This interaction is an exhibition of the casual nature at which men in positions of power believe that everything belongs to them including women's bodies as they're merely just trying to do their job.'

In response, Freeman issued a long semi-apology in which he emphasised that he did not believe that his behaviour should be called harassment: 'All victims of assault and harassment deserve to be heard. And we need to listen to them. But it is not right to equate horrific incidents of sexual assault with misplaced compliments or humour. I admit that I am someone who feels a need to try to make women – and men – feel appreciated and at ease around me. As a part of that, I would often try to joke with and compliment women, in what I thought was a light-hearted and humorous way.'

Is the pushback against Freeman's 'compliments' a sign that the #MeToo movement has gone too far – that women are being too sensitive in cases when men are trying to be light-hearted and humorous? Do men need to re-learn what compliments are and how to deliver them? In a world where we're truly sensitive to sexual harassment, can anyone say 'nice haircut' to anyone else ever again?

THE TROUBLE WITH COMPLIMENTS

It's not an unfamiliar experience for many women, I'm sure, but when I think about what I'll call The Trouble With Compliments, I remember in particular a man of my acquaintance who I used to run into socially three or four times a year, which is to say that we knew each other, but not well. Every time I saw him he would greet me with an enthusiastic: 'You've lost weight!'

Rather than make me feel good about myself – which I genuinely think was his intention, rather than to fat-shame me (each time he saw me, I'll note, my weight had hardly vacillated) – this always made me feel bad. 'How heavy did I look last time I saw you?' I would wonder, and also, 'Why is the size of my body the thing about me that you find most worthy of a remark?' It would never have occurred to me to comment on his measurements in return.

A compliment is defined by its intent, not by its receipt. That is to say, just because you make a remark to someone that is intended to be a compliment doesn't mean that the recipient will understand it as a compliment – and it certainly doesn't mean that the recipient is obliged to receive it as a compliment. Or, at least, it shouldn't. But, for a long time, that hasn't been our collective understanding.

Rather, for time immemorial, it's been a commonly held view in Western culture that women should be flattered when men pay them compliments – that it's an important tradition not just of flirtation and romance, but of chivalry. Women who have negative reactions to compliments from men are often chided for being ungrateful. But, in the post-#MeToo era, one of the things that we're having to consider is how often statements that are intended to flatter can be undermining or harassing, or even abusive. Now, women are putting their hands up to say, 'I don't want you to tell me that I look hot.' It's been a long time coming.

HE DOES IT BECAUSE HE LIKES YOU

For many women, our toxic understanding of compliments goes back to childhood, when so many of us learnt that male attention was, in itself, complimentary, regardless of the form that it took. 'He does it because he likes you' is still a too-common explanation to young girls when their male peers are unkind to them. By that logic, if negative attention is just a reframed compliment, then not only should we tolerate it, but we should be downright enthusiastic in our acceptance of any positive male attention. No matter who it comes from, or when.

These are narratives that gaslight women – that tell us how to feel instead of acknowledging our real feelings, and the primordial nature of these stories mean that they're hard to shake off. Just a couple of years ago, I was slapped on the bum by a stranger riding past me on a bicycle while I walked my dog. When I recounted the story to friends (after I called the police), they all commiserated, but more than one of them added, 'Of course, he probably did it because he thought you were attractive.' I'm sure this was intended to comfort me, but it was a reflection of how much people want to believe that women should consider any sexual attention to be positive attention – even if it's literal assault.

Compliments are at their most problematic when they're insincere, and the truth is that most of them are, especially in professional contexts. When a man who has no real (or appropriate) romantic designs on a woman compliments her on her appearance, her body or her sex appeal, it shows the opposite of sincerity or reflection. It functions as a signal of his understanding that she is a woman, that the way she looks or the degree to which he considers her sexually attractive is his primary interest. More broadly, it signals that this is how they think about women in general. Some men do this because they know no other way to relate to women (perhaps Freeman, as a man over eighty, falls into this category). Some men do it because they want to put women in their place – to remind us that they consider us as ripe for their consumption, no matter the reason for our engagement.

THE END OF COMPLIMENTS?

French actress Catherine Deneuve led a backlash against #MeToo, claiming that it would spell an end to sexual freedom. 'It's as if someone finding you attractive is an insult,' she complained. 'I beg to differ: I'm complimented if someone is attracted to me. The only question is: am I allowed to say no?' The shortcoming of Deneuve's argument is in the assumption that every display of attraction is a compliment. The question is not just whether a woman is allowed to say no to a sexual invitation, but whether a woman is allowed to reject an expression of attraction itself because it's unwelcome, regardless of the reason that it's unwelcome.

No one is saying that compliments should be banned. But now is a good time for a reconsideration of their appropriateness – for us to rethink how men talk to women and vice versa. In general, compliments about the physical appearance of someone with whom you don't have an established level of emotional intimacy run a high risk of being inappropriate. Telling someone you've just met that you find them attractive will rarely put them at ease – it instantly flags that you are assessing them primarily as a potential sex partner. Even if, like Freeman, you think you're being nice.

This is particularly the case in a professional situation, but I'd say that it's even the case in a scenario where people may be more open to a romantic connection: going up to a stranger at a party or a bus stop and saying, 'You're hot!' is far more likely to evoke an eye roll than a phone number. A good rule of thumb is to ask yourself: would I make this remark to someone who I didn't consider a potential sexual partner? Where lines are crossed become pretty clear thereafter: if you are a heterosexual man and wouldn't tell another heterosexual man that you admire his legs, it's creepy to say it to a woman outside of an explicitly romantic situation in which you know that your interest is reciprocated.

Does that mean that no one can be made to feel appreciated and at ease anymore? Of course not. It's just a matter of showing that appreciation through compliments that call out positive attributes of a person that have nothing to do with sex – like their intelligent conversation; their great sense of humour; how good they are at their job; how they're kind to other people. These sorts of compliments indicate that you admire someone as a whole person – that you're considering more than the body that they inhabit. But it's also important to remember that these kinds of compliments are not accompanied by entitlement, either – if your compliment doesn't elicit the response that you desire, the recipient is not to blame. Gratitude is earned, not an entitlement.

When we talk about imposter syndrome, we need to be intersectional

IMPOSTER SYNDROME IS OFTEN SEEN AS A GENDER-BASED SCOURGE, BUT WE RARELY LOOK INTO THE PART RACE PLAYS IN FEELING LIKE A FRAUD

BY YOMI ADEGOKE

Discussions surrounding imposter syndrome are more often than not hinged on gender – when we talk about it, our imagined sufferer is usually an overachieving, under-confident white woman in a corporate setting, questioning her legitimacy at every given moment, while her male colleagues jostle about with ease, never once worrying about their lack of credentials.

But rarely do we examine the part that race plays in making individuals feel like frauds, despite their achievements; ethnic minorities are constantly battling imposter syndrome, and when you're at the intersection of both race and gender – as women of colour are – the feeling can be doubly hard to shake.

This idea was outlined by a piece in The *New York Times* by Kristin Wong, Dealing With Impostor Syndrome When You're Treated as an Impostor, which looked at the idea that not only are ethnic minorities more likely to feel like imposters in their industry, role or position, but that it's linked to the continued treatment that tells them they are such by their peers.

Kevin Cokley, a professor of educational psychology and African diaspora studies at the University of Texas, published a study in the *Journal of Counseling Psychology* and found that impostor syndrome can compound the already existing discrimination some minority groups may feel, adding to their anxieties. The study also found that African-American college students had higher levels of anxiety and discrimination-related depression when they had significant levels of so-called 'impostorism'. He was inspired to conduct the research when, as a black academic, he felt as though he was suffering from feelings of inadequacy, too.

'Can we say discrimination causes impostorism? No, but we know there's definitely a link between the two,' he told the *New York Times*. 'Feeling like an impostor can exacerbate the impact of discrimination. This is what we found with African-American students in our study. I suspect that discrimination can also exacerbate the impact of impostorism.'

The default person expected in positions of power is, as we are well aware, well-off white men. This means anyone who is from a poor background or female or from a BAME background or a multitude of other things often questions their right to be in spaces that were not created with them in mind. And, too often, we assume gender is the only thing that impacts how credible we feel in these places – when you type 'imposter syndrome' into Google, an onslaught of articles crops up wondering why women suffer from it so much, with very few asking why minorities (especially female minorities) do, too.

'I have written eleven books, but each time I think, "Uh oh, they're going to find out now,"' novelist, poet and civil-rights activist Maya Angelou once famously said. 'I've run a game on everybody and they're going to find me out.' And, while many women of whatever colour are likely to relate to this sentiment, many may miss that she was likely to have felt like an imposter not just because she was a woman, but also because she was black.

The *New York Times* article recommends different approaches for minorities to tackle feelings of inferiority: joining an affinity group in order to find workers with similar backgrounds and experiences, recruiting a mentor and taking stock of your accomplishments. But another memorable quote, from another woman of colour, is also worth noting – simply, 'Why not me?', the ever-relevant motto of actor and writer Mindy Kaling.

Sex should not be an extension of team sport

THE MANY STORIES OF GROUP SEX AND MALE SPORTS TEAMS REVEAL A PACK MENTALITY THAT APPEARS TO DEHUMANISE WOMEN

BY RACHAEL SIGEE

There is a rape trial underway in Cardiff. A twenty-four-year-old man has been accused of assaulting a nineteen-year-old woman after she had consensual sex with his friend. The prosecution has told the court she protested, 'What are you doing? You can't pass me around.' They have alleged that it did not deter him: 'He proved he had no respect for the complainant – because his friend had had sex, it was OK for him to do so, too . . . He passed her on to his friend as if she were chattel.'

The lead detail in most of the coverage is that both the men involved are professional swimmers. This has become a noticeable pattern: successful young sportsmen in the dock on charges of sexual violence.

But another pattern is how many of the cases involve more than one defendant or, at least, circumstances involving more than one man – multiple young men whose 'promising futures' and 'exciting careers' can be mourned.

And in these cases, it is not his word against hers – it is their word against hers.

Even when no crime is found to have taken place, the sexual practices, language and power dynamics in these cases are worrying. For example, the rugby players found not guilty in the Belfast rape case exchanged WhatsApp messages that read 'There was a lot of spit roast last night' and 'It was like a merry go round at the carnival'.

After the verdict, one Irish sports journalist wrote of stories he had heard during his time on the beat: 'a female running from a hotel room when players emerged from a wardrobe; Olympians secretly filming themselves with an unsuspecting lady; a woman fleeing the country in shame after a night demeaned by rugby players'.

In June 2015, Leicester City football club sacked three players over a video of them engaging in group sex with Thai sex workers while racially abusing and humiliating the women. The three naked men high five each other in the middle of the action.

We know the problems with sport fuelling rape culture. How being fiercely competitive in games and trying to win 'at all costs' can translate to blanket entitlement off the field. How sporting success is equated with being sexually desirable to women. The way that misogynistic language is a mainstay of locker rooms. That sportsmen are celebrated as heroes and notoriously difficult to knock from their pedestal.

A great article on the topic comes from an unlikely source – the *Daily Mail*, back in 2014, when Ched Evans was released after serving half of his prison sentence for rape and before his conviction was quashed and a retrial found him not guilty. Sports journalist Martin Samuel wrote about how football's culture of denial affects players' behaviour off the pitch. He talked about the way footballers never accept responsibility for mistakes on the pitch and how damaging that approach is when it spills over into real life. In light of Evans' acquittal, the piece is dated. But it is still a sharp observation.

And even Evans' version of events includes him being casually messaged that his friend and fellow footballer Clayton McDonald had 'got a bird'. Both men had sex with her while Evans' younger brother and another man watched from the window and tried to film what was happening.

The finger can obviously be pointed at pornography, where women are routinely shown to be degraded, humiliated and used. The majority of porn accessed online does not prioritise a woman's autonomy, desire or enjoyment when depicting sex, and what might be considered violence or abuse in real life is shown as simply part of sex between men and women.

The popularity of search terms like 'extreme gangbang', 'bukkake' and 'double penetration' illustrates that the sexual set-up of men outnumbering women is being normalised.

But everyone can access this stuff, not just sports players – there is more to this.

Group sex involving professional sportsmen is not about 'one night of madness'. It is routine. It is not a story of sex positivity, thanks to a progressive approach to sex or a liberal attitude to pleasure. Often, this willingness of male sports teams to participate in group sex with each other is present in sports with appalling records on homophobia and few or no out gay players. There is absolutely nothing wrong with consensual sex that incorporates more than one person, but the frequency of these cases suggests that professional sportsmen are uncommonly keen on the group aspect and less than bothered by the consent element.

It is the result of a pack mentality on the pitch encroaching on real life and real women? Male sport teams are fuelled by hypermasculinity. And what better way to prove one's machismo than to literally demonstrate one's sexual prowess, in front of teammates?

Sports teams spend an inordinate amount of time with each other compared with other professions. They share locker rooms, hotel rooms and showers. They are absolutely familiar with each other's bodies. What they also seem to share is the notion that sharing women is acceptable. That they can help themselves. That they are entitled to it. It might not always be a crime, but it is a culture.

Work

LAUREN LAVERNE | CAROLINE O'DONOGHUE
ROBYN WILDER | HARRIET MINTER
MARISA BATE

Why single-tasking can make everything better

IT'S MADE LAUREN LAVERNE CALMER AND MORE FOCUSED, PLUS
SHE CAN ACTUALLY GET MORE WORK DONE IN LESS TIME

BY LAUREN LAVERNE

Last week, I bumped into an old acquaintance. We got talking and realised we hadn't seen each other for a decade. This is one of those things which seemed unimaginable when I was young, but has begun happening to me with alarming frequency as I hurtle towards my forties. A bit like dinner parties, 'shapewear' and being called 'Madam' in shops.

Anyway, we started catching up and it was as if no time had passed at all (another feeling that seems to come with bona fide adulthood). My friend revealed the many profound changes that had taken place in her life in the decade since our last conversation. She had moved countries (continents, actually), got a divorce, found someone else, changed tack in her career, taken some risks, tried, failed and ended up in a better place. She was happier than ever, which she put down to working out, living in a cool town close to nature and also, er, magic mushrooms. 'And how are you?' she asked.

How was I? Good. 'Good,' I replied. Because I am. I'm good. But then I stopped, because there was nothing I could offer that could match the dramatic hurly-burly personal odyssey she had just described. I was living in the same house, with the same partner, the same priorities, doing a very similar job. The last psychedelic mushrooms I saw were on an episode of *The Magic Roundabout*. It wasn't that nothing had changed – a lot had happened to me, too. But none of the fundamentals were different since she'd last seen me. She was depicting a new landscape. I would have been describing a tree that was ten years older than the last time you saw it. Bigger, stronger, weathered some storms . . . but same tree.

Does this make me boring? The part of me that still loves the makeover movies I grew up on (from *Calamity Jane* to *Legally Blonde* via *Grease* and *Thoroughly Modern Millie*) thinks so. The drama of the Damascene conversion is appealing; the idea of transformation romantic. Even so, I know that, when it comes down to it, drastic changes aren't my style. Literally – I've been wearing different iterations of the same ten items of clothing since I was fourteen (I prefer to see this as consistency, rather than a lack of imagination).

Not only that, everything I've ever done that worked started small, from this piece you're reading right now (which developed out of a conversation about a website over a cup of coffee with Sam Baker) to my family set-up (technically, the product of a fling with a colleague that seems to have lasted fifteen years). I've always preferred evolution to revolution – the small changes that can dramatically alter our lives.

I'm quite sure that the best small change I ever made was deciding to start doing things one at a time. These days, productivity experts call this 'single-tasking' and it's an approach that has been proven to reduce stress, increase productivity, improve focus and decision-making and even help keep your brain healthy.

Ten years ago, however, when I first began to attempt to juggle a busy work life and a young family, 'multitasking' was the watchword. It was, people said, the modern way to have it all, get everything done and (what a lucky break for a lady with too much to do!) women were supposed to be naturals. So, I dutifully dived headfirst into the new, confusing, Sisyphean list of tasks each day brought.

I did as much as I could, the best I could, for as long as I could, then slept for a minuscule amount of time before being woken up by a tiny child dressed as Lord Voldemort, standing silently at the bottom of my bed. This went on for about five years and was absolutely successful in that everyone remained alive, I remained employed, the washing got done and life went on. It was, however, absolutely exhausting and eventually – towards the end of 2012, after a horrible bout of shingles and the realisation that I was so busy all the time I hadn't looked out of a window for about a year – I'd had enough. I was stressed, overworked and exhausted. I loved all of the things in my life, but I had to find a new way to fit them together, or I was going to lose it completely.

It was my mam who suggested single-tasking. She didn't call it that, of course. She just told me that in her hectic thirties (that time of life another friend of mine memorably described as 'when everything in your life just feels like it's on fucking fire'), she learnt to cope by forcing herself to focus on the task at hand, to the exclusion of everything else. So, no working at home, no homing at work. Choose what the moment is, then be in it.

This life-saving advice came at the perfect time, because I needed it to help me with the phase my own life was in, but also because, by then, the age of digital distraction was really kicking in. For the first time, it was normal to have numerous communication streams – social media, text, email – going at once. Multi-screening was now a thing (why watch TV if you're not also tweeting about it?). Everyone was recording and broadcasting every moment. Among my peers, the expectation was that you should suck up news like a Hoover, before issuing opinions on everything with all the consideration and tact of a leaf blower.

While these digital pile-ons could be fun, more often they were stressful, distracting and obstructive to what I actually needed to do. I decided to make doing one thing at a time my (lone) New Year's resolution. It's one of the few I have stuck to and I've never regretted it.

I get more work done in less time, and have got better at managing my time and prioritising the things I need to do. My focus improved and kept improving (like anything else, single-tasking gets easier with practice). Of course, I'm not perfect. When events crowd in on me and I'm stressed, I still catch myself flapping around and trying to do everything at once and accomplishing nothing at all. The good thing is I'm better placed to deal with those moments when they come around. I know I need to stop (collaborate and listen), prioritise, work out a plan and stick to it. I also make sure I block in time to mess about, browse and chat to friends online. I still love doing that stuff – I just want it to be an elective activity, rather than my default setting. Similarly, I make sure I have space to do switch off and do nothing, which I'm absolutely convinced helps me get more done in the long run – that old adage about how you eat an elephant turns out to be true after all.

Dear Millennials . . . This is what employers really mean when they say they want a 'grafter'

AN ARTS CAFE TARGETED MILLENNIALS IN A RAGE-INDUCING JOB AD

BY CAROLINE O'DONOGHUE

When I was younger, greener, and earning just under £18,000 a year, I had a boss that asked me to do a spreadsheet. Not just any spreadsheet, mind. This was a spreadsheet detailing the tea and coffee preferences of everyone who worked in the office, to be stuck up in the staff kitchen. I did it, and at the end of the day, I found myself at the wrong end of a conversation about The Problem With Young People.

'You see this,' he said, pointing at my spreadsheet, where 'HENRY – 2 SUGARS' was curling under his finger. 'This is what is wrong with your generation.'

He set me a task, he said, which I completed. His problem, however, was that I didn't 'throw' myself into it – I made a list, but I wholeheartedly failed to do anything 'interesting with the colours or the fonts'.

'It's all about going above and beyond what is being asked of you,' my boss explained.

I don't think this kind of thing is uncommon. Hell, maybe you're an employer reading this right now and thinking: well, why didn't you give everyone's name a different font? Show a little pizzazz, for God's sake.

Maybe you even agree with the people at arts cafe Tea House Theatre, who, after having a series of short-lived 'millennial' employees, posted the following job ad on the Arts Council website. The ad, which started with a mighty 'Dear Millennials', questioned if young people 'are taught anything about . . . the real world' and lamented that 'it shouldn't be this hard' to find a 'grafter, who can commit' to do a full-time job worth £15–20k per year.

Everything about this makes me want to scratch my own skin off, and apparently, I'm not alone. The job advert has touched a nerve with job-hunters and millennials alike. Twitter is thick with 'er, excuse me?' reactions, as well as stories from people who have worked or have interviewed at the Tea House Theatre, and are just as unimpressed with the hiring staff as the hiring staff are with the outside world.

This story has burrowed under my skin. Not because it's so outlandish and bizarre: but because it's so perfectly one-hundred-and-ten-per-cent believable. Here's the fact of it: in my experience employers – not all, but many – tend to treat anyone under twenty-five as though they're the human equivalent of anti-bacterial hand gel. Necessary, cost-effective, but slightly distasteful to deal with. There's a long-held belief that if you want a 'start' or a 'leg-up' in any career – particularly if that career is arts-adjacent – you have to be a 'grafter' who 'can commit'.

'Grafter' is possibly the word that irritates me the most here. 'Grafter' is part of a lexicon of words people use to talk about work that is intended to shame anyone who gets ideas above their station (by, say, asking for a pay rise, or leaving on time at 6pm) and to soothe anyone who stays in their place. 'Grafter' is used as a weird, backhanded compliment in the work place, and when I worked in recruitment, it was a word I heard a lot. When someone is looking for 'a real grafter', it means they are looking for someone peppy, preferably young, and willing to do more work than they are being paid to do. Grafters are perpetually grateful for any job, of any size, and always smile when they do it. Grafters are basically the shoemaker elves of the employment world, in that they are rarely seen, but you just missed one, ten minutes ago. Oh, you didn't see her? Our last girl was a real grafter. Unlike . . . well, you.

(See also: 'all-rounder', 'willing to get her hands dirty' or someone who is 'willing to make the job their own'. Young readers, please note, if someone would like you to 'make the job your own', it means that you will be expected to sleep under the copier.)

And maybe the language of the grafter made sense a few years ago. Maybe asking someone to dedicate their days, nights, hearts and souls to a lowly paid job was fine when you could promise a clear career trajectory, a benefits package and a gold watch on retirement. But that's not the kind of deal on the table for the much-loathed 'millennial' worker, and so there's no reason for them to give it. It's something for nothing. Or rather: it's everything you are in exchange for £15k at an arts cafe.

When someone fails to be a grafter, they become part of The Problem With Young People. The problem with young people is that they're all bone idle. Or, the problem with young people is they expect too much. The problem with young people, according to one twenty-seven-year-old business owner I recently interviewed, is that they want a 'free roast dinner for lunch every day'.

The funny thing here is that places like Tea House Theatre – and I honestly don't think the arts cafe is unique here, merely expressing publicly what many employers already say privately – will lambast young people while still insisting that only a young person could do the job that they're advertising. The ad reminds us that 'one old lady used to run the whole of Mountview Academy with an IBM computer, it shouldn't be this hard', but fails to recognise that the old lady probably had decades of experience before going to Mountview in the first place. There's two assumptions here, and both of them are nasty: one, that a twenty-something fresh from university should know exactly how an office environments works, and two, that an 'old lady' is somehow the least impressive species of employee.

It's gross, lazy ageism, and it cuts both ways: we're not going to pay enough to employ an older person with actual experience in office admin, but we're not going to take the time to train a young person to do a job they are not yet qualified to do.

No, we're just going to take aim at millennials. We're just going to bitch.

Maternity leave: the reality versus the expectations

NO, YOU WON'T FINALLY WRITE THAT BOOK . . . THE TUMULT OF CHILDBIRTH, THE RELENTLESSNESS OF PARENTING AND THE LACK OF SLEEP WILL DOMINATE MATERNITY LEAVE

BY ROBYN WILDER

Breastfeeding picturesquely in a stripped-pine rocking chair. Long, serene walks with the baby on Hampstead Heath. To say my expectations of maternity leave were unrealistic would be an understatement, especially since using my rocking chair is like sitting on kindling, and it'd take me nineteen-and-a-half hours to walk to Hampstead Heath from my house. But, when I got pregnant in 2014, I didn't know any better. None of my friends had babies and I fell between NCT catchment areas, so all my points of reference were clichés. Essentially, I thought it was a slightly more maternal version of annual leave. I expected to spend it looking radiant. 'Hey, maybe I'll even have time to write that book,' I thought.

The first hurdle to my dreamy maternity idyll was that I only qualified for statutory maternity pay, though. For me, this worked out as 90 per cent of my pay for six weeks, then £139.58 for thirty-three weeks, then nothing. My husband doesn't earn the big bucks as a journalist so, in the months leading up to the birth, I developed A Realistic Plan.

First, I'd work right up until my waters broke (I was on staff at BuzzFeed, so I was relying on being captured on camera so that I and my flowering uterus could be catapulted to international fame as a lucrative meme). Next, I'd have the baby, look after the baby, move out of London, no big deal. Finally, I'd return to work the second my maternity pay dropped off, six weeks later. I mean, it'd be tight, but people did it. It was just a baby. How hard could it be?

Shockingly, it turned out that this plan was as farfetched as the rocking-chair one. At six months pregnant, a series of pregnancy illnesses took hold, forcing me to take maternity leave early. By the time my son, Herbie, arrived – traumatically, and with a Kent postcode – the bulk of the pay was gone, and now there were three of us.

Which is how, ten weeks after giving birth, I found myself filing my first piece for this website, sobbing, at 3am. I'd discovered, you see, that you can freelance to subsidise your maternity pay, so my new money-making plan was to take the full fifty-two weeks' maternity leave and freelance throughout.

But, oh, it was hard. I live hours away from my friends, I don't have many family members who can help out and Herbie wouldn't sleep alone, so I'd basically work whenever my husband could take him, while he napped on me, and through the night when I should have been asleep myself. Plus, the tumult of childbirth, the relentlessness of parenting, the lack of sleep and the insidiousness of postnatal depression had turned my brain to mulch, and writing – which is, after all, my livelihood – was (and still often is) like dragging cats out of a lake. Each commission would take me three all-nighters and a total meltdown to complete. And, though the money was rolling in slowly, I was pretty much hallucinating with tiredness.

Until, suddenly, it actually began to work. I found we could scrape together enough to pay a nanny to take Herbie during a couple of mornings a week while I worked.

Conversely, the idea of returning to work felt increasingly unnatural. Almost twelve months of motherhood had blurred together and it seemed that we'd only left hospital a day ago. The prospect of spending ten hours a day away from Herbie felt biologically offensive to me somehow, as though our umbilical cord was still invisibly attached. So, in the end, I quit my job and turned freelance.

Of course, this isn't everyone's maternity-leave experience. Tillie Newnham, a learning and development trainer, found herself pinched during her maternity leave, despite saving for it, and planning not to return to work after having her first child, when an unexpected redundancy and an unwell husband drove her back into employment just four months after giving birth: 'Going to job interviews and trying to convince employers you are motivated to leave your baby at home is not easy,' she tells me. 'I landed a part-time role when my daughter was six months old. I cried most days driving to work.

'I tried expressing at work in a meeting room with paper taped over the window, but it just felt too uncomfortable, especially being the new person. Struggling to find a balance was so exhausting that I ended up having a very serious accident which put me in hospital. As I hadn't passed probation, I wasn't entitled to sick pay, so my pay was even lower.'

Things are better now, says Tillie: 'I adore my business. My colleagues are supportive, understanding and encouraging.'

'But,' she adds. 'I find it scandalous that the government is urging businesses to pay employees a living wage, yet statutory maternity pay is nowhere near the living wage.'

So, here I am now, writing this at my kitchen table while my family sleeps upstairs, and it feels like the right choice.

None of this is what I expected of maternity leave when I stroked my pregnant belly and dreamed of being Katherine Heigl. But then maternity leave isn't really leave, is it? It's a chrysalis. And when you emerge, you are a different person.

Is Lean In still relevant five years later?

WHEN SHERYL SANDBERG'S MANIFESTO WAS
PUBLISHED IN 2013, IT BECAME A GLOBAL HIT.
HARRIET MINTER EXPLORES ITS RELEVANCE
IN A POST-#METOO WORLD

BY HARRIET MINTER

About five years ago, I sat in a Tube carriage on my way to work and counted three women reading the same book, *Lean In*. What had started out as a TED talk encouraging women to 'sit at the table' in business meetings had ended up as a bestseller, a worldwide network and a launch-pad to fame for the speaker, Sheryl Sandberg. It came just after the UK government announced a review into the number of women sitting at board level and while everyone was speculating whether Hillary Clinton would be the first female president. For me, at the time an aggressively ambitious middle manager in a team dominated by men, it felt like the first time that someone had pointed out that the world of work might not be an entirely equal playing field.

It's easy to write off *Lean In* in today's world. When it was first published, its critics pointed out that it completely failed to cater for any woman who couldn't afford or didn't want full-time childcare, that it taught women how to survive in a structure that was built for men, rather than how to change that structure, and that it never stopped to question whether this alpha-male, uber-capitalist description of success was really what we all wanted. I remember discussing it with friends over dinner one night and one of them pointing out what she saw as a major flaw in the text: the book dealt with work and with family, but there was no mention of a life beyond those things.

'When does she just go for pizza with her mates?' my friend asked. 'It all seems awfully tiring and not really a lot of fun.'

I can confirm, in fact, that life at Sandberg's pace is definitely hard work. A few years after *Lean In* had come out, I invited her to take part in a live Q&A at the *Guardian*, where I was then working. She accepted and what had been a small, intimate event suddenly spiralled to a full-scale production. Each morning, I would wake up to a long list of questions from her team – could I tell them the exact size of the car lift in our building, because they needed to make sure it matched with the dimensions of the people carrier she would be arriving in? Could I let them know what the changing rooms were like, how much space would she have? She'd like to have turkey salad sandwiches to eat before the event – please ensure it's turkey not chicken.

I tell this not to suggest that she's hitting Mariah Carey levels of divadom for having a favourite sandwich filling (although why would you go with turkey over chicken?) but to explain why *Lean In* feels as though it was written for a different world – it was. For most of us, that will never be reality, but it was for Sandberg and it was the aspiration for the women she was writing for. Because, the most troubling aspect about *Lean In* – the one that even when I first read it I couldn't quite get over – was that it seemed to require women to be the ones who did all the work in order to finally get to a place where someone else ordered your sandwich for you. Women had to flex to fit the male structure, women had to explain why they worked differently if they wanted their boss to understand them, women had to *Lean In* merely to be seen at the table they'd pushed forward to sit at. What were the men doing during all of this?

When I ran that event with Sandberg, the date turned out to be her wedding anniversary. Her husband was still alive and he'd flown over to be with her on the day, even if she still had to work. During the audience Q&A section, somebody asked him how much of the household admin he did and how much she did. He estimated it was still 60 per cent to her. Even the woman pushing for gender equality at work couldn't get her husband to sort out parents' evening. It was a clear sign that *Lean In*, while a career manual for women, was definitely not a life manual for men. It left everyone in the room questioning whether that was really good enough – we know now that it wasn't.

Today, women aren't pushing to sit at the table – they're standing on the table, waving placards and shouting to be heard. #MeToo can often feel like a reaction to *Lean In*, a rebellion against the head girl who so desperately wanted us all to succeed, but by following the rules, not by breaking them. The problem was that *Lean In* started a debate that it could never win.

Sandberg being the most famous woman in tech didn't challenge the boys' club culture, it didn't encourage culture change in those laddish start-ups and it certainly didn't help women get the same level of support and funding that the guys did. *Lean In* encouraged men to support women, but it failed to ask them to take a good, long look at their own behaviour. And, in the end, those women who Sandberg had urged to stand up and be heard got tired of shouting into the void. They got tired of reading books about how to negotiate better, how to ask for more, how to play the political game. They got tired of being told they weren't good enough as they were, so they did the only thing left to do: rather than sitting at the table, they upturned it, burned it and danced on its ashes.

Is *Lean In* still relevant five years later? I'd argue yes. It's relevant because it shows all of us clearly exactly how the power structure is set up to support men and discourage women. It's relevant because it challenges us all to take action in our own lives and not settle for less than we're worth. And it's relevant because it started a discussion about women and work without which I'm not sure we'd be where we are today. But it also didn't go far enough. It didn't challenge the status quo – it expected women to be the ones to change and it told us that success was still entirely dependent on what we achieved at work.

The heartbreaking reality of pregnancy and maternity discrimination

AS NEW GOVERNMENT FIGURES REVEAL AN INCREASE IN DISCRIMINATION, WOMEN ANONYMOUSLY SHARE THEIR STORIES WITH *THE POOL*

BY MARISA BATE

When we put out a call for women to share their stories of discrimination *The Pool* was inundated. Here are just a few, but ones that articulate common themes that cropped up again and again. For advice, visit Pregnant Then Screwed, a pressure group working to help pregnant women and new mums who are facing discrimination.

'WOULD YOU SAY YOU WERE THE . . . ER . . . MATERNAL TYPE?'

I had a good relationship with my MD; I enjoyed my job and I'd been promoted or given pay rises every six months during my four years there, so was fairly senior by the time I announced my pregnancy. He was visibly shocked and said awkwardly, 'Would you say you were the . . . er . . . maternal type?'

To be fair, no I really wasn't. I had every intention of coming back to work full-time post-baby, and told him so. It was a small company and I was aware that I'd only be entitled to statutory maternity pay, but he privately told me that he'd work some kind of special package out for me as long as I kept it quiet. The agency was 90 per cent women aged twenty-three to thirty-five and he was unwilling to 'set a precedent', he said.

Throughout my pregnancy I tried to pin him down as to what this package might be, but he was evasive, saying he needed to speak to his lawyer – the atmosphere between us had grown increasingly hostile. Eventually he told me he'd decided I wasn't in need of extra pay as my partner had a highly paid job in finance and I'd just bought a big house. Also, I'd probably want to have another child anyway and obviously wouldn't want to work by then. I'm embarrassed to say that I didn't pick him up on any of this; partly because I was so shocked but also because I was actually still keen to carve out some kind of deal. Plus, we had no HR.

No 'deal' ever materialised and I was stuck on £500 a month, so was keen to return to work and reclaim my salary after the baby. Unfortunately, this proved even more difficult as he refused to let me work flexibly from home (despite others in the agency doing so) and eventually I gave up. I considered taking him to court, but I just wanted to move on. I now freelance from home and am much happier doing so, but I still feel furious about how difficult he made things.

I CAN'T PROVE ANYTHING . . . BUT I KNOW I'M BEING PUSHED ASIDE

I've always had a good working relationship with my boss. She pushed me forwards in my role and I always felt that I had a champion in her. Everything has changed since I got pregnant.

I told her really early on in my pregnancy because I didn't want to mislead as an opportunity for progression was in the works. So when I found out at four weeks pregnant, I pretty much told her straight away.

Everything seemed fine at the time and my job role progressed as expected despite the pregnancy.

However as time has gone on, things have changed. She has started to nit-pick at things and micro manage me whereas in the past she always trusted me and left me to it. She undermines decisions I make as a manager; for example, while on leave she changed what I had asked my team to do in my absence. She has taken duties off me and given my work laptop to another member of staff (months before my mat leave), and now I am unable to work from home when I need to. She has made comments that my pregnancy has 'gone on forever' and that she did not expect me to have children at this time, as she didn't know that was in my plans.

While I was off sick a major decision was made which affects my job and nobody told me. I found out third-hand from a colleague and had to enquire directly with HR myself to confirm. My boss has still not told me herself.

Everything I do is questioned and a lot is done via email or text, never face to-face. My return to work after being off went fine and all of my supervisions are standard stuff. When things need to be 'by the book' they are followed through in a standard way.

At first I thought I was being paranoid and put it down to hormones. But when my husband and friends saw the messages and emails they agreed that she was being difficult.

It's made me really down as I can't prove anything and they've not done anything illegal. I just feel as though I'm being deliberately pushed aside. I know they can't fire me or discriminate against me but I'm being made to feel like I'm not wanted there.

I have a short time to go until my mat leave and I'm working up to close to my due date to help them with cover. I'm exhausted by the whole situation and dread what my position there will be after baby arrives.

'SHE'LL BE OFF HAVING BABIES'

This isn't actually my story, but when I worked at a local authority, we were interviewing for a new officer in the department and it was basically between one man and one woman. Both scored exactly the same in the interview, both had great references etc., there was nothing to separate them. Both were mid-to late twenties.

I overheard my manager, who is female in her mid-thirties, say 'Well obviously we've got to go with him, because she'll be off having babies within a year.' It was passed off as a joke when I expressed my shock, but sure enough, they went with the man.

I MISSED OUT ON THE PAY RISE AND THE BONUS

I had a horrendous boss, who bullied and belittled me throughout my pregnancy. When I told him I was pregnant, the first thing he said was 'Maternity is such a pain for business'. During my pregnancy he told me I was 'pregnant not ill' when I was in the throes of morning sickness; he told me that his wife (who had recently given birth) had 'sailed through her pregnancy'. I gave birth six weeks prematurely, a fact not unrelated to the stress I was under at work, and when I called to say the baby had arrived he asked me if I had 'got my dates wrong'. We had discussed a pay rise prior to my pregnancy which never materialised and I also missed out on the bonus related to the year I had worked prior to delivering my child. He has now been promoted within the company. I received a pay rise within weeks of my new boss arriving. I'm now pregnant with my second child and am concerned about how this will stagnate my financial progression.

I'M NOT ON ANYONE'S STATISTICS . . . THESE GOVERNMENT STATS MUST ONLY BE THE TIP OF THE ICEBERG

I worked in one of those enviable creative industry jobs that people intern and volunteer for years to get. I'd done my time and finally had my salaried position.

It was promoted as very family friendly, as our audience was made up of that demographic, but like most venues like ours, the economic downturn and a Tory government had taken its toll. We worked on a shoe-string and staff went above and beyond our paid hours.

When I found out I was pregnant I knew I wouldn't be able to come back full-time. To be honest, it didn't even make much sense to come back part-time. Nearly all my salary went on childcare, but as a family we reasoned that even if that was the case for a few years, I'd worked too long and hard to finally crack into the industry. That a break in employment would be to damaging in the long term.

The organisation did everything that was legally required. The trouble began when I came to return. The return to work meeting was dreadful. They offered me (at same job title and salary) another role in the department that was much junior. They knew the days of me working a twelve-hour day were over. Then they packaged up this new role with, 'it will be great because you won't have to think'.

When I returned to work I told myself that it was some sort of maternal rite of passage to cry in the toilets every day. Looking back now I can see it wasn't me, it was bullying.

While on mat leave they advertised a job that looked startlingly like my own. It had a slightly more senior job title and a tiny wage increase. I queried it and they encouraged me to apply. But didn't answer my question of how my role would fit alongside this new one.

I didn't get it.

Upon my return they informed me that there were departmental changes and my current role wasn't needed anymore.

They operated with guidance from HR and offered me a new role. But now they wanted me to work weekends, where previously I had been Monday to Friday. It was totally impossible for me to get childcare then.

I spoke to friends and took advice, but I was so utterly heart-broken that every time I spoke to anybody it was through embarrassing big, snotty sobs.

They all firmly encouraged me to take it further legally, but I felt so utterly defeated. I wasn't sleeping, I had two pre-schoolers at home. The thought of taking on another battle was something I couldn't face. And then I would think on how I was letting the sisterhood down. Cue more tears.

I'm not on anyone's statistics. It's not logged anywhere what happened to me. These government stats must only be the tip of the iceberg. How many other women, like me, couldn't face the fight when we were entering such a difficult new season in our lives?

Friendship

LAUREN LAVERNE | MARISA BATE
LYNN ENRIGHT | VIV GROSKOP
SALI HUGHES

The six types of friends you don't need

REFLECTIONS ON THE 'BAD FRIEND'. HOW TO AVOID HER. AND HOW TO AVOID BECOMING HER

BY LAUREN LAVERNE

Can I start this by saying I love my friends? Good friends are like clothes. Technically speaking, you can survive without them, but life would be very cold, very strange and a lot less fun. When everything else is going wrong, a night out with my closest female friends makes the world feel the right way up again. I value them beyond price, and count myself lucky to have fallen (platonically) for each and every one. As Albert Einstein put it, 'However rare true love may be, it is less so than true friendship.'

Having said that, it would be wrong to pretend that the road to true friendship always runs smoothly. Like any relationship, being a good mate takes commitment, empathy and care from both parties. Sometimes, though, it doesn't work out that way. Things can turn sour. And, while it often takes a lot longer to realise a friendship is dysfunctional than it would a love affair, being trapped in a bad friendship can be just as damaging. So I'm listing my deal breakers – the unacceptable behaviour that indicates a friendship might be on the rocks. Everyone is entitled to mess up now and again, of course (I'm with Doris Lessing on that: 'Trust no friend without faults, and love a woman, but no angel') but, when bad behaviour becomes habitual, I reserve the right to move on. These archetypes represent friends I wouldn't want to have, or to be.

①

THE PASS/AGG DRAG

Passive aggression is like a carbon monoxide leak – chronically poisonous, but a bugger to detect. It's quite easy to accidentally become friends with someone who is an expert at this type of indirect hostility – they seem OK on the surface but, pretty soon, life with them is one long exhausting headfuck sigh-fest. Though she doesn't have much to moan about, this friend has somehow become a joy-Hoover. Negative, sullen, occasionally catty (a specialist in critical 'jokes' that aren't really jokes), she is adept at making you feel inexplicably responsible for her misery and guilty about any happiness you may experience. Avoid.

(2)

THE HAIRDRYER

What's one of the most important ingredients in a good pal? Do you know the easiest way to make connections in the first place? Which ingredient is the most important for an interesting life? Curiosity, of course! See what I did there with all those questions? You'd be amazed how many people never ask questions. Ever. So it is with the hairdryer, whose only setting is 'out'. Of fulsome ego, they can be funny and charming, which can go a long way to make up for their lack of interest in your life. But, while it's great to be regaled with their adventures up to a point, finding yourself three hours into a dinner date during which you've barely spoken isn't so copacetic. Luckily, hairdryers are relatively easy to fix and naturally robust, so they won't take offence when you try to change their behaviour. If you want to salvage the relationship, take a gavel out with you and bang it every now and again, so that you get a chance to speak.

(3)

THE THROWBACK

This friend is set to #TBT ATT, and may need to GTFO. A good pal with whom you share a long history knows who you are, but The Throwback only knows who you were. She's stuck in the past and there's something uncomfortably controlling about her unwillingness to move on. Throwbacks enjoy bringing up old stories more than you do – indeed they may delight even more in dredging up memories that make you uncomfortable. Unwilling to change, they refuse to try new places or seek fresh experiences. Loyalty (yours) is a laudable quality, but remember: it isn't unconditional. As Alice Walker wrote, 'No person is your friend who demands your silence, or denies your right to grow'.

(4)

THE BOGOF (WHOSE PARTNER COMES EVERYWHERE)

Hooray for love! It's a beautiful thing, and even better when a pal's new squeeze can become a friend of yours. But, while I'm generally of the more-the-merrier persuasion when it comes to socialising, there is something disconcerting about couples who can't do anything separately. In the starry-eyed, first throes of love, this kind of behaviour is forgivable (if occasionally nauseating). When you find yourself two years down the line and having to explain to Sarah that no, actually, Barry can't come to your hen do, you know you've got yourself a BOGOF, and my deepest sympathies.

(5)

THE TAKER

As the saying goes, when you're up, your friends know who you are; when you're down, you know who your friends are. Takers are friends you're likely to meet when life is going well. They're out for what they can get and prepared to give as little as possible in exchange. When the chips are down, they're nowhere to be found but, when you're high on the hog, they're suddenly back in the picture, but their presence comes with strings attached. A close friend's Taker experience takes some beating – the lady in question was AWOL during her house move, pregnancy, birth, divorce and book deal. Then, when the book proved a huge hit, suddenly reappeared, asking my mate to lend some social-media support to her new 'hipster teapot' business. Reader, she didn't.

THE ONE WHO'S JUST BEING HONEST

They say honesty is the best policy, but they are idiots. What purpose are friends if not to cushion you against life's unyielding edges, to shield you from the harsh facts? This friend does neither; in fact, she does the opposite – making a virtue of her tactlessness, she seemingly takes pleasure in her lack of care over the feelings of others. I take a strong position on this behaviour. 'Just being honest' is an asshole's get-out-of-jail-free card, but only for people too stupid to realise that anybody can tell the truth – real friends know when it's kinder to lie.

A letter to my friend: you are experiencing emotional abuse

AS THE COERCIVE-CONTROL OFFENCE LOOKS SET TO COME INTO ACTION SOON, MARISA BATE TELLS A FRIEND SHE'S NOT ON HER OWN

BY MARISA BATE

It started two summers ago. We met for drinks on a warm, sunny Saturday afternoon. You looked different. I couldn't quite put my finger on it. It was you, beautiful you. But the glow from that wide grin was ever so slightly dimmer. The mischievous glint in your eye was slightly harder to spot. We drank and chatted.

The next time I saw you, we went to a fancy pop-up restaurant with friends. Where had your body gone? That tiny waist. Those elegant shoulder blades. Your body was hidden in a curtain of beige drapes. No trace of your signature red lips. And why weren't you drinking?

I met with a mutual friend and mentioned that your clothes had changed. They'd become more middle-aged than mid-thirties. Am I overreacting, I asked. 'Hmm, maybe. You know she likes things not too tight.'

And then came the arguments. What was it about this time? It didn't really matter. It was always your fault, according to him. You deliberately scraped the new wardrobe on the bedroom walls when you were moving it in. You purposely spilt water on his iPad. You absolutely, intentionally lost his bike light. You were stupid and careless and arrogant. You were probably drunk. You didn't care and you certainly didn't care about him. So you apologised.

I'd speak to more friends. 'All couples fight', they'd tell me. 'Haven't you seen how well they get on? He's so charming.' They'd look bemused; I came across as paranoid, maybe even jealous.

And there was – on the surface – plenty to be jealous of. Friendly, smart, smiley, good-looking. You now have a beautiful puppy and a beautiful flat. He's a lawyer. He knows about Things. He's smarter than you. He's smarter than everyone. He knows best. On paper, he was perfect. Think of the life you could have with a man like that. His charm was like a jagged piece of metal in the sun: the reflection was blinding and distracting.

It was summer again. This time, it was a Sunday morning. Our bikes locked up, coffee and newspapers. There's been another argument, you'd finally admit. He did what? He threw the contents of your handbag into the street.

We met last week. He'd done the same again except, this time, he threw a cold cup of tea in your face, too.

You know all of these events. You know them – and the others you haven't told me – far better than I do. You've probably replayed them in your mind over and over and over. But what you don't seem to know is that this is emotional abuse. This is the cruellest form of abuse – the blink-and-you'll-miss-it abuse. This is the abuse that is *almost* invisible (no wonder he scrubbed the walls clean of the cold tea. Other people could see that). So almost invisible that you're not sure if it's even actually happening. And, with a wry smile, a bunch of flowers and a slight retelling of events, he'll erase it entirely.

But it *is* happening. The textbook hallmarks are there, scarring and staining, far worse than the tea: controlling, jealous, gaslighting, degrading, mocking. I'd add 'isolating you from friends', but I simply won't let that one happen.

The House of Lords introduced the new offence of coercive and controlling behaviour in late 2017, put forward by the then-home secretary, Theresa May. Quite how they intend to police this, let alone prosecute anyone, especially as our authorities so inadequately respond to domestic violence cases as it is, remains a bit of a mystery. But this is a step forward. Because this invisible abuse, that no one else can see, hidden behind the bravado of a charming man, buried under layers of crushed self-esteem and fear and a sense of failure and humiliation – this kind of abuse has finally been recognised in the eyes of the law, not just worried friends and family.

Part of the nature of the abuse is the doubt that it's even happening. It permeates the silence, the feeling that somehow you've caused it or provoked it, that you're doing something wrong. I want you to know that what is happening is very real. You don't need a bruise or a hospital visit. And I don't mean to be facetious when I say, if this continues, that will come next.

I can only love and support you, believe you and help you. I can't quite dispel his myth yet – overwrite the hope and the promise he still presents to you. I feel like you are in the middle of an Indiana Jones-esque rickety rope bridge, high over a rushing river. He's behind you, coaxing you back with guilt and manipulation. I'm in front of you, arms stretched out, telling you to be brave. I won't give up on you. Don't give up on yourself.

Mourning the loss of intense female friendships

LYNN ENRIGHT SPENT HER TWENTIES IN INTENSE FEMALE FRIENDSHIPS, PASSING WHOLE WEEKENDS WITH THE WOMEN SHE LOVED MOST. ALL THAT CHANGED ONCE SHE TURNED THIRTY

BY LYNN ENRIGHT

For me, one of the most notable features of ageing is how predictable it is – how utterly unremarkable; how I age exactly the same way as everyone else.

When I was younger, I was quite convinced that I was unique, special, one of a kind, but now, aged thirty-two, I realise I'm just a very slight variation on all the others. I age reliably, hitting foreseen markers like all those other thirty-two-year-olds. It's all exactly like they said it would be: most Topshop stuff looks ridiculous on me; I'm very interested in soft furnishings; I worry about dying more frequently than I used to; I'm a little bit richer and fatter than I was in my twenties; my garlic press is impressively efficient; I only rarely get messily drunk.

Oh, and I also don't have as many intense best friendships as I did in my teens and twenties.

I thought that one was just me – I'd felt sort of simultaneously embarrassed and forlorn about my shrinking friends list, worrying that it was a personal failing, but it turns out that having no friends is just another predictable side effect of getting older. Last week, *nymag.com* even published an article headlined, 'Science Assures it's Fine to Have Fewer Friends In Your 30s'.

So, it's not just me, I thought, a little relieved – it's an age thing. Then I wondered which of my friends I could share the piece with, but, like I said, I don't have very many friends these days, so I emailed it to my boyfriend.

My boyfriend, I suppose, is one of the main reasons I'm feeling so friendless. We moved in together in May, which has been mainly lovely, but when I signed a lease with him, I left a flatshare I had been really happy in for two years or so. I'd lived with a very nice guy (often out, he worked in the evenings) and another woman in her early thirties, and although we hadn't known each other before we lived together, she became a good friend.

We'd potter round the house a couple of evenings a week, talking about our work and our worries and our lives – about our relationships with other friends and with men, about ageing, about politics, about the countries we'd left to set up lives in London, about our mums, about everything really. We'd sit in pyjamas, watching *Game of Thrones*, the intimacy easy and the chat soothing and restorative.

Now, when I want to see her, which I often do, I have to consult a diary, email her and arrange to meet her for brunch somewhere. And brunch is nice, of course, but I'm sad that we're never going to shoot the breeze in our pyjamas again.

If all goes well with my boyfriend and we do all the next steps like people do, I might never chat and laugh and cry with another woman while we both wear pyjamas ever again. When I was in my twenties, I wore my pyjamas around my best friends all the time. We often went the whole hog and slept in the same bed.

There was the friend who always fell asleep before I did, while I was mid-midnight anecdote. She lives in Los Angeles now and just got engaged. We said we were going to Skype recently, but we didn't. I last saw her more than two years ago, because flights to and from LA are very expensive. And that expense is something I used to prioritise when I was single and didn't spend my money on kitchen utensils. But somehow it's like I've grown out of dropping a grand to fly to the other side of the world to see a friend.

There was the friend with whom I could easily share a single bed; after years of practice, our bodies slotting into each other perfectly, our ease with each other allowing us to sleep top and tail, feet in faces. She and I seem to have fallen out, a decade of suspicious competition and complicated admiration for each other finally petering out into something fractious and awkward.

Another friend usually used the right-hand side of her bed for storage but would shift her clothes and books and magazines to the floor when I came to visit. Now, I see her as often as we can manage, which, because we live in different countries, is about twice a year. There's the very, very best friend whom I still see at least once a fortnight, but haven't slept alongside since around the time of my thirtieth birthday.

My twenties were defined by those close female friendships; yes, I had relationships and I was building a career but, like the characters in Greta Gerwig's *Frances Ha* and Edna O'Brien's *The Country Girls*, I was mainly made up of the friends I surrounded myself with. And, like the characters in those stories, it became impossible to sustain the giddy intensity of those friendships, as age and its boring side effects bore down.

There has only been one falling out (and even that one hasn't been particularly dramatic, and might be mended yet), but having a job with greater responsibility, and a relationship that I hope to make last forever, has meant that my priorities shifted and friendship – once the most important aspect of my life – now sits lower on my list, occupying a snatched Sunday morning, rather than an entire weekend.

I could try shifting it up, and I do make efforts to see my friends as often as I can, but to get 'friendship' to number one seems impossible, going against the well-tread march of ageing.

Nora Ephron once said, 'Oh, how I regret not having worn a bikini for the entire year I was 26. If anyone young is reading this, go, right this minute, put on a bikini, and don't take it off until you're 34.'

Well, if anyone young is reading this, go and hang out with your friends this weekend. In your bikini or in your pyjamas. You won't live in a houseshare forever and you won't fit in a bed, snug like two little worms, forever. So, embrace the decade that prioritises friendship while it lasts. And embrace your friends. Soon enough, you'll be emailing your boyfriend about not having any.

When did all my friends get too busy to see me?

YES, IT'S AN URBAN CLICHÉ – BUT ARRANGING TO
GO FOR A DRINK WITH A FRIEND SUDDENLY FEELS
LIKE A LOGISTICAL IMPOSSIBILITY

BY MARISA BATE

I have arrived at the place I swore I never would, standing on the platform of a station I promised myself I'd never get off at. And even though older friends warned me, and in recent years I've seen it starting to happen around me, I still didn't *really* believe it – I thought it was all an unnecessary charade. For years, I naively and confidently assumed that my life simply wouldn't fall into the same middle-class narrative that sounds like nails on a blackboard. But here I am. I have officially arrived at peak I'm-too-busy-to-see-you-until-October-2019.

Seeing friends has become a logistical minefield; arranging plans comes with all the agony of trying to park in central London. They are busy, I get it. They have jobs and lives and plans. But once I was intrinsic to those lives and plans. We saw each other because that's what we did. It was a given – pubs, brunches, coffee, walks, dinners. We were each other's lives.

Now I'm a bit older, that's all changed. For starters, often you're not just scheduling to see one person but two. Partners show up and add all sorts of chaos, claiming dates and weekends for events with people you've never even met. Your friends' partners have families and friends and needs, and they've basically friend-blocked you until August. Like trying to get Beyoncé tickets, you're left wondering, 'Damn, how did they get in there so quickly?'

And so you start to arrange dinner between six of you. Dates are thrown around like confetti – all hope and good meaning to begin with, but useless and discarded as it seems more and more likely you'll have to be content conducting this friendship on WhatsApp. Because everyone is booked up already. And when I think too hard on it, that actually becomes an unsettling notion. Everyone uses every bit of time they have and they fill it with something and I'm not sure why. Yes, it's hard to get balance. My friend called the other day to say she's been neglecting her fiancé, but how, she wondered out loud, could she make time for everyone equally – her friends, her family and her new business venture? But I also think, in our era of hyper-connectivity and hyper-loneliness, we have got collectively very nervous about empty spaces in diaries or time unallocated to a person or a plan.

Obviously, the arrival of children throws all this to the wind, but for those of us without, have we become scared of being by ourselves in a world that both makes us feel forever in a crowded lift but also always slightly outside of the conversation other people are having, watching lives from a filter, not ever really feeling in the centre of our own? I'm currently poring over the pages of a book called *Alone Time*. A *New York Times* journalist visits cities and examines the experience of doing so by herself. Apparently, more people are doing this than ever, but she still writes about it with a tone of fascination – as if it's an entirely alien project to not have plans with other people, to not have plans at all. Have we forgotten how to let time settle, as if dust in sunlight, and simply see where it falls?

And so now it's summer and friends have weddings and holidays and family visits, and I'm trying not to take it personally when my close friends give me a look of, 'Well, you should have booked earlier,' as if I was trying to rent a beach hut in Brighton on a bank holiday. My natural aversion to planning of any kind is increasingly problematic and means I resent the idea that I have to be on a waiting list – that life can't be about spontaneous decisions and last-minute texts and an openness to adventure that isn't compatible with weekend plans booked months and months in advance.

In many ways, I wish I lived in small place. Or, I wish it was like how it so often is on TV, where someone just pops by, knocks on the door, sees if you're in your house in that moment (and not available for brunch in ninety days' time via Doodle). I wish you could have someone over for a cup of tea or a glass of wine for an hour or so before they went on their way. Living in (south) London means that many friends live an hour away – and, anyway, they don't seem to have left any evening free just to pop by. The sound of the door knocking is always a worry – a local campaign group, religious group, someone trying to sell you something, never the potential of a friend 'just seeing if you were in'.

We fill up our lives like we fill up our homes with framed photographs and our Instagrams with filtered pictures – 'Look how full our lives are,' we try to tell one another. And we believe a full life is a happy one – people, experiences, connections. But what are we letting slip through the gaps? I don't resent friends for their busy lives, but I miss the way we used to let life lead us a bit more. Afternoons tipped over into evenings; dinners turned into discos; coffee became lunch. I miss the flow and surprise that free time allows to blossom. We're often told not to wish our lives away, but maybe we shouldn't plan them away, either.

Who is fanning the flames in your friendships?

FRIENDS AREN'T THERE TO BE FULL-TIME LIFE COACHES OR THERAPISTS. INSTEAD, FRIENDSHIP IS A TWO-WAY STREET WHERE YOU TAKE IT IN TURNS TO SUPPORT EACH OTHER

BY VIV GROSKOP

Will Smith may seem an unlikely guru (although I can think of worse and he is certainly more charismatic than David Icke). But in a series of online videos he revealed an extraordinarily zen and useful take on life. In one, he asks a question. Or, I should say, he gets away with asking a ridiculously earnest question by virtue of being Will Smith. The rest of us would feel very silly asking this question, but he can style it out: 'Who's fanning your flames?'

His argument is that it is not worth having anyone around you who is pissing on your bonfire. (I paraphrase.) Instead, we should all focus our energies on people who can help us keep the flame of self-belief burning bright. It sounds hippy, but we all know what he's talking about. Why invite people in to your life who are just going to rain on your parade? (The whole concept is very anti-water.)

On *The Pool*'s podcast 'Dear Viv', one of the questions we get asked the most is whether to cut ties with 'toxic friends'. I think this idea is closely related to this anxiety. It's really hard for us to avoid someone when we suddenly realise that person is running us down, making us feel horrible about ourselves and doing the opposite of 'fanning the flames'. After all, if they're really such a negative influence, why have we had them around all this time? But we all choose how to spend our time and choosing to spend our time with people who don't support us – let alone champion us – is an act of slow self-destruction.

There are, of course, limits to this. On the one hand, as Will suggests, you have got to have good people in your corner. On the other hand, our friends are not necessarily there on-call 24/7 to be our mentors, coaches, therapists and cheerleaders (although you should definitely get some people to play these roles in your life). Sometimes, we need to put up with friends who are having a bad time and can't be very helpful to us right now. In fact, they may need us to be helpful to them. That is what friendship is: a two-way street where you take it in turns to fan the flames.

Sometimes even excellent friends will behave – very occasionally – in a way that is borderline 'toxic'. None of us are perfect. And it's wrong to cut people out of your life for one mistake or just because they're not 'useful' to you anymore or because they don't appreciate just how amazingly you are 'crushing it' on social media. So, there's a fine line between cultivating positive, nurturing friendships – and putting up with people who, in the long term, drag you down and always take but never give back.

With all the focus on the new kind of 'friends' we've all made in the last ten years over social media, I think this is a useful distinction. In real life, people divide into those who make you feel warm and fuzzy even if you can't quite say why (cultivate these) and those you come away from feeling like there's something wrong with you even if you can't quite say why (avoid these). Likewise online. There are people who are generally supportive and happy. And people who only connect to put you down or big themselves up. It's just as important to be able to tell them apart as it is to work out which group – in the eyes of others – you fit into yourself. See you at Will Smith's house. Bring bellows, and definitely no water pistols.

The importance of maintaining a girl gang

SALI HUGHES RELIES ON HER FEMALE FRIENDS FOR PROFOUND TRUTHS AND RAUCOUS, LIFE-AFFIRMING LAUGHS

BY SALI HUGHES

Tomorrow, I'm off for Christmas lunch with the girls. When I say 'the girls', what I actually mean is a group of women, all of them very grown up, who get together on a quarterly basis to get blind drunk, moan about government and the difficulty in finding frocks with sleeves, then hatch upwards of four plans to change the world, all of which are forgotten by the time we fall through our respective front doors. Last month, another group of women travelled to my house from South Wales, Manchester, Leeds and London to laugh, dance, eat and drink to excess for three days, during which time, literally no subject was off limits – the filthier the better. Between Christmas and New Year I'll be brunching with yet another girl gang who meet every three months for fried eggs, bloody Marys and a giggling debrief of life since the last.

It's only in the last ten years or so that I've come to realise I need regular women-only company like I need food and lodging. There was a time when just the sound of a girls' night out in the street genuinely made me feel a bit frightened and anxious. A childhood of being bullied by a gang of mean girls almost certainly contributed to my tomboyishness, as did an upbringing surrounded entirely by brothers and a single dad. But also, I was less considered and considerate, consumed by pretty crap romantic relationships with men, and generally sought female friendships only with women who'd also run a mile from a hen night. But somewhere around my late twenties, something shifted. Big changes were happening in my life – marriage, children, an acceleration of my career – and I needed the shared experience, insight, empathy and counsel of other women to make sense of the madness

Nowadays, I can't imagine life without the scaffolding of female friendship groups. If someone's toddler won't sleep, someone in our gang can provide personal assurances that everything will become dramatically better in precisely eighteen months. If another is having husband trouble, we've about 110 years' of combined relationship lessons on which to draw. When one of our own is enduring job trauma, we rally to remind her how completely ace she is. But crucially, there's much more than unanimous encouragement.

A highly important function of female friendship groups is to step in when someone is either in the process of, or about to make, a really bad decision. It's a firm but kind and caring intervention, in which women who want only the best for one another sit you down and say 'Delete the tweet', 'Write that book or you will cry', or 'Babe, buying eyelashes for your car headlights suggests a dark premenstrual episode – here, lie under this soft blanket with a Babybel'. It's a sisterly talk down from the ledge, a protective measure to stop one of your own making a hash of things, or an absolute tool of herself. I've lost count of the number of occasions on which I've read about some mortifying or tragic incident involving a female celebrity and immediately thought, 'Where the hell are her girls!?'

There's a unique and almost magical dynamic between women who love and respect one another that I'm not sure can ever exist between a mixed gendered group, much as I adore my male friends in a different way. Certainly, none of my exes has ever had an equivalent of his own (and they've all been reliably stunned by the level of detail and depth of emotion shared between my girls). I wonder how men navigate life without that same spiritual crash mat, because for me, seeing no upcoming girl-only engagements in my diary is like opening the fridge and finding no milk. I rectify as a priority because I know that without women time, the world begins to look the wrong way around. I need a reason to get out of my writing pyjamas and put on some heels and a good bag, or to laugh until I'm barely able to breathe, or to feel the release of bellowing out the lyrics to 'Like a Prayer' in a drunken chorus of bawdy, like-minded broads. It's not just fun, it's positively necessary for my continued mental health. It resets the dials on my life.

Yesterday, when I asked some girlfriends why they felt the same, we reached unanimous agreement that our friendships with other women allowed us to better connect with ourselves. We all love our partners deeply, but there's something about a female-only gathering that reminds us of who we are when briefly not someone's wife, mother, boss or employee. With my women, I'm just me, and that's intoxicating. I can swear as much as I want, say how I really feel about things, sneak a cigarette, sing badly and dance like an idiot, remember that I'm good at telling jokes and OK at dispensing advice. I'm loved, accepted and under no pressure to impress. I feel free, equal, positive about myself and my life outside of the group. I invariably return home to my house full of beloved boys and men with deeper appreciation and renewed vigour. Until six weeks later, when my soul starts clucking for a top-up.

Body

YOMI ADEGOKE | LOUISE MCSHARRY
ALEXANDRA HEMINSLEY | POORNA BELL
AMY JONES

Do you remember when you first began to judge your body?

THE POOL TEAM SHARE THEIR MEMORIES OF THE FIRST TIME THEY FELT SELF-CONSCIOUS ABOUT THEIR BODIES

BY YOMI ADEGOKE

Many women are so accustomed to feeling bad about their bodies, it's difficult to pinpoint where and when it began. In a world where a woman's worth is often measured in direct correlation to how she looks in a bikini, a constant dissatisfaction with how you look sometimes seems like it's just part and parcel of the female experience. According to a study, 90 per cent of British teenage girls are unhappy with their bodies. Journalist Vonny Leclerc challenged tweeters to chart their relationship with their self-image by asking a simple question: 'When did you start judging your body?'

Some respondents were as young as eight when their body issues first began, with insecurities ranging from tummies, height, thighs and whatever else can be criticised on a woman's body, which is, well, anything. For me, it was my boobs. Up until around age fourteen, my chest was verging on concave. It wasn't particularly of note to me, until one of my friends mentioned them (or lack of a 'them') in the changing rooms. While for her it was a passing comment, for me it fuelled months of self-consciousness and, after some time, self-loathing.

I was so concerned about my small breasts, I quite literally called on supernatural help, dedicating my nightly prayers to asking for a pair of massive knockers, promising God I wouldn't use a DD cup for ill. Eventually, I was granted a pair that wouldn't stop growing. After some time, they temporarily culminated at an E, which sat awkwardly on my then size six frame. I soon realised this was a 'blessing' that came with back aches, unsolicited comments from strangers and unwanted stares from men twice my age, as well as a brand new worry about their perkiness. I was screwed either way. And it didn't help when I realised I had in fact made the wrong request and that bums were actually the coveted body part in my community.

Despite them feeling ubiquitous, problems with body image don't form in a vacuum. Following on from Leclerc's thread, *The Pool* staff share their memories of when they first began to judge their bodies.

EMILY BAKER

My body developed a lot quicker than my friends, meaning I had fully fledged curves and boobs when I was around fourteen. I was also quite a bit taller, so I stood out – literally. It was the age we started going out to parties and my friends would always compliment me on how I filled out dresses. It's not a necessarily negative story, but it's the first time I realised my body was up for discussion and meant something more than just functionality.

AMY JONES

I can't remember a time when I didn't judge my body. I think it would have started when I was seven, when I moved to a new school in a different country – as well as being teased for being nerdy and having a weird accent, I was teased for having a bigger body than everyone else. It really kicked up a gear when I was eleven, though – in secondary school, my group of friends were obsessed with making me lose weight. I remember them taking my lunch money so I couldn't eat and my bus money so I'd walk home and get more exercise, and then making me give them piggybacks and run around everywhere to try and lose weight. Spoiler alert: this didn't work, and has destroyed my relationship with food, my body and exercise so much that I think it's beyond repair, as even therapy hasn't mended it.

ZOË BEATY

I'm tall – six foot – and I have always been this way. Excruciatingly so, as a teenager. Aged twelve, my friends were all teeny tiny put-me-in-your-pocket petites, and I towered over them, all arms and legs and angles and awkwardness. I lost a lot of weight to try and make my body fit the norm. I wanted to be feminine and dainty and all the things I believed made a woman attractive. I wound up too thin and still 'bigger'. It wasn't until my twenties that I learned first to say 'fuck fitting in', and second that I actually enjoy being a minor giantess.

LUCY DUNN

I can't remember the moment I started judging my body – that's because I am old – but the one time I remember properly feeling ashamed was when I was nine months pregnant, literally about to pop. I was sitting in a hospital waiting room, waiting for the doctor to decide whether they were going to induce me, when I bumped into another mum-to-be who had been in my NCT class a couple of months before. She took one look at me and said: 'Oh my God, you're huge, HUGE. ENORMOUS!' She wouldn't shut up, and my lovely glowy little pregnant world was shattered in an instant – and suddenly I was flooded with guilt, shame and concern. Was I huge? Was that wrong? Would that be dangerous for the baby? Twenty-four hours later I gave birth (by caesarean!) to a ten-pounder – a lovely, bonny pink scritchy bundle who has been the constant joy of my life for the last seventeen years. Those thoughtless words still ring in my ears . . .

DEBORAH CASTLE

I think I became self-conscious about how I looked when my dad called me 'a great lumptious girl' (he's from Dorset) when I was about fourteen. From that point on, being tall for my age, I always felt 'big' and cumbersome around my contemporaries.

FRANKIE GRADDON

I was around thirteen or fourteen when noticed that my thighs were bigger than a lot of my friends. I remember thinking a lot about it and feeling self-conscious in my PE shorts. Not long after that, I got hips. It was before a lot of the girls in my year so that was hard. I remember a boy in the year above me telling me I looked wide from behind. Dickhead.

HANNAH VARRALL

I probably first started to judge my body when I was about thirteen and other girls at school started developing boobs. I was really disappointed in myself for being so flat-chested for such a long time. I used to think I might get a boob job when I was older, which looking back is horrible.

KUBA SHAND-BAPTISTE

I started judging my body as soon as I started to go through puberty in year four. I was one of one or two other girls whose bodies had started to change visibly, and it was the first time other boys in the class started to comment on my body – an incident in which a boy told me I could no longer go braless because of my 'big tits' springs to mind. I don't think I'd ever felt shame like that in my life, or realised that others expected me to treat my body as a source of shame. And, as you can imagine, it all got ten times worse when I went to secondary school and realised that my chubby body wasn't exactly desirable to others, either.

JADE HUTCHINSON

I vividly remember being in Youth Club (around eleven) and one of the men that worked there pointing out I had chubby knees. (Side note: he was an overweight male in his late forties . . .) I didn't think it bothered me at the time, but as I've got older I've become increasingly paranoid about them and you'll now never see me wearing anything above the knee outside of very close company.

When I was little, I don't remember being aware of judging my body. When puberty hit though, I started to feel more uncomfortable. I remember being on a school trip when I was about fifteen in Cornwall where we had to get into our swimming costumes to go in the sea. Being in front of my whole class with so much of my body on show felt excruciating and it was the first time I really started comparing my body to others.

Why I didn't lose weight for my wedding day

WOMEN ARE URGED TO SHRINK DOWN FOR THEIR BIG DAY. IT'S SINISTER AND UNNECESSARY

BY LOUISE MCSHARRY

I was a fat bride. I understand if this reads to you like one of those horror-show headlines on a certain type of women's magazine. 'I breastfeed my dad', that kind of thing. For many women, it would be a nightmare, and entire industries exist around that fact. 'Diet diaries' emblazoned with phrases like 'Slimming down for the gown', 'Gotta squat before I tie the knot' and the slightly less elegant 'Don't listen to your inner fatty she's an evil bitch' are purchased every day. I, however, did not slim down for the gown, and on my wedding day I was approximately a size twenty.

When I got engaged I thought about losing weight too. 'I just want to feel my absolute best on the day,' I told a friend, 'I don't want any distractions, and I certainly don't want to be thinking that I wish I'd lose weight.' In the end, I lost several stone in the year after I got engaged, and I didn't even have to try. Cancer, in the form of Hodgkin's lymphoma, took care of it for me. Fortunately, my experience with cancer also transformed the way I felt about my body, so

I was OK with the fact that by the time my wedding rolled around, I had put the weight back on.

That doesn't mean that I didn't have some negative body thoughts in the run-up to the big day. The idea of losing weight for your wedding is not one that any bride can avoid. In fact, I would say that being a bride is one of the most body-terrorised times in a woman's life. There are the people who assume you're losing weight, and ask you which diet you've decided to go with. There are the moments when shopping for your wedding dress, you are forced to squeeze yourself into dresses that don't fit you and told to 'imagine' what it might look like in your size. While scheduling your dress fittings, sales assistants reference the fact that there the dress will likely need to be taken in shortly before the wedding because 'most brides lose a lot of weight'. The message is clear. Your body isn't good enough as it is. The strange thing is it really doesn't matter if you're already a slim person, if you're getting married, you're going to lose weight.

Lots of women do lose weight, of course. I have a friend who lost several stone ahead of her big day, because she felt that she would always look back on the photographs wishing she had made more of an effort if she didn't. Now, a few years down the road, she looks nothing like the woman in her wedding photographs and feels ashamed of the fact that she hasn't maintained her weight loss. I try to remind her of how miserable she was during those months when she existed solely on grilled fish and carrot sticks, but all she can see is her thinness, and all she can think about is how thin she isn't now. I can't help but think that she'd be happier looking at those photographs if she'd just stayed the way she was, at her body's natural shape and size. Perhaps she'd look at the pictures and see how happy she was, rather than her size.

That's what it comes down to for me when I look at my wedding photographs. I am fat, yes, but I have always been fat. I was put on my first diet at age seven. If I had devoted all my time and energy into becoming a thin person for my wedding day (and that's what it would have taken, like all fat people I have tried), I wouldn't have been myself. I wouldn't have looked like myself. I might have felt delighted to be thin, but I wouldn't have been able to maintain it, because my body is not built to be thin. I would be looking at my wedding photographs today unable to recognise myself because I am a fat person. I have accepted that. And so, I was a fat bride. I was a fat bride, with three size eight bridesmaids, and still I was the star of the show, because I was so happy.

It didn't matter that I had hardly any hair after six months of chemotherapy. It wasn't important that I was several sizes larger than many women would deem acceptable for a bride. I glowed. I laughed. I danced until five o'clock in the morning. I was beautiful. I was a size twenty, I was beautiful and I was myself. Because I am not a work in progress. I am not a thin person trapped inside a fat person's body. I am not waiting 'until I lose the weight' to live my life. I have no 'inner fatty', because I am my inner fatty and my outer fatty and every kind of fatty and that's OK. Even on my wedding day.

When did we lose sight of a regular size 12?

DO YOU HAVE THE FAINTEST IDEA WHAT A HEALTHY BODY LOOKS LIKE?

BY ALEXANDRA HEMINSLEY

A study released by Public Health England revealed some pretty bleak statistics about how many of us are either overweight, too inactive or drinking too much. A whopping 80 per cent of forty-sixty-year-olds are in this boat as a result of lifestyles being squeezed by family responsibility, commutes and sedentary jobs, and the repercussions are serious – particularly regarding type 2 diabetes. But one line in the report rang louder than any other: 'Many people no longer recognise what a healthy body weight looks like.'

This is entirely true, and never is this more starkly illustrated than January when the fitness and diet industry swings into its annual frenzy of 'New Year, New You' promises. It's not just that there are swathes of us convincing ourselves that if everyone we know is unhealthy, it ceases to be unhealthy – it's that there is also an entire industry trying to convince us that anything above the super-clean, gleaming blonde size eight female is equally unhealthy.

The usual avalanche of new year books, DVDs and YouTube programmes is about to descend and while I am sure there are many involved who truly want to help others, it is a profoundly unhelpful and deeply depressing industry. Largely because the images we are presented with are as detached from what a normal, healthy body shape is as anyone who is overweight and in denial about it. These are two tribes looking at a fairly regular size twelve and believing it to be a bizarre and faraway land, never to be visited in this lifetime – it's just that they are looking at that place from opposite ends of the scale.

The double whammy of images and promises grinning at us from the books and DVDs rammed into aisles of the so recently sausage-and-stollen-decked supermarkets seem so friendly, so positive, so 'there for you'. But they're not. Because the reality is that you don't need to be a new you. You are enough. And even if you do need to make adjustments to your lifestyle, or even if you want to take on an impressive challenge, you don't need to be a different person to do it.

One of the industry's favourite tropes is the DVD with dual, before-and-after images – inviting you to see the old person as one to be discarded, or one that the 'real' person was trapped inside of. There is no time during the accompanying PR interviews for analysis of the (considerable) speed at which the weight was lost, or the (considerable) emotional ramifications of an entire nation confirming to you that the person you were last summer was ghastly or the (ongoing) commitment it takes to carry on being the 'real' you when the support team vanishes.

So when us regular punters see these DVDs, books and websites, and the magical results therein, the vast majority of have thought, by the 17th of January, that we'll never be like that, that we're being truer to ourselves if we stay the way we are, and that none of it's worth it anyway. And so the cycle continues.

But while it is never worth trying to become a new you, it is worth making some small changes. It could simply be walking half an hour a day, cutting back on some food, drinking on only certain days of the week or aiming to try a Couch to 5K programme once spring comes around and you've got yourself comfortable with regular walking. No one knows what private insecurities each of us harbours, what or why our fears about our bodies are, and no one deserves to tell us that we are worth merely the distance we can run or the number on our scales. These are selling tools, pure and simple. Half an hour outside a few times a week is of immeasurable value compared to the soulless trawl around the health food shops for ingredients bought every January and ignored by March.

In studies released in the last year alone it has been shown that a little exercise transforms the cellular nature of fat cells into ones that are metabolically active, it can alter our actual brain cells making us more mentally agile and can change our gut microbes in ways that can aid weight control in the long term. Stopping exercise for just ten days alters the flow of blood to the brain, but we can turn that around so much faster than we can become another person.

None of these actual scientific studies specified that you had to run a certain distance in a formal event, rock a one-shouldered unitard or obtain the arse of an Instagram superstar. Indeed none of them said you had to be a new you. Because no one needs to do that: we just need to move around a little more, and to do that, we have all we need within us already.

No body type has a monopoly on confidence

POORNA BELL HAS BEEN BOTH SKINNY AND
OVERWEIGHT – AND IT'S TAUGHT HER THAT THERE
IS NO GUARANTEED LEVEL OF HAPPINESS, WHATEVER
SIDE OF THE FENCE YOU FIND YOURSELF ON

BY POORNA BELL

Here's something I've never, ever confessed: when I was a kid, my nickname was Mowgli. Not because I was brown, conversed with orangutans or wore red underpants, but because I was so ridiculously skinny.

It turned out, a lot further down the line, that I was probably that skinny because I had a then-undiagnosed heart condition that has now been fixed. But, at the time, I remember being obsessed by the thinness of my body. All I wanted was to be normal and look like the other kids.

At university, I remember travelling to some grimy London club with my usual wolf-pack. One of the newer guys in the group didn't think I could hear him and made a comment about how scrawny my legs were. He may not have called me Mowgli, but there I was, transported back to 1988.

I stopped being skinny in my twenties – mainly due to a balanced diet of chips and alcohol – and evened out to a normal body weight (by science standards). And, eventually, my heart condition was fixed. But in the last few months, I have been in full reverse-Mowgli. I've been on a seven-month sabbatical and, in the time between when I left and returned to England's shores, I've put on about ten kilograms.

There is no amount of 'love yourself', 'eat whatever the fuck you want' ideology that is going to make that alright for me. There is no getting around the simple science that it is too much weight for my height and that it was the result of eating a cheeseboard almost every day for three months. There is also no getting over the fact that, at the age of thirty-seven, I feel like my body has slightly died in its ability to tone up or drop weight. I also know too much about nutrition to ever consider going on a crazy diet – like just drinking Cup-a-Soups.

Something had to restore a sense of balance about my body and, unexpectedly, it came in the form of a Reddit thread that asked: 'People who have been both fat and skinny at some point in their adult lives, what is the biggest difference you experienced?'

The conversations were illuminating. Some people said that they felt they were taken more seriously at work when they were over-weight, others said they found the same only after they had lost the weight. Some said being skinny meant they felt the cold more easily, while others said being overweight impeded their breathing and levels of exhaustion.

Some said that when they got skinny, people were nicer to them. Women said men approached them more. But they also said that their friends were not very nice to them once they dropped the weight, and others said that when they tried to tell people how they lost it, they were called liars. One was even accused of having HIV.

A common theme in this thread was also around confidence – and no particular body type had the monopoly on that.

The conclusion is that there is no guaranteed level of happiness whatever side of the fence you find yourself on. Hankering after a particular body type in the hope it will make you finally love yourself is not the thing that is make you going to love yourself.

After all of these conversations, the central realisation is that people have to do what is right for them. At some point, there was an internal dialogue that may have started with weight, but finished with their understanding that being happy is more than just your kilograms.

It provided a valuable lesson about my own issues with my body. What do I really want from it? Do I want it to look a certain way or fit a certain size of clothing because that will actually make me happy? Or do I want to be able to eat a balance of foods I like and be strong enough to lift heavy things?

Of course, it's the latter. And being skinny had never made me happy, so why was I striving so hard to get to a place I had no real desire to arrive at?

There's a saying, 'Don't compare your insides to someone's outsides,' but I think the reverse can be true. Equating another person's body weight to how you feel about yourself inside is a loser's game. Your insides have to gain an equilibrium with your outsides for you to feel good about yourself.

It's a shame it has taken this long, but I think I am finally learning that lesson.

Where is the #fitspo for fat, fit women?

FAT PEOPLE CAN RUN, SWEAT AND MOVE, TOO – SO WHY IS FITSPO SO FOCUSED ON THIN, CHISELLED BODIES?

BY AMY JONES

Last week, I signed up to run a half-marathon. This doesn't sound like much, but let me give you some context: I signed up a mere twelve hours after I did the very first session of Couch To 5K (an app that aims to help unfit people start running), which I have tried and failed roughly eight times in my life. I currently have to lie down and pant after running a mere three kilometres and in five months I have to run seven times that distance.

There are a couple of reasons I did this incredibly stupid thing. First, I'm running the half-marathon to raise money for Refuge and I thought that doing something I am genuinely, truly going to hate would compel people to donate. But the thing that made me feel like I had even a gnat's sweatband of a chance of doing it in the first place was watching Bryony Gordon and Jada Sezer running the London Marathon in their bra and pants. Seeing them doing this incredibly challenging thing with the same thick thighs, belly rolls and big boobs that I have gave me hope. If they can do it, then maybe I can, too?

See, I'm a fat woman who struggles with exercise. Not struggles physically – although, yes, chugging yourself round a park when you're carrying six stone more than the NHS says you should be isn't particularly easy – but mentally. I feel sick and ashamed of myself for not being like the sleek, smooth fit people I see exercising around me and that mental barrier is far harder to blast through than any physical one. That spark of hope Bryony and Jada gave me was all it took to get me going, but I know that the only way I'm going to keep going is if I keep that spark alive. Problem is, it isn't easy.

When I looked online for fitness inspiration or running tips, searching #fitspo hashtags on Instagram and 'women running inspiration' on Pinterest, all that were getting served to me was images of thin, strong (usually white and blonde) women, bodybuilders or 'before and after' pics demonstrating the huge amounts of weight people had lost since they started training. These bodies seemed so far removed from my reality that there was no point even trying to aim for them – I'm like a different species and I feel simultaneously enormous and very, very small when I look at them.

I started looking specifically at tags relating to fatness and fared better. Ish. #fatbutfit showed me some bodies that looked like mine, but also lots of women showing off their perfect six packs in a gym mirror. When I searched #fatgirlsrun on Instagram, I got just over 2,000 pictures – compared to the 25,000 you get when you search for #girlsrun. The body-positivity and fat-acceptance communities online have been so incredible in helping me feel positive about my own body and it was incredibly frustrating that I was struggling to find a similar space specifically related to fitness.

Look, there's nothing wrong with lots of photos of slim, incredibly fit people showing off their slim, muscled bodies. I can see why these photos are inspiring to a lot of people – after all, when you buy a cookbook you want beautifully styled food photos, rather than the blurry iPhone snap you're probably going to upload to Instagram when you try it – and people should absolutely be proud of the hard work they're putting into their fitness. I just wish there was more space given to fat bodies that exercise, too, in a way that wasn't focused on weight loss.

I have big thighs, a wobbly belly and everything jiggles when I run – but I can run, as my training is showing me, and I can swim and do yoga and lift weights with my body looking the way it is now. I just didn't believe it until I saw other fat women doing it first. Exercise is about more than weight loss, and fat people deserve to get its benefits without feeling like they have to strive for a chiselled body to be able to do it.

Love, sex & relationships

BRYONY GORDON | SALI HUGHES
DAISY BUCHANAN | LAUREN LAVERNE
ROBYN WILDER | POORNA BELL | ARIFA AKBAR

How my relationships with men were affected by my mental illness

WHEN BRYONY GORDON WAS STRUGGLING WITH HER
MENTAL HEALTH, SHE WAS ATTRACTED TO ABUSIVE
OR UNAVAILABLE MEN. THEY WEREN'T BOYFRIENDS REALLY,
BUT MARKERS OF HER LACK OF CONFIDENCE

BY BRYONY GORDON

When I started to write my memoir of mental illness, I expected many things. I expected it would not be easy, that churning up my experiences of Obsessive Compulsive Disorder might be a little uncomfortable: the time I became convinced I was dying of AIDS, for example (I was twelve), or when, as a seventeen-year-old about to sit my A Levels, a voice in my head started to tell me I had killed someone and blocked it out. I knew that writing about my bulimia would be difficult, and that it would not be a walk in the park writing about my cocaine dependency in my twenties. But what I had not expected was to realise that most of my life could be defined by the relationships I'd had.

As a staunch feminist and (I like to think) reasonably intelligent woman, this shocked me. I don't know why, given that reasonably intelligent women are perfectly capable of doing stupid things like taking coke three to four times a week to dampen down the voices in their head that tell them they are the worst human being ever to have walked the earth. I had never linked my mental health with my relationships, even if a cod psychologist could make it out a mile off. I had always seen my attraction to bad boys as an inevitable part of trying to grow up in the hurly-burly world of London media.

If anything, I had seen it as a sign that I was a strong, independent woman, because I didn't need a stable man, I was doing just fine on my own! All cultural references I had – Bridget Jones, basically –

told me that it was perfectly normal for me to go out with shits. This was just the way the world worked; it was simply something I had to endure as a woman. I suffered fools gladly, because didn't everyone? But as I wrote my book, it became almost impossible to untangle the relationships I had from the state of my mental health at the time. Did everyone go out with men who flew into violent rages and left bruises on them? Did everyone sometimes sleep with men out of a warped sense of politeness? Did everyone have affairs with married men and cry themselves to sleep at night, or worse, cry themselves out of sleep until they finally managed to get out of bed in the morning? As I wrote *Mad Girl*, it became clear to me that the answer was probably no. Not everyone did this. My relationships, and my approach to them, had not been normal or healthy.

So here I am at thirty-five, finally unpicking my 'love life' (bluerggh) in the hope that it might help another woman out there enduring a shitty relationship because she has somehow convinced herself it is normal. Because these men I am about to describe were not boyfriends, not really . . . more accurately, they were reflections of my diseased brain; markers of my self-esteem and confidence or, moreover, my lack of it.

THE VAMPIRE

By the age of twenty, there is one thing I haven't achieved – I haven't fallen in love. Curiously, given my cripplingly low self-esteem and my love of vomit, I have yet to find a man who wants to share my special journey with me. These just aren't the things that someone puts down on their list of attractive qualities when searching for Mrs Right, and if they are, you probably don't want to date him. Take it from me, you really don't.

His name was Paul*. I'm about to make him sound awful but the sad truth is that people like him – bloodsuckers, vampire-boyfriends, wife-beaters – have to have some really redeeming features in order to get away with their otherwise piss-poor behaviour. They have to draw you in with something, be it charm, good looks, a cracking sense of humour or, as in Paul's case, all three. These things are their foils.

They are what make men like him so very appealing yet dangerous. The question we often ask of people in abusive relationships is, 'Why doesn't she just leave?' And this is why – because she can't. Because she's stuck in his beautiful, glistening web.

He was charming from the offset, and exceedingly handsome. I couldn't believe that he wanted to talk to little old me that night, of all the girls in the room. There were glamorous ones, confident ones, cool ones, and yet he chose to attach himself to the shy, retiring, mousy one standing in the corner. I now know that these are exactly the qualities a man like Paul is drawn to. Had I been glamorous or confident or cool he wouldn't have been interested for a moment because a glamorous or confident or cool woman would have soon found him out for what he really was and told him to sling his hook. But back then I was just flattered. Not to mention thankful. God, I was thankful.

Relationships like this creep up on you slowly. Like praying mantises, they dance seductively in front of you to lure you in before biting your head off. They work by stealth, and before you know it you are declaring undying love to a man who seems sometimes to hate you. Except what you're feeling isn't love, not really. It's fear. It's fear of him, fear of yourself, fear of being alone. It feeds on every single one of your myriad insecurities. It feeds on them, and then it uses them as a breeding ground to create even more. Things you didn't even know bothered you start to become an issue. The way you walk. Your habit of breathing heavily when you sleep. The sound of your cry, which has become so normal you almost can't hear it any more.

A few months after we move in together, he leaves his mark on me for the first time. I am, unbeknownst to me, 'late' home from a night out, and he has lost his keys. He sits on the front door growling, grabs me and drags me into our flat where he rips the jewellery from my neck and leaves his fingerprints in purple bruises on my arms. Another time, he slams my hand in the garden door and then locks me outside as . . . what? Punishment? Our relationship soon takes on a familiar pattern. I do something wrong, he becomes aggressive, tells me he is leaving me, we make up, repeat to fade. It is never, ever me who threatens to go. It only ends after a couple of years when he swings for me in public, and the horror of my friends means I cannot stay any more. A few months later I see him at a party, where he tells me I am fat, and says that nobody will ever love me the way he did. Thank God for that, I think. Thank God for that.

* Not his real name.

When it comes to sex, sometimes we just need to crack on

IN A LONG TERM RELATIONSHIP, SEX CAN FEEL LIKE A CHORE. BUT WE NEGLECT IT AT OUR PERIL

BY SALI HUGHES

A new study published in the journal Archives of Sexual Behaviour (imagine the prize crossword) has concluded that American adults, on average, were having sex less often in the early 2010s than they were in the late 1990s. The research, conducted by San Diego State and Widener Universities, analysed data from almost 27,000 men and women (the vast majority of them heterosexual) and attributed the drop in sexual intercourse to a variety of external factors, both positive – like the increased empowerment of young adults over their sex lives – and worrying – an overall increase in working hours and in digital distractions like social media and at-home entertainment-streaming. It would seem that 'Netflix and chill' is often far from a euphemism for sexual contact, but displacement activity to avoid it. It stands to reason that the less we have to do, the more we make our own fun (and babies – more are conceived in the cold, dark, tedious months than in autumn, spring or summer), and so, conversely, when we have too much to do, sex becomes less of a priority. Quite simply, we may be too busy tweeting and watching Narcos to have sex with our partners.

The studies were of particular interest to me, since I have several friends who complain about not having enough sex, and the academic research rather legitimised my often scoffed-at belief that their partners should regularly make time for it – whether or not both parties completely fancy it at the moment opportunity presents itself. It's not a question of stoically 'lying back and thinking of England'. But, in a busy, demanding life, sex is like going to the gym or putting out the bins – we may not always feel motivated to do it, but we should look at the wider, long-term benefits and crack on.

This is a deeply unpopular view, I do realise. By today's standards, sex should be wonderful, romantic, sexy, adventurous, athletic, mutually climactic. Both parties should be wholly focused, thoroughly warmed up and equally turned on. I worry our expectations of Hollywood-style 'good sex' have become so heightened that we've forgotten the importance of a swift, good old-fashioned maintenance shag. The sexual equivalent of making a slice of toast, rather than cooking a full English, this sort of straightforward quotidian seeing-to has few frills, bells and whistles, but can be just as satisfying and necessary for sustenance. It's this sort of convenient, timely sex, not the fairy-tale, soft-lit, sensual marathon (which, let's face it, happens only on high days and holidays), that acts as oil to the cogs of the relationship machine. We neglect it at our peril.

For most of us, sex is important not just because we need it, but because it represents a unique, conspiratorial connection between two people that has nothing to do with our friends, kids or colleagues. As importantly, it makes us more forgiving of myriad infuriating things that would, without shared physical intimacy, make us want to hack up our partner's jumpers with a breadknife. The crude reality is that it's hard to be furious about an empty rinse-aid dispenser or a damp towel on the floor when you've recently been given head. For the sake of continued or renewed harmony, it's invariably worth turning off the telly or putting down the iPad to get naked for a bit (my friend S says sex with her husband of fifteen years is like going to the cinema: 'Every time I do it, I thoroughly enjoy it and wonder why we don't go more often'). One may not instinctively be in the mood but, within the confines of a loving, mutually respectful relationship, one rarely regrets having sex, only avoiding getting started. When it's all over, one is usually delighted and relieved to have gone for it, even if it hasn't begun as enthusiastically for one or both of you.

Naturally, some relationships simply don't need sex to survive or even thrive. Amiable companionship, kissing, hugging and shared interests are enough to sustain many marriages, no doubt. Often, one partner's difficult labour and breastfeeding, or either party's physical or mental health, forces sex out of the relationship, either temporarily or long-term, and people make the best of a bad situation, as they essentially vowed to do in marriage. But when there are no mitigating factors – merely laziness, disinterest or the distraction of everyday life – the success of a sexless relationship depends on the serendipitous likelihood of both partners feeling exactly the same way. How often are two people so completely in synch as to want very little or no sex? Much more likely is that one half of the relationship is tolerating the other and would very much like it in their lives (I most often hear of men not putting out, but your mileage and social group may, of course, vary) or, worse, feeling wounded, rejected and dissatisfied.

Some ebb and flow in sexual appetite is normal, but I know from experience that too much ebb can be terminal. A month becomes three and, before you know it, over a year may have passed. It's not fair to withdraw sex from someone's life without consultation and consent. It's a bit like coming home from the office and announcing that you've decided you'll never again go on holiday, or eat in a restaurant, or travel anywhere by car. And, yet, it happens frequently. Instead of simply compromising to bridge the perfectly manageable gap between two libidos, people just stop having sex altogether.

I don't believe many of us want that. But kids, work, extra-curricular activities can get easily aid in our avoidance. Flopping on the sofa to watch a box set can seem a more relaxing way to spend rare downtime. It's easier to lie in bed waiting for an available wireless network than to reconnect with your partner. But it's also unrealistic to always expect the mood to strike both of you at the same moment, and at a time when sex is even practical. What is realistic is to mentally flip through your household's calendar and think, 'This maybe the last chance we have this week,' before squeezing in a swift one before the kids get home from LaserZone. There's something bonding and actually pretty funny about saying, 'We can't be arsed to have sex, but we really need to' and mucking in for the good of the relationship, even if it's with an eye on the clock and an ear to the front door. If you hold out for Occasion Sex, you may find it becomes fatally occasional. Don't underestimate the relationship-sustaining power of the routine rooting.

I Want A Wife – why a 46-year-old essay is still shockingly relevant

FEMINIST JUDY BRADY WROTE ABOUT THE ROLE WIVES
PLAY IN THE SMOOTH RUNNING OF LIFE BACK IN 1971.
IT REMAINS DEPRESSINGLY APT TODAY

BY DAISY BUCHANAN

'I want a wife who knows that sometimes I need a night out by myself.'

'I want a wife who will take care of the details of my social life . . . [and] the babysitting arrangements. I want a wife to keep track of the children's doctor and dentist appointments.'

'I want a wife who takes care of the children when they are sick . . . My wife must arrange to lose time at work and not lose the job.'

Where does this wish list come from? It could be something that emerged from one of the murkier, MRA-leaning Reddit forums. It could be part of a four-pint conversation between tipsy, self-defined alpha males in a raucous City bar. It could be the internal monologue of Paul, Julia's husband in *Motherland*, who is conveniently 'right behind' Julia but forever elsewhere, ordering a latte or careening around a corner on a go-kart when Julia is in the throes of a childcare crisis. But it was written by feminist activist Judy Brady in 1971 for Gloria Steinem's *Ms.* magazine and just republished by *New York Magazine*.

Brady opens by explaining that a newly divorced male friend was on the search for a brand-new wife, and it occurred to her that she too could do with a wife of her own. With a wife, she could return to her studies, become better qualified, get a new job and become financially independent while her wife committed all of her energies to making her life as pleasant as possible. Brady would be liberated from childcare, domestic problems and all hospitality responsibilities. Her essay is now forty-six years old, and it's barely aged.

I'm a wife. I'm thirty-two, and my husband and I don't have any children. With my hand on my heart, I think I can say that our domestic responsibilities are split fairly evenly, and yet, maybe they aren't. On Friday, we're hosting a small dinner party. I organised an online shop, planned a menu, and asked whether my husband would make something for the main course. As I asked, I felt an odd pang of guilt. I had a strange feeling that I was shirking my duties, that somehow this should all be falling on me – and also, that my contribution to the cooking, dessert and side dishes, was less worthwhile and impressive than his efforts would be. It reminded me of when we first moved in together, and I discovered that he would buy ready-chopped vegetables and microwavable mashed potatoes. For most of my childhood, my mother didn't go out to work, and made me feel as though there was something vaguely lazy and sinful about spending an extra thirty pence in order to get out of scrubbing and cutting your own carrots.

I am writing this on Thanksgiving Day, and I wonder how many men and women are splitting the chores and responsibilities fairly and equally. I wonder how many husbands are telling their wives that they'll put out some snacks or entertain their children just as soon as the game is over, or as soon as they've finished this beer. I wonder how many wives have been planning a meal for days and weeks, spending hours shopping, prepping, looking at recipes and curating Pinterest boards because they've felt responsible for the day, not just for feeding a family but making the day feel cosy, emotionally satisfying and perfect. Over here, in a month, we'll get a go. I think of my own parents, and how I grew up seeing them and their friends and their parents produce this pattern.

We see these images on every advertisement, saturating every part of pop culture. We even have a prime minister who divides domestic labour into 'girl jobs' and 'boy jobs'.

There are exceptions that prove the rule. I know men who cheerfully identify as househusbands, wives who work as breadwinners and get home after a long day in the office to a hot dinner that was prepared by someone else. Still, so many of us feel that as wives, our main job, and the one that has the greatest value, is to be an emollient, putting the smooth running of our families' lives before success and progress in our own. My most enlightened, feminist friends will make pained jokes about male partners who don't know how their vacuum cleaner works. 'Do fathers have to pay nursery fees' is a Google search with nearly three million results. According to the Office for National Statistics, women's earnings peak when we're thirty-four, and men's peak when they're fifty. When do we start families? When do most of us have to take a year out of our careers? When do so many of us discover that economically and practically, it makes more sense for our partner to work full-time, while we go part-time or find childcare such an expensive struggle that we don't go back at all?

According to Brady's essay, to be a wife is to be a sponge. Wives absorb every problem, obstacle and distraction and ensure that a husband's path to success and self-fulfilment is set in a smooth, straight line. She ends by asking 'Who wouldn't want a wife?' Indeed. We tell our girls and young women that they can do everything, but we need to start spreading the message that they really don't have to. They should be able to pick and choose. Now, being a wife still means that we're often putting in a double shift at work and at home, and being manipulated into the latter because we're told it's a labour of love. I don't want a wife. I want every woman with a partner to be met in the middle, to never feel as though it's entirely on them to ensure that everything is clean and everyone is fed. I want to make sure that in thirty-two years' time, my niece never feels residually guilty about not making a main course, or cutting her own carrots. I'm pretty sure that I don't need to worry about my nephew.

When 'bad boys' no longer appeal

ONCE WOOED BY THE KIND OF MEN WHO DIDN'T RETURN PHONE CALLS OR BUY CHRISTMAS PRESENTS, SALI HUGHES HAS LONG SINCE MOVED ON TO NICER TYPES

BY SALI HUGHES

I was in bed watching my favourite programme, *First Dates*, the other night, when yet another young, female participant described her ideal type as 'a bad boy' (seriously, there's one practically every week). My boyfriend groaned, complaining he'd met dozens of women – platonic and otherwise – who'd told him this almost as soon as they'd met.

I was surprised to hear it. I suppose that having been in long-term relationships with two emotionally unavailable, sexually messed-up, power game-playing, commitment-phobic narcissists in my distant youth, I had rather optimistically assumed that the appeal of the bad boy had died the moment I finally came to my senses. A little research and I find to my horror that the appeal of these men isn't just prevalent – it appears also to be scientific fact. A study at Durham University into the bad boy phenomenon, showed that female undergraduates (I suspect age is a big factor here) were more likely to be sexually attracted to men possessing 'the dark triad' of narcissism, psychopathy and Machiavellianism. Common traits of this type include 'a desire for attention, admiration, favours, and prestige; the manipulation, exploitation, deceit and flattery of others; a lack of remorse, morality concerns and sensitivity, and cynicism'.

As baffling as this seems, I know these traits all too well, and also how, within a relationship, they can gradually trick you into a skewed sense of what's normal. And 'bad boy' makes it sound much more jolly than it is, as though these men are lawless teen-idol types like James Dean. The reality of life with a bad boy, however, is a drip-fed diet of gentle criticism and push-pull affection to keep you exactly at clutch-biting point – even if it means being routinely chucked out of bed post-coitus because 'I'm not ready for a girlfriend', or being dumped on your birthday, only to be asked back a week later when he's bored and lonely.

It can mean not receiving a Christmas present despite investing several years of your time, because it's all 'just conformist crap', or enduring a cavalier attitude about monogamy because he would not be confined by the dreary societal norms you've swallowed unquestioningly (reader, all these things actually happened to me), all apparently defended by beat writer clichés and dreary sob stories about how his dad didn't love him. It's not always this dramatic, of course. The tiny, insidious stuff has even greater effect. Missed dates and putdowns, days without so much as a text, failing to show because something better came up, the constant reminders that one shouldn't get any ideas above one's station.

Ask a bad-boy chaser why she persists in courting these dreadful men and she will very often say, 'Nice guys are dull, I want someone who's not a pushover', as though men can't possibly be expected to stand up for themselves unless they have a cruel streak (try telling a nice cardigan-wearing nerd that his awful trainers need binning and see weapons-grade stubbornness in action). Nice people are dull insofar as they're reliable. Reliable is wonderful. Reliability is knowing that someone would never stay out all night without calling to let you know they're not getting laid or murdered.

Reliability is someone who doesn't equate one's request for a lift from the station after dark with a desire to be married and impregnated with triplets. It's frying you some bacon, ensuring his own phone is switched on, not leering after your embarrassed friends and neither noticing nor caring that you've gained five pounds in Christmas brie. It's a returned text, a sincere expression of emotion without ulterior motive, it's deciding he really likes someone and making the uncomplicated decision to see lots of them. Reliability is being told you're lovely and not being too terrified to say it back.

Unhelpfully, our culture buys into poor behaviour as some romantic idea. The internet is awash with 'fun' features about how we all love a bad boy, many of them dispensing advice on how to conduct oneself around someone who already doesn't deserve us. This advice around the treatment of bad boys – as though they somehow have special needs – is absolutely infuriating because it basically encourages women to join in the game of emotional dysfunction.

Don't sleep with him on the first date! Don't return his calls! Don't say 'I love you'! Wait at least one hour before replying to a text! But despite the gazillion Google hits suggesting the contrary, here's the crucial thing one learns: you will never change him. Not because he's some untameable free spirit, but because he's an arse with arrested development, who has learned over time that you will put up with behaviour that erodes who you are and what you think you're worth. He either doesn't like you enough, doesn't like himself enough or both. He might, deep down, be capable of good, but it's too late for you to be on its receiving end.

The way one actually deals with bad boys is far more organic. One becomes hopelessly, irredeemably bored. The occasional laughs and memories of once-great sex become piecemeal in a tedious and lonely existence of tongue-biting, second guessing and constant, low-level ennui. One becomes too embarrassed to discuss his behaviours with friends, too fatigued by this parallel universe of headfucking, outside of which, other people are just hanging out and watching telly with their loved ones, feeling annoyed about real and enviable stuff like unemptied dishwashers and disappointing takeaways. Ordinary, unexciting, emotionally healthy and undramatic lives become almost pornographic in their appeal, until one day: enough. Off you pop.

Then you look at yourself and ask how you ended up with someone who treats you like a nobody, and whether you've been unconsciously trying to prove to yourself that they're right. Are you persistently pursuing men who will reinforce your own ambivalent feelings about yourself? If your lady boner is activated by someone

treating you as unworthy of love, attention or care, then some stereo-
typical bad boy is the least of your worries. He's just a sideshow and
a distraction from the real hard work: that which must be done on
ourselves.

What do weddings have to do with marriage?

THE BIGGER THE ROCK THE ROCKIER THE MARRIAGE? LAUREN LAVERNE ON THE JOY OF SMALLER WEDDINGS, AND SAVING THE BIG PARTY FOR A BIG ANNIVERSARY

BY LAUREN LAVERNE

When Valentine's Day is done for another year, and spring is almost
here, for Britain's betrothed, the season of 'wedmin' begins. I only just
found out about wedmin, from a friend who is about to get married.
I couldn't relate, because my wedding was old-school, analogue. I was
among the first of my friends to get married, way back in 2005. I
often forget that Mr Laverne and I have been together so long, but
then something will happen that reminds me. It might be a photograph of us when we first got together (there aren't many and all of
them are physical objects). Remembering that the first mix he made
me was on minidisc. Driving down our old street (our first flat was
cheap – we had silverfish, a flatmate I called Naked Brian and a DJ
booth in our dark purple living room). It was also on Primrose Hill.
The Bulgari group recently redeveloped the site and are now offering
apartments (like ours, only not) for between four and twelve million
pounds. It's fair to say we hooked up in a different time.

I'm glad about this for several reasons. One is that we got married
before we knew how you were supposed to do it. Wedmin and bri-
dezillas did not exist. Nobody had Facebook, let alone a wedding
website. The average cost of a British wedding now is £21,000.
The British wedding industry is said to be worth a mind-boggling

£10 billion. In 2015 *You & Your Wedding* revealed 50 per cent of brides were prepared to go over budget to get the day of their dreams and 20 per cent were prepared to go into debt. 87 per cent of brides planned to lose weight before the big day. 37 per cent had their teeth whitened. 57 per cent were going long haul for their honeymoon. 59 per cent of brides did their wedding planning alone. Most engagements last one-and-a-half to two years. The statistics make creating a perfect big day sound like long, hard, lonely work.

Our wedding was not like this. Mr L proposed to me on my birthday and twelve weeks later we got hitched at the same church my parents had thirty-two years before. I didn't go on a diet or fix my teeth. An arty friend helped us make our wedding invites (featuring a childhood pic of each of us in fancy dress – him as a cowboy, me as Hiawatha). We printed them off ourselves. I decorated our wedding cake. Friends DJd at our reception. The venue was half-price because it was Bank Holiday Monday. Our favours were a CD of our wedding playlist. The morning of the wedding I went for a run, put on my dress (which as far as I was concerned had cost a fortune) and after we said our vows we had a big party with an open invitation to all our family and friends. Everyone thought I would cry and was keeping tissues handy in case I did. In the end I laughed – pretty much all day. My dad and I giggled all the way there in the car. The ceremony, the speeches and our first dance (which we had both been dreading) to The Beatles 'Here Comes the Sun' all turned out to be enormous fun. We did it the way we wanted, which of course is as it should be. If a blowout wedding is your heart's desire, I suppose that's fair enough. But I wonder whether ours would have been quite so joyous if we'd bankrupted ourselves (or our parents) to do it?

Interestingly, recent research has suggested that there may be an inverse relationship between weddings and the longevity of the marriage that follows. 'The larger the rock, the rockier the marriage' as *MarketWatch* put it. Nobody knows why: sky-high expectations created by a 'fairytale'? The resultant financial burden? Perhaps it works the other way round: maybe lavish weddings are just part of a self-obsessed culture and that's what makes it harder to stay together. I have no idea (I'm only eleven years married, after all. I'm not pretending to be an expert).

In the years that followed our wedding, most of my friends got married, with dos that ranged from the DIY to the spectacular, and quite a few divorced. I still love weddings, but I have come to understand that they don't really have a lot to do with marriage. They're the bang of the starting pistol – the two of you run the race yourselves. Having had a relatively spontaneous, relaxed wedding, I'm also starting to see the appeal of a big do. I'm just wondering if we have them at the wrong time. If we're lucky in eight years' time Mr L and I will have been married twenty years, despite his penchant for tinny Italo Disco and my refusal to check the cupboards before doing the online shop. That really will be worth celebrating with the mother of all parties. We'd better start saving now.

How the hell do you have sex when you've got young children?

FINDING THE TIME IS HARD ENOUGH WITH ONE CHILD, BUT HOW IS IT EVER GOING TO BE POSSIBLE WITH TWO

BY ROBYN WILDER

Do you know where I can get my hands on a Tardis? Because I might want to have sex again one day and I don't think I can have sex anymore without a Tardis.

No, I don't have a Doctor Who fetish – although that's almost certainly the next thing I'll Google – I just have two small children, which means that neither my time nor my space is my own. I don't even get to visit the loo without my toddler demanding to know if 'your wee is yellow or a poo', so I think it will take the help of some sort of extra-dimensional doohickey if rumpy-pumpy is ever to enter the equation again.

And, without being indelicate, rumpy-pumpy used to enter the equation all the bloody time. Not constantly, obviously – my husband and I aren't Olympians – but we did used to enjoy a sex life as healthy as anyone's. That's how we ended up in this mess in the first place. Quite often, these days, I will look at my husband and think, 'Gosh, what an attractive man,' and allow myself the smallest admission of lust. But then I'll remember that I have a deadline and a soiled nappy to deal with, and that I'm wearing yesterday's clothes and haven't even brushed my teeth today, and I am already covered in two other people's bodily fluids and the Venus flytrap (if you will) will inevitably snap shut.

Also, there is the problem of my recalcitrant vagina.

Even among all the sleeplessness, stress, postnatal depression and sheer volume of muslins that we endured when my first son was small, sex was still something could happen between chores – so long as it happened quickly, quietly and without too much of a run-up. These days, however, I'm all about the run-up. My second son's labour progressed so quickly and was so painful that my nether regions are now extremely suspicious of unexpected visitors. I might need a bottle of wine before any unclenching can happen. Some soft lighting. Definitely a shower. Certainly nothing that can be achieved during a baby's nap time.

Yesterday was my husband's and my first Valentine's Day as the parents of two children and it was the first Valentine's Day in our entire relationship that sex was entirely off the table. Neither of us even expected it. We exchanged gifts and messages of love at around 6.30am, in between exhausted but important memos about the bins. Then we went about our working day, looked after our children and ended proceedings with a pizza, the Chris Rock Netflix special and a pre-10pm bedtime.

At no time was there any expectation of clothing removal. I think, perhaps, at one point one of us squeezed the other's arm, but that was it. And, in yesterday, I saw our future. A future of living sexlessly, possibly until our kids move out. At which point, we try and figure out a) whether we still find each other attractive and b) where all the bits go. I don't really like the sound of this future and I'm beginning to think it's nature's way of stopping us having more children. Nevertheless, I have considered our other options. These are they:

1

DRUGS

In which I just neck a bunch of muscle relaxants so I can have a quickie and not care. This also runs the risk of rendering me a) unconscious for the act itself and b) incapable of childcare. I haven't run this past my husband yet, but I'm assuming it would be a mood-killer for him, too.

2

HOTEL SEX

Oh, the ideal. Just checking in somewhere dark and plush for the night, luxuriating in a bath that doesn't still have foam letters lurking in it, daring to put drinks on low surfaces, eating a meal without a baby drooling on my knee. All of that sounds amazing and I haven't even got to the part where I have sex. Unfortunately, we aren't in a financial position to stump up the cash for this sort of thing once, never mind every time we want to have sex.

3

GETTING A FAMILY MEMBER TO WATCH THE CHILDREN SO WE CAN HAVE SEX

Clench!

BEING THE SORT OF COUPLE WHO ARE 'JUST REALLY OPEN ABOUT THIS SORT OF THING' AND HAVE SEX WITH THE DOOR OPEN, WHILE THEIR KIDS, WHO ARE WEARING KAFTANS AND WERE POSSIBLY ALLOWED TO NAME THEMSELVES, ARE IN THE OTHER ROOM

Clench!

(5)

NOT HAVING SEX

Which we have discussed.

(6)

HAVING SEX WITH OTHER PEOPLE

Which would at least solve the problem of who's going to look after the children.

No, sorry, none of these will do, I'm afraid. It's going to have to be the Tardis. What's that? The Tardis is fictional? Well, that's just great. Now, I have to add 'invent Tardis' to my list of things to achieve. Honestly, as if I don't have enough to do.

Now he's gone, should I give up my late husband's name?

POORNA BELL CHANGED HER SURNAME AFTER SHE GOT MARRIED. COULD IT DEFINE HER FOR EVER?

BY POORNA BELL

The first time I took another boy's name, I was fourteen. The words 'Mrs Dan Cox' were scrawled all over my blue General Note Book. (He didn't even know I was alive.) My friends had similar notebooks, with the names of different boys circled in red hearts. I doubt the boys down the road were doing the same; they were probably tonguing whoever was available in Smokers' Alley, the patch of land that separated our two schools.

Ten years on, over violently blue fishbowl cocktails, I found myself discussing with my female friends whether we'd change our surnames when we got married. I adamantly said I wouldn't. It felt like a betrayal of women's rights, and I didn't see why I should have to give up a name I'd had all my life when a guy didn't have to. But also I think it was because Shakespeare was wrong. There's a lot in a name, and especially when you come from a non-Western culture. A name can immediately tell you many things – what area of the country your parents are from, your religion, your historical context.

My maiden name was Shetty, and I was very proud to be a Shetty. Shettys come from the south of India, we are usually clever (admittedly not humble); most of us end up working in the professions as doctors or lawyers. We can get a bit fighty after a few whiskies but the women especially have a particular mould – resilient, strong, fiery, warm, kind. So of course, while drinking fishbowls and tripping from one crappy relationship to the next, I couldn't imagine giving my name up for some guy.

But four years after that conversation, I met Rob, who confounded my expectations of men, and surprised me so much, I agreed to marry him despite not ever really being bothered about getting married. When we discussed it, I said: 'So, I expect you think I'm taking your name?' He just looked at me with this casual, easy way of his, and said: 'Honey, it's your name. And you choose to do whatever you feel is right.' And in that moment I knew I was going to take his name. Because it didn't mean that I was giving up being a Shetty. It meant I was capable of making my life experience something bigger. And because I knew I was marrying someone who respected my family, and who wouldn't ever force me to do something I didn't want to, I wanted to honour that.

And I knew this was the only person I ever wanted to spend the rest of my life with so why would it matter?

But I imagine a lot of people's fairytales begin like that – with utmost hope and expectation. Why get married if you're going to be Eeyore-ish about the outcome? The reality, of course, is that a lot of marriages don't end the way they should: old, wrinkly, a life well lived together. A lot of them succumb to divorce, or in my case – less common – your spouse dies young and you are left to ponder: 'What's in a name?'

When the ending is acrimonious, that's easier: changing your name back to its original form is a powerful way of reclaiming who you were. But when the ending is sorrowful yet respectful of the love you once had for each other, where does that leave you?

It's a question I was asked a lot in the first year after Rob died. Was I changing my name? Vehemently I said no, but it was also complicated. It was my married name, and I was no longer married . . . but my maiden name was like a stranger's house and the locks were changed. I am no longer that person anymore. And I felt by changing my name, I was erasing him from my life, when the absence of him was already so huge.

There was also brutal practicality to consider. I changed my name before my career took off and now I was expected to change it to a nobody's name, as if it was a pair of socks? But on the other hand, this huge, life-changing thing had happened and it was fighting between my work and personal life.

A colleague, who swapped her maiden name for something a lot harder to pronounce, was left wondering the same after her divorce.

At the time, as it did for me, it seemed like such a monumental deal. It seemed like one of the most important decisions she could ever make. Was she going to be saddled with this painful reminder that it didn't work out? This name that signified a future where now there was none? In the end, she kept her married name.

When the break-up is raw, and you want to banish everything and anything that reminds you of them, because when the grief and sadness is too weighty an anchor, it's tempting to reach for the things within your control. And like a radical new haircut, a name is certainly one of them. But the thing I realised, is that yes, names are powerful things. But whatever power we have is what we give them, and it is possible to shape that into something with a different purpose and meaning.

Some might say – well why bother with changing it in the first place? I understand people are worried about losing themselves but I think we're capable of a bigger experience than that. That it is possible to be all of those things – the girl who wrote boys' names on a notebook, the woman who held a man's hand while they said their vows, the wife who buried her husband – and still be yourself.

Someone asked me if I got remarried, would I change it again? And I think quite possibly if that happens, I would. Because my name is a capture of who I was, who I am and where I am going. And I don't think Rob – as proud as he was that I took his name – would want me to not move forward.

On marriage – the second time around

AFTER A DIVORCE, SALI HUGHES WAS BATTLE-SCARRED AND THOUGHT SHE'D NEVER MARRY AGAIN. BUT THEN SHE REALISED THAT LOVE WILL ALWAYS COME WITH RISK

BY SALI HUGHES

I'm getting married again. I might as well say it, since I've failed so pathetically to make a proper announcement for the past couple of months. It's easier to type it on a black and white Pages document than it is to say out loud that I'm rolling the dice again, having truthfully sworn I never would, after my first marriage ended pretty agonisingly in divorce. Announcing it is just so . . . optimistic, isn't it? There's a vulnerability in going public in your belief that everything will be OK this time, that love and humanity will prevail when you know it so often doesn't. Safer to stay in the bunker. It's the reason I refused to join the right-minded chorus of 'Trump will never be president! Britain will never leave Europe!' for a full eighteen months until, well . . .

It may seem an unromantic analogy for such a personal and extremely happy development, but it's also impossible to disentangle my decision to remarry from the global and domestic events of the past couple of years. When untouchable chaos rules, one wants to shelter under the wings of what is meaningful and true: my family, my friends, our collective kids, new puppies, daft jokes, birthdays, walks to town for a new pencil case or to cafes for scrambled eggs. I can no longer believe in much else. As the news got worse, my boyfriend's solid goodness became even more pronounced, an increased sense of permanence became more appealing. And so I finally said yes to the man with whom I already intended to grow old (who also had no intention of getting married himself until last year), and swapped the ring I didn't quite love for one I very much did, and kept it in a drawer until I could bear to admit to anyone but my kids that I was putting myself back on the line.

I know how unromantic it sounds, but my fellow first wives will understand. It's not that you lose your sense of romance or sentiment when divorced. You still cry at the films, books, other people's weddings (even if you do shamefully wonder which 50 per cent the happy couple will ultimately fall into). You still squeal when your friends become engaged. You certainly still glance over to your boyfriend on the sofa and feel purest love and exciting lust, or across a restaurant table and think how lovely this is, how much more often the two of you should do it. But these are moments, not a long-term reality you can invest in without considerable risk. You don't fantasise about a proposal, or see it as the grand finale of a dream courtship, but as the beginning of a bigger challenge the past has told you you're not up to. You immediately wonder how you'd cope if it went wrong. However truly happy, you're battle-scarred, reluctant to reopen the wounds.

Besides, my boyfriend and I were already married, for all intents and purposes. We'd happily accepted this was it, so there seemed no point in expensively gilding the lily just because society expected it. Nothing was broken. We are one another's favourite person. We laugh at exactly the same things and respect one another's careers. I like big noses; he likes small people. We both love doing nothing as much as – if not more than – doing something. We already share a home and just bought a massive new telly from which neither of us would ever blithely walk away. What would really change? Statistics show that, more than ever, divorcees choose cohabiting over marriage and, for several happy years, I've been one of them. My children are happy, settled and secure in their two blended families, with parents, a stepmother and stepfather they love. I don't believe in God, will never again want a joint bank account and white clothes makes me look like ham. Why mess with as close to perfection as I can imagine?

This is what I said to myself for several months, during which time my youngest son got gravely and terrifyingly ill, and stayed in hospital for a month. At Christmas, when he was home and well, and I finally began to process the trauma, I recalled my son lying weakly on Dan's lap in A&E, looking up at him gently catching Pokémon on his behalf with one hand, stroking puke-clumped hair with another. It was this memory that made me realise he deserved to be a legitimate part of our family, how lucky we'd be to welcome him, and how much we all needed a party.

And so we're doing it, this autumn. Not that I'm ignoring past lessons or throwing caution to the wind. Just as one shouldn't take love and time for granted, let tiny resentments fester and breed, allow sex and jokes to dissipate or problems to go undiscussed, one should also never be without a pre-nup and running-away fund, whether the first, second or eighth time down the aisle. But I've decided that cynicism is no longer a place of safety, and fear should never drive major life decisions – it's never been allowed to in any other area of my life, so it should no longer have a casting vote in the most important. While I firmly believe it's healthier to know that bad endings lurk in the bushes than it is to dismiss them as an impossibility, I've decided that I can no longer carry around the weight of divorce on my back. Yes, divorce should be scary and no one should imagine themselves so in love as to be above it. Romanticised complacency, not marriage, is the real state of danger. But fear of divorce should only make us try harder, not refuse to get into the race.

The value we place on romantic love can feel tyrannical – especially if you're a single woman

WE'RE CONDITIONED TO SEEK OUT ROMANTIC LOVE, BUT TOO OFTEN OVERLOOK THE BEAUTY OF OTHER RELATIONSHIPS

BY ARIFA AKBAR

I saw an elderly couple on a commuter train recently who looked like they were grumbling, but she must have said something that tickled him because he broke into a laugh and blew her a kiss. There, just then, the rush-hour clouds parted and the sun shone down on them.

That's what romance is. Whatever our age, however long we've been a couple, it is a tender, transformative or exhilarating moment. But it is just a moment and yet so many of us pin our hopes and dreams on it, and consider ourselves failures if no one blows us kisses on a train.

I am not being cynical or anti-romantic. Quite the opposite. I'm all for love, but that's exactly my point. There are so many kinds of love that we often overlook when we talk about 'love', which have their own satisfactions and joys, and while it's not a competition, these loves aren't as controlling or possessive or as occasionally blind as romantic love can be, and they don't demand breakfast in bed or handwritten love notes. So, why do we fixate on romantic love as the best, highest, giddiest, which will apparently make us feel the most alive?

Firstly, romance doesn't always amount to anything deeper than a dopamine-filled head rush and, even when it does, it's wrongly assumed to be a permanent feature of love, when it's more a thing that comes and goes, like a gust of wind or the seasons.

Secondly, romantic love is not the be-all. As a serial single person, there have been times when I've struggled with being on my own, when all around me are pairing up, but I have never been 'unloved'. Yet throughout my twenties and thirties, I was constantly being asked what I was doing to find love, as if I had a gaping hole inside until the man of my dreams turned up to fill it. It's too easy to internalise this question – 'Why haven't I found love yet?' – and became miserably fixated by it.

The value we put on romantic love can become tyrannical – 'Have you found love?' my married friends have asked, with concern written on their faces. 'Is there any love in your life?' Yes, I want to say. There are friends who'll come around for lunch and we'll talk until dinner and they'll stumble home after midnight. The friends who are pillars of strength, who'll carry me in moments of crisis.

And all those other kinds of love: of children, of nieces and nephews, the love of work and art and nature and the endless supply of unconditional love from parents which makes everything we do interesting to them, whatever our age. None are substitutes for romantic love – they are equals and I wish we could be released from thinking otherwise.

When I say 'we', I mean particularly women, because the expectation of romantic love is something we're fed from an early age and told to aim for as our ultimate goal through fairytales and pop songs and girl-meets-boy films and happy-ever-after novels. So many brilliant and beautiful women I know strive for it and, if they don't achieve it, they feel not quite whole because they've internalised the myth that if you don't have romantic love in your life, it is somehow a reflection on you – a failing.

There is a part of me that hopes to become the couple on the train, to grow old with someone, but it is not something that I think tops all else. And if romantic love is supposed to bring us the most intimacy and companionship, it's not always the case in reality. Some couples don't seem to know each other all that well; others feel more alone together than if they were alone. And some have lost their own boundaries and no longer see themselves as a 'me' and 'you', but as an 'us'. I'm not arguing against the joy of coupledom – I'm just saying that the grass isn't always greener.

I'm not undermining romantic love either, with its fizz and butterflies and miraculous spark. But I wish we'd acknowledge other kinds of love alongside the erotic a bit more. They add such richness and pleasure to our lives. Let's show these loves a bit more love.

Wombs

ZOË BEATY | ROBYN WILDER
CAROLINE O'DONOGHUE
KUBA SHAND-BAPTISTE | SALI HUGHES
JENNIFER RIGBY | KAT LISTER

The vaginal tape scandal putting women's health in danger

HUNDREDS OF WOMEN ARE SUING THE NHS AND MANUFACTURERS OF THE TRANSVAGINAL MESH TAPES WHICH PROMISES A 'QUICK-FIX' TO INCONTINENCE – AND IS LEAVING THEM IN AGONY

BY ZOË BEATY

'If this hadn't happened to me, and someone told me about it, I'm not sure I would have believed them. It's like a bizarre horror story.' We're 36 seconds into our conversation and Kath Sansom has already reached 200 words per minute. She has unwittingly become the face of the latest scandal in women's health – and she is desperate to be heard. Kath is one of thousands of women in the UK – and all over the world – speaking up about transvaginal tapes, often made of mesh, being used in NHS surgical procedures. They are sold as the quick fix to end incontinence and pelvic organ prolapses (POP), which has left thousands of women reeling in pain. The story hit national headlines, and Kath, a local newspaper journalist and campaigner, has been at the heart of it. 'I've seen some crap in my time,' she says. 'But this has blown me away.'

Transvaginal tapes made of mesh have been used by the NHS since the mid-nineties, when they were introduced as time and cost effective way to treat women suffering from stress incontinence and pelvic organ prolapses. The device is a polypropylene (plastic) mesh strip or panel, which is cut to size and then surgically placed through the vagina or abdomen. The twenty-minute operation was seen as a 'simple' way to alleviate taboo symptoms often suffered by women after childbirth – a fast alternative to the more invasive, lengthy procedures of the past. It proved popular. Between April 2007 and March 2015, some 92,000 women were treated with vaginal inserts.

Some women do have positive results from the surgery. And it feels like it should be a positive initiative for women. When it comes to talking honestly about the effects of childbirth – and incontinence, and the menopause, and pretty much any other topic surrounding the intricacies of women's bodies – taboo still threatens to silence women's voices, and often they are left to suffer alone. This should be a way for women to take back some control. For those who have positive experiences, it is.

Yet, even limited research shows that at least one in eleven women has experienced failed procedures, resulting in severe repercussions and chronic pain. Now, according to the BBC, at least 800 UK women are suing the NHS and manufacturers of the panels (Johnson & Johnson are one of the main producers), and the repercussions are wading into public life: Owen Smith MP announced he would hold a Parliamentary debate on the issue, and ordered an investigation. In Scotland, a 2014 inquiry following a petition prompted MPs to suspend NHS use of mesh implants pending safety investigations. The subsequent report stated that mesh must not be routinely offered to women with POP and ordered mandatory reporting of all procedures and adverse effects.

Women have described intense pain on waking from the operation, struggling to urinate, the plastic cutting through the wall of their vagina, and even, in many cases, through the urethra. Many are left unable to have sex, due to pain or use tampons, or been left reliant on a wheelchair due to the pain. Some have said their partners have been cut by the tape during intercourse. The physical and emotional repercussions have left some women feeling suicidal. A woman speaking out on the *Victoria Derbyshire* show had lost the use of her bladder and bowel as a result of the procedure. When I mention the news to my friend, an NHS physiotherapist, over dinner last night, she says she can think of at least four patients she's treated in just a few months who have all had the same failed surgery, and were suffering chronic pain.

For Kath, it was intense pain, the inability to walk and a feeling that her feet had been cut off at the ankle. She had the device taken out, but, despite leading an incredibly active life before her twenty minutes on the operating table – she was a keen highboard diver and cyclist – she is now unable to run, or even kneel down to garden for any period of time. Her experience led her to set up the Sling The Mesh campaign, and she's been campaigning tirelessly ever since.

'I started getting this cheese-wiring pain inside my vagina,' Kath explained. 'And in my pelvic area. It felt like someone was cutting me, from the inside, with knives. I put it down to being post-op, but it didn't end. I was freelancing, I had to get back to work as I'm a single parent. I don't know how I got through it. I had to keep getting up from my desk, hang my head over the sink and sob. I didn't know what to do with myself.'

But what makes this mesh so harmful? 'The overriding problem with it is that it shrinks,' she says. It's widely reported in medical journals that the material does shrink and can erode once inside the body, and that can lead to vaginal scarring as well as pain and other complications. She says that surgery guidelines state that materials which change over time should not be used as devices to be inserted in the body. 'It should remain the same until the patient dies. But there are studies which show this fabric can shrink, and twist and the edges can fold, it can degrade and have fragments drop off, and it can go brittle or really hard.'

I'm still trying to verify the 'surgical law' which Kath cites. But there are harrowing indictments that this device and procedure have long been considered unsafe which date back to the 1990s. Just three years after transvaginal tape made of mesh was introduced in 1996, one of the first products – ProteGen Sling, as it was known – was recalled due to safety concerns. In 2008, the first public health safety notification about the products was issued in the States, a measure which was 'updated and strengthened' in 2011. By the same year, at least eight of eighteen devices evaluated by the watchdog US Food & Drug Administration (FDA) had been removed from the market, and the FDA announced that transvaginal tape made of mesh was 'high-risk' for women. That warning was reconfirmed by them as recently as 2015.

That's not all. In Australia, a senator compared the scandal to Thalidomide as one of Australia's worst health scandals. In the US, a class-action lawsuit over the devices – involving a reported 54,000 women – settled for $12.3m and new cases are still coming forward. There is little knowledge about long-term effects of the tape, though some women have had positive outcomes, only to experience debilitating symptoms when the material morphs up to a decade down the line.

The scale of the scandal is huge. Yet, it's also sadly unsurprising. It's indicative of the lack of respect we have for women's health – and how little we care for women's bodies. The frustrating thing, Kath says, is that women are often not well enough informed of the risks before the procedure, nor are they being listened to when they speak up about the after-effects. 'No one wants to take it seriously,' Kath explains. 'Still surgeons are purporting that the surgery is more beneficial than risky. But what we should be doing, instead of rushing women into procedures like this, which are obviously not working well enough, is looking towards preventative measures.

'In France, women are given physiotherapy as standard to help repair their pelvic floor after giving birth. That works. This does not.'

Calls are now being made for the tape made of mesh to be banned, but Kath says her main objective is to tell as many women as possible of the real risks, and help them make an informed decision about their bodies. 'I don't want anyone to go through what I – and thousands of other women involved in my campaign have – been through,' she says. 'This has to stop.'

I shouldn't have to defend my right to a caesarean – all births are real births

ROBYN WILDER WAS DENIED THE PLANNED CAESAREAN
SHE WANTED FOR HER FIRST BIRTH AND ENDING UP
HAVING A DISTRESSING EMERGENCY SECTION.
SECOND TIME AROUND, SHE WON'T BE BOWING TO PRESSURE

BY ROBYN WILDER

It is late 2014. I am in the obstetric consultant's office, my knees shaking so badly that all thirty-six pages of the NICE guidelines I've printed out and brought with me keep falling to the floor. I'm picking them up as elegantly as a heavily pregnant woman can when the consultant says:

'So, tell me why you are requesting a caesarean section for this birth.'

'I have mental-health issues,' I reply. 'Specifically, a severe panic disorder I was diagnosed with at twenty-one. It has significantly impacted on my life – at one point, I was housebound for four years – and I'm concerned that I won't fare well, mentally, during an induced birth.'

I have gestational diabetes in this pregnancy, so birth is to be induced at thirty-eight weeks. I will be admitted into hospital and given drugs to start labour, which should take effect over the following three days. My midwife has already warned me that induced contractions are especially painful, and has basically said I should ask for an epidural as soon as I'm on hospital grounds. This effectively means being tied to a bed for three days with a question mark hanging over my head, and I can't see any of my breathing techniques combating the panic attacks that this might trigger.

I explain this to the consultant, adding: 'Since there's a 22 per cent chance of an emergency C-section associated with inductions,

I'd like to request an elective to mitigate any ill mental effects and make the birth as smooth as possible. According to these NICE guidelines, I'm entitled to one,' I pass the consultant my now crumpled and sweaty stack of papers. He does not read them.

'Hmm,' he says. 'Birth is a scary thing, but there's really no reason to panic.'

'Right, but that's not really how panic attacks wor—'

'We will take very good care of you,' the consultant gets up and ushers me to the door. 'Don't worry about a thing.'

'So can I have a C-section?' I ask, confused now, trying to push from my mind the family friend who disapproves of my asking for a C-section "because it's not like a real birth". 'Because the NICE guidelines state that—'

'No, we won't be doing that,' the consultant smiles and holds the door open. 'Goodbye, Miss Willdo.' The door closes.

For fuck's sake.

'You're panicking, I can tell,' the midwife is telling me, not unkindly. 'Try and calm down. It's important for the baby's heart rate that you calm down. Calm down.'

'I'm trying,' I tell her. Then I vomit into a kidney dish and cry. I am thirteen hours into my induction. I started dilating as soon as the drugs were administered, and the contractions rolled in one on top of the other. They were so painful that I kept hopping round the room, and it took three goes to get the epidural needle in. But, for the last ten hours, I've just laid here, labour stalled completely, while I lost myself alternately to utter panic and the oblivion of pain meds. Finally, I start shaking and vomiting and the baby's heart rate goes through the roof. I have gone into sepsis, it turns out, and the baby is tachycardic, his heart beating four times a second.

'Leave me, save the baby!' I call melodramatically as I'm wheeled into surgery for an emergency caesarean which, at three minutes from incision to birth, is the least traumatic part of all this. My son is limp, purple and silent when he is born. They take him to an adjacent room because he's not breathing. Time stands still. Then my husband runs in, and proclaims 'He has a massive ballsack!', and

I realise all is well. By the time they put him on me he is already regaining his colour. I smile at him and gratefully pass out from blood loss.

It is 2017. I am sitting a different consultant's office, pregnant with my second child – this time with my NICE guidelines in a neat plastic folder – and a take-no-shit expression on my face. My knees are still shaking, though.

'Right,' the consultant begins. 'What sort of birth are we looking a—'

'I would like an elective C-section,' I bark, almost. 'I am legally entitled to the choice, I have considered the alternatives and I would like a C-section.'

'Gosh,' the consultant says in surprise. 'I should think you do. It says here that you developed PTSD from your first birth – which isn't surprising, reading your notes – and you ended up having an emergency C-section anyway. Frankly, Miss Wilder, I'm surprised we didn't offer you an elective in the first place, given your mental state.'

'Well, yes,' I stutter, the wind slightly gone from my sails. 'I was, too.' Then I tell her the story of the The Tale of the Door-shutting Consultant.

She doesn't say anything for a while and then she says this: 'I'm sorry. I'm really sorry. In the past, we haven't done mental health very well here. I know that doesn't make up for anything, but I am sorry. For what it's worth, I am recommending you for an elective caesarean, and referring you for two different lots of perinatal mental-health support. I want this process to be as easy on you as possible.'

The family friend I mentioned is present when I tell my loved ones the news. She wrinkles her nose sympathetically: 'What a shame you still won't get to experience a real birth.'

'C-sections are real births,' I tell her. I point at my two-year-old son, playing happily with his trucks and dinosaurs. 'He is a real child. All births are real births.'

All births are real births.

38 per cent of women ignore gynaecological cancer symptoms, hoping they'll go away

AND I WAS ONE OF THEM

BY CAROLINE O'DONOGHUE

I had never met a speculum before May of this year and, when I explained what it looked like later that day to my best friend, I described it as 'the skeleton of a duck puppet'. You can see where I was coming from: long metallic beak, quacking away in the opening of my cervix. It was my first time at the gynaecologist and, barring a few routine STD tests at uni, the first time a government worker had looked inside my vagina. I'm twenty-five, so while I had received my NHS letter about a smear test, I hadn't *quite* gotten around to it. When the duck re-emerged, it was covered in blood. My doctor furrowed her brow.

Immediately, there was talk of cells spreading, of malignancy, of swabs, of scans, of potential risks. Words and phrases that I recognised from film and TV as being 'Cancer Chat', and I was scared. And, moreover, I was kicking myself for not having made an appointment sooner. I'd had painful, troubling symptoms for months that were beginning to ruin both my social and my sex life, but still I had held off. I had just started a new job and didn't want to be That Girl – the girl who takes loads of time off for mysterious appointments, when the business she has just joined is trying to get off the ground. Vaginas, I knew, were mysterious. They went through moody phases, cast strange spells, had a different understanding of the world than I did. It was best to leave it to its own devices. And, in the back of my head, I was kind of worried that I secretly had an STD. After all, I'd only had three sexual partners in the last four years. Why I thought that was relevant, I still don't know. Like one in five women, I had made a link between gynaecological health and 'promiscuity', and wasn't quite able to understand the outcome: I had been 'good', after all.

When I told my family about the incident at the gynaecologist, they weren't so secretive about their thoughts. 'That's the clap,' my dad said decisively, before passing the phone back to my mother. 'Has Gavin been honest with you?' said my mum. 'Lots of men play around at the beginning. Hedge their bets.' My sister weighed in, speculating that maybe I had dirty period habits.

Every possible explanation felt like my fault, somehow. I know now that my family wanted to simplify the problem, to will the problem into being some routine infection, and not a deadly cancer.

This story, it turns out, is fairly identical to two-fifths of British women. 39 per cent of women believe there is generally a stigma associated with that type of cancer, while one in five links gynaecological cancers with promiscuity. A further 38 per cent believe that their symptoms will go away if they ignore them. When it comes to breast cancer, we're more than happy to run a half-marathon in a pink bib, while someone hands us a leaflet on the five ways to check our breasts for tumours. But, when it comes to the complex system of levers and pulleys that operate our reproductive system, it all gets a bit medieval. We will put on a brave face, pee blood and tell no one. Or, in my case, faint in the bathroom of a Japanese restaurant and tell no one. At twenty-five, I also fell smack into the 41 per cent of women under thirty-five who believe they're 'too young' to get cancer.

This is all information from The Eve Appeal, which has developed this research to launch Gynaecological Cancer Awareness Month (GCAM). Awareness and education need to be a priority around gynaecological cancers – particularly when 71 per cent of women have experienced symptoms.

There's a happy end to this story: I didn't have cancer. I didn't have an STD either, so that's Gavin absolved in my mother's eyes. I had a routine infection that was killed off with several courses of antibiotics. I like to think I've learned from my mistakes, and should the duck puppet rear its ugly head again, I'll be a little more clued up this time around.

Young women are ignoring worrying period symptoms due to social stigma

AS A NEW PLAN INTERNATIONAL UK SURVEY REVEALS FOURTEEN- TO TWENTY-ONE-YEAR-OLDS ARE STRUGGLING TO UNDERSTAND THEIR OWN BODIES, KUBA SHAND-BAPTISTE EXPLORES HOW A MENSTRUATION 'WALL OF SILENCE' IS HAMPERING THEIR TREATMENT

BY KUBA SHAND-BAPTISTE

Teenagers and young women are avoiding seeking help for severe period-related symptoms due to the social stigma around menstruation, a survey of fourteen- to twenty-one-year-olds by Plan International UK has shown. As many as 79 per cent of girls admitted that they hadn't sought help from a doctor or health professional – despite experiencing worrying symptoms.

Over a quarter of girls and young women also said that they felt too embarrassed to raise their concerns with a doctor, while almost one in ten attributed their failure to disclose their menstruation-related issues to their doctor because there were only men available.

The survey of over 1,000 girls also revealed that 29 per cent of respondents said they had experienced heavy bleeding, while 38 per cent of young women had dealt with severe pain due to their period. Others also mentioned depression and irregular periods as issues they had to grapple with in relation to menstruation.

The NHS recommends that patients see their GP in the event that they 'have severe period pain or your normal pattern of periods changes – for example, if your periods become heavier than usual or irregular'. In addition, 'symptoms of secondary dysmenorrhoea, such as intense pain or heavy or painful periods' are also cited as grounds to make a visit to a health professional. Yet, 54 per cent of young women said they had avoided going to their GP because they assumed their symptoms 'normal', while 13 per cent had been told that they were exaggerating their issues.

As I write this, I'm in the midst of an unbearable wave of cramps. I know just how discouraging it can be to drag yourself out of bed and to the doctor only to be handed a prescription for mild painkillers or instructed, for the umpteenth time, to try a new form of contraception in order to ease the pain.

Just a few months ago, a new doctor at my local surgery told me – after I'd complained about a series of worse-than-usual symptoms – that things would improve drastically once I have a family. 'But, I bled for nearly two weeks,' I told him, the desperation in my voice moving him to throw in an extra box of tranexamic acid – a pill for treating heavy bleeding.

But, as helpful as the various cocktails of medication I've knocked back have been where my monthly onslaught of cramps, nausea, diarrhoea (yes, really), fatigue and heavy, clotted blood are concerned, I wasn't after another 'thing' to take. I wanted to be heard. I wanted my pain – and by extension, the pain of thousands of other women – to be taken seriously.

It's not a surprise that young menstruating women are finding it so difficult to be open with their doctors about these issues. Just last year, the National Institute for Health and Care Excellence (NICE) reminded the NHS that it 'must listen to women . . . if they have symptoms including continuing pelvic pain, severe period pain, pain during sex or they suffer from infertility'. It also said that 'endometriosis must not be ruled out' or ignored if a patient 'continues to say she has symptoms when examinations such as ultrasound scans are negative'.

Whether doctors are taking the steps to really educate themselves about the range of symptoms that women can experience as a result of menstruation remains to be seen. Anecdotally, at least, finding a doctor who genuinely respects what women have to say about their pain can be extremely difficult. And, if you're lucky enough to find one, there's no guarantee that the referrals they make for further testing – if any – will be able to produce anything resembling a silver bullet for years of period-related complications.

Thankfully, more organisations are dedicating their time to understanding more about periods. As the *Huffington Post* reports, Plan International UK is launching a first-of-its-kind report about the stigma around periods in the UK, as well as period poverty and the ways in which people are educated about menstruation.

Speaking to the *Huffington Post*, Tanya Barron, chief executive of Plan International UK, said, 'The stigma and taboo around periods is creating a wall of silence, with girls struggling to understand their own bodies, and feeling too ashamed to speak out when they think there's a problem.

'Better education for both boys and girls is needed to bust taboos and make sure girls know when the symptoms they have are healthy and normal or when they need to seek medical advice.'

Our ongoing denial of period poverty is a stain on the entire nation

IT SEEMS INSTINCTIVELY IMPLAUSIBLE THAT PERIOD POVERTY COULD BE GOING ON IN THE UK, BUT FOR THOUSANDS OF OUR SCHOOLGIRLS, IT'S A HUMILIATING REALITY

BY SALI HUGHES

Imagine having to attend school with a handful of scrunched-up toilet paper wedged precariously in your knickers. Or having to sit in lessons, praying that, when the bell rings and you have to get up from your desk, you won't leave the chair bloodstained for your classmates to see. Or consider how gross you'd feel if you had to make one tampon or towel last the whole day, willing it to remain secure and dry enough to not show through your uniform, purely because you couldn't afford a fresh one. Imagine having to then replace it with an old sock or folded scrap of newspaper, and concentrate on maths. Or consider not even being able to attend school at all, because your inability to buy adequate sanitary protection makes learning, seeing friends, playing games, talking to boys or indeed doing anything but sitting at home on a plastic bag just too shameful, impractical and humiliating.

It seems positively Dickensian and instinctively implausible that this could be the reality in our country. Some people even believe the concept of period poverty in modern Britain to be a lie. But, in fact, the problem among our schoolgirls is such a shockingly huge one that in 2018, on World Menstrual Hygiene Day, London mayor Sadiq Khan called on the government to eradicate an issue that prevents girls from engaging fully in education, sport and their communities. The mayor was acting on new City Hall research that reveals that 17 per cent of women aged sixteen to twenty-four say they have experienced period poverty (that figure doesn't even take into account the girls under sixteen, the vast majority of whom will already have started their periods). Other research by OnePoll.com concluded that some 137,700 girls missed school last year because they couldn't afford sanitary products. More than a fifth of parents have gone without other essential items in order to buy their daughter towels or tampons, and 11 per cent of girls admit to wearing sanitary protection for longer than they should in order to save money, despite that posing a risk to their health.

Horrifying though the situation is, these figures come as no surprise to the many of us working in the volunteer and charitable sector in an attempt to alleviate what amounts to a public-health crisis, albeit a discriminatory one. At Beauty Banks, the non-profit collective I co-founded with Jo Jones, we hear of every single scenario described here, happening everywhere across England, Wales and Scotland. Teachers – men and women – tell us they've been using their own wages to buy essential sanitary towels (still 5 per cent VAT inclusive) for their poorest female pupils for several years. Food banks and charities working in the most deprived communities tell us there's a desperate need for towels and tampons among their client families. Charities like The Red Box Project and Bloody Good Period are devoted purely to an issue that has worsened exponentially since the austerity cuts to benefits and local authority spending.

Cuts, unemployment and economic instability are certainly the drivers (food-bank usage is at its highest rate on record, according to the leading network, The Trussell Trust). The problem of period poverty obviously centres around exactly that – the severe shortage of money for period products among Britain's poorest families. But this particular issue is in no way helped by the continuing shame and silence around the subject of menstruation. Just discomfort around the word 'period' remains significant, without the added humiliation of not having enough cash to stay clean and dry for three to five days per month. The unhelpful taboo of what is part and parcel of most girls' lives literally causes their education and consequent prospects to suffer and arguably perpetuates the cycle of poverty. A secondary-school teacher told me recently that some ordinarily well-behaved girls now rebel, acting loudly and antisocially, in the hope of being marched out of class and into the privacy of the corridor, where they can apologise and ask 'Miss' discreetly if there's any chance of a towel.

This is precisely the issue the Guides are hoping to tackle. Girlguiding, who have been raising awareness around this crisis among girls for some time, announced last week the introduction of a dedicated Period Poverty badge, challenging their young members to engage with the problem of period poverty, assisting their classmates and fellow Guides, talking openly and learning about alternative methods and best practices. Critics accused them of 'going too far' in naming the badge so explicitly and in singling out what should be an unremarkable part of life. But periods are only unremarkable when they're invisible, not forming a puddle on a canteen chair.

Besides, it's hard to see how anyone could take issue with a badge awarded to girls who demonstrate an understanding of, and sisterly care towards, those affected by an inexcusable lack of sanitary protection. Or how open, frank conversations among friends and responsible adults could do anything but alleviate anxiety, banish shame and normalise the process of menstruation – whether or not a girl is lucky enough to afford to do it in dignity.

It's hard to imagine how arguments against teaching children to be socially aware, empathetic, physically unembarrassed, more confident and kind could be in any way compelling, least of all if they centre around an impulse to shush about women's bodily functions in a way that makes period poverty not only about financial embarrassment but also about physical shame. It's perhaps harder still to imagine not having three quid for some towels. It's time for people to try. Because our ongoing denial of period poverty, and our pathetic squeamishness around menstruation, is a stain on the entire nation.

The truth about post-birth vaginas

LET'S STOP GOOGLING SYMPTOMS IN THE SMALL HOURS AND WHISPERING IN THE PLAYGROUND. IT'S TIME WE TALKED ABOUT OUR VAGINAS

BY JENNIFER RIGBY

Elaine Miller is a stand-up comedian, but she doesn't tell knock-knock jokes. Instead, her show is about pelvic floors, pee and pregnancy.

'I make jokes about people wetting themselves,' she says.

In fact, Miller's show – which even features a 'clench-along': a jolly song the audience is encouraged to exercise their pelvic-floor muscles in time to – is an attempt to highlight a massive issue affecting tens of thousands of women every year. It's an issue that is somehow, astonishingly, rarely discussed: the long-term, often debilitating, physical aftermath of giving birth, not just weeks afterwards but years and even decades later.

The conditions range from long-term pain to incontinence, sexual dysfunction to prolapse (a condition where the internal organs slip down or forward – it's been in the news recently because one of the treatments for it, vaginal mesh, has caused major suffering).

'There's a lot of, "Oh, you've had a baby – what did you expect?,"' says Miller, whose show was motivated by her work as a women's health physiotherapist – or, as she describes it, 'fishing about in fannies'.

She adds: '50 per cent of women have prolapse. If 50 per cent of men had their scrotum falling off, something would be done about it. This is not something we are shouting about, but we should.'

Instead of shouting, many women are whispering – confiding quietly in fellow mums as their kids go down the slide, Googling their symptoms in the small hours or writing about it online.

In part, this is because many feel abandoned by the NHS once their baby is safely out. After a cursory six-week check at the GP that is mainly focused on the baby and whether the mother is coping, and which often does not involve a physical exam of any kind, most women are then left to themselves.

That's despite the fact that huge numbers of women suffer some serious injury in birth, which can, and often will, cause long-term repercussions. 90 per cent of first-time mothers tear or are cut during birth, and around 9 per cent of the tears are third- and fourth-degree, which involve the vagina, perineum and anus.

As a result of these injuries and the other physical stresses of pregnancy and birth, including weakening of the pelvic floor, around one in three women experiences long-term urinary incontinence, and one in ten has faecal incontinence. Up to 30 per cent have pain during sex. But experts at organisations like the Birth Trauma Association and Mothers with Anal Sphincter Injuries in Childbirth (MASIC) suggest that the real numbers are much higher – and, moreover, that these conditions can last for much of the rest of women's lives if they don't get help.

New research from *Mumsnet* released exclusively to *The Pool* backs this up. The team there surveyed 1,224 women as part of their campaign for better postnatal care, because they wanted to find out more about long-term problems after coming across discussions on the topic on their forums every single day.

They found that, three months after birth, 36 per cent of women still found sex painful or uncomfortable, and 42 per cent said that birth had contributed to incontinence or worse pelvic-muscle control.

'We're not really surprised,' says Justine Roberts, *Mumsnet* CEO. 'However, while we're not surprised, it's sad that the long-term impacts are so bad for many women . . . Of course, it's important to say that this doesn't reflect most mothers' experience – but it is a significant minority.'

Stacey Baker, who is twenty-five, is one of them. The birth of her two-year-old son, Alfie, was traumatic, ending up with a ventouse delivery – the use of a vacuum device to help get the baby out. Her epidural failed, leaving her with just gas and air for the pain.

Baker tore, but her injury was misdiagnosed and badly repaired. Her pelvis also dislocated and, since birth, she has suffered with bladder, bowel and womb prolapse. Her mental health has also suffered.

'I try not to let my problems stop me from being active with my son, but I really suffer with severe pain, and the prolapses mean finding a loo everywhere we go is first priority,' she says. 'Mentally, I don't think I will ever recover, to be honest.'

But the most shocking part of Baker's story is the care she has received – or, rather, not received – since birth. She was supposed to see a health visitor and a psychiatrist, but did not get appointments. The wait to see a consultant was six months. She now sees a physiotherapist, but she was told at her local hospital that she is too young for any further procedures or surgery.

'I feel very let down,' she says. 'It's like problems during and after birth are treated like nothing. It feels like because I'm young and chose to have a child, they don't care.'

Her story is not a one-off. Mumsnet also asked its users about the care they had received for their post-birth problems. In fact, just under 10 per cent had the same experience as Baker – asking for help and not getting it.

'There are a few possible explanations, not least the pressures faced by the NHS,' says Roberts. 'Most enraging is the fact that we've seen some accounts of women who've approached healthcare professionals only to be told that mothers must expect everything to be different after birth, or "so long as your husband can penetrate you, it's fine".'

'This is misogyny, pure and simple,' she adds, suggesting that women in this situation seek a second opinion.

But there is another issue too: many women just don't come forward, either because of embarrassment, a lack of time or a belief that your own health, as a mother, isn't the priority. Mumsnet's numbers show that up to three-quarters of the women affected by incontinence or pain during sex had either not asked for or not received any care.

Their fears about the NHS's attitude to their problems may also have been a factor, the numbers suggest: 56 per cent of women in the survey said that they didn't think the NHS would focus on their issues either because of its financial constraints or, more concerningly, because clinicians either only cared about the baby's health (17 per cent) or because there was an institutional attitude that 'birth equals worse sex for women and mild incontinence – that's just the way it is' (15 per cent).

'There's always a thing that brings people to clinic – something so embarrassing that it's less embarrassing than showing their bum hole to the NHS,' says Miller.

'For me, it was wetting myself in the mums' sack race at school sports day. It was alright because I was in the sack, but I wouldn't come out of the sack. And all the mothers got it.'

But this culture of silence is profoundly damaging, because studies show that many of the problems women face after birth are treatable. For example, 70–80 per cent of women could cure stress incontinence with physio. And it does seem to be more of a problem in the UK than elsewhere – for example, in France, women automatically see a physiotherapist after giving birth.

That's the least the UK should do, say Helen Lauer and Lyanne Nicholl, two campaigners who set up a Facebook group to support other mothers and, ultimately, convince politicians that something must be done. Nicholl says she only feels able to talk about these issues because she hasn't had long-term health difficulties; she sought treatment privately.

'There are ten times more studies done on Viagra than women's health/prolapse,' says Lauer. 'That's about where we are in society in terms of the importance women have.

'If this was pain in any other part of the body, after a car accident or a procedure, people would be dealing with it. But you've just delivered a human and the NHS is going, "Ah, well . . ." – that's not good enough.'

It's not. Which is why, first and foremost, we need to keep telling the truth about post-birth vaginas. Because, ultimately, we deserve better.

My desire to become a mother is a patchwork of loss, longing – and intermittent hope

THE PSYCHOLOGICAL IMPACT OF INFERTILITY

BY KAT LISTER

The strange thing about trauma is the little things you remember. I can still recall the burble of *BBC Breakfast* and the numbered ticket I clutched in my hand. A six-year-old boy whose high-pitched screams alerted hospital staff to a McDonald's balloon jammed precariously between two plastic seats. The gentle sobs coming from examination room B and the coolness of gel between my legs.

Every day, countless women walk into ultrasound rooms across the country and, with a dampness in their gusset, walk out harbouring an empty feeling, deep inside, where a heartbeat should be. The six-year-old is still running riot, the television continues to burble and yet, in the midst of all the everyday chaos, something has been irrevocably lost. The waiting room is still the same, but your compass has imperceptibly shifted – quietly, acutely, behind a closed door.

Retracing your steps past the pregnancy bumps and foetal-development charts on that lonely walk to the elevator, anguish distorts into a strange kind of shame.

My story doesn't begin with a singular experience of miscarriage at my local early-pregnancy clinic – that's not how infertility works. Like my scattered memories, this one event, like a random scrap of quilting fabric, constitutes only a tiny piece of an ever-expanding patchwork of loss, longing – and intermittent hope. Over the last four years, my desire to become a mother has coaxed me, incrementally, into a strange kind of no-man's land, concertinaing time. In 2015, ovulation apps were swapped for hormone injections and a poorly graded embryo in a petri dish. Last year, my 'non-viable' pregnancy ended in a surgically managed miscarriage. Science doesn't always have all the answers – this much, I've learnt. Uncertainty breeds anxiety; prescribed fertility hormones intensify the lows.

Yet, despite its pervasiveness, we rarely talk about infertility in relation to long-term psychological wellbeing – and when we do, the conversation is too often hijacked by scaremongering headlines challenging the detached 'ethics' of assisted reproductive technology. As *VICE*'s wellness website, *Tonic*, pointed out last year, 'fertility treatments take a toll on mental health.' In the UK alone, between 1991 and 2016, there have been over 1,100,000 IVF treatment cycles in UK licensed clinics. And yet, despite the numbers, when it comes to engaging with infertility – and, most importantly, treating it – mental health isn't always an instinctive focus of concern.

'People can feel incredibly socially isolated,' Catherine Hill, communications manager at Fertility Network UK, tells me. We're discussing the everyday psychological impact that 'trying' to conceive can have. 'The effect of fertility problems on a person's mental health are severely underestimated,' she says. 'Not being able to have a baby commonly triggers a life crisis in both women and men. It impacts on so many different aspects of how you live and can be absolutely devastating.'

In 2016, Fertility Network UK uncovered just how devastating living in limbo can be. Their survey of over 800 respondents found that 90 per cent felt depressed and, shockingly, 42 per cent experienced suicidal feelings as a result of fertility problems and/or treatment. When the charity published their findings, they warned how it painted a 'stark, distressing picture of what it is like to experience fertility problems in this country'. Key recommendations at the time called for greater education among GPs and funded counselling to support those experiencing high levels of distress.

When I underwent IVF in 2015, I was able to access unlimited counselling via the NHS – therapeutic sessions that, at particular points during my gruelling cycle, offered me a lifeline amid the stinging needles, bruised thighs and yo-yo moods. I was one of the lucky ones. Mental-health support is mandatory if you're going through fertility treatment, Hill tells me, but that can be just one session, something she says can be 'far from enough'. And, although the government last week announced increased funding to care for the mental health of new and expectant mothers, it is worth highlighting that those struggling to conceive are still falling between two stools.

With NHS budgets being squeezed, Hill tells me that 'the counselling that's needed isn't in place as it should be'. The same could be said for equitable fertility provision in England: last year, it was reported that thirteen areas of England had either restricted or completely halted IVF treatment to couples trying to conceive. 'We're fighting at the moment to enable women and men to be able to access IVF in England – it's very much a postcode lottery,' says Hill. With IVF rationing spurring increasing numbers of vulnerable would-be parents to overseas clinics, lured by bogus success rates (some as high as 98 per cent), now is arguably the time to demand greater protections for those seeking invasive treatment without the necessary support to guide them along the right path.

In the absence of fairness and cohesion, it is essential that we coax the conversation away from coarse headlines and towards a holistic, nuanced understanding of what that much-used acronym TTC (for the uninitiated, 'trying to conceive') really means. The psychological strain felt by those seeking fertility assistance is emotional, social and financial, Fertility Network UK underline – and the practical and existential questions raised by such assistance can be hugely overwhelming to tackle on your own. We often talk of sadness in regards to infertility, but we rarely talk about the worry, the anxiety and the frustration, the strain on existing relationships and the devastating social alienation it can cause.

Infertility isn't restricted to the confines of an NHS waiting room – it spills out into everyday life, defying hospital walls. Over the years, I have watched friends traverse smoother paths, met their new partners and watched households expand from three, to four, to five. It never gets easier – and perhaps that's my point. The truth isn't always what you permit it to be; what appears is seldom what is. Appearances can be deceptive – and I should know. Days after my miscarriage, I placed my hand on my friend's swelling bump and smiled.

Mind

DAISY BUCHANAN | LIZZIE POOK | ZOË BEATY
NATASHA DEVON | CATHERINE GRAY
ROISIN AGNEW | JUNO DAWSON | POORNA BELL
ROWAN HISAYO BUCHANAN

Depression is not a battle that can be won or lost

SALLY BRAMPTON'S HEARTBREAKING SUICIDE WAS DUBBED BY MANY AS 'LOSING HER FIGHT' WITH DEPRESSION. BUT THOSE WORDS ARE WRONG

BY DAISY BUCHANAN

Sally Brampton's words first reached me when I was in my teens, and I've been carrying them with me ever since. Sometimes she'd appear in British *Elle*, the magazine she launched. I was addicted to her advice columns, from the sex and relationship advice she offered in the *Daily Mail* to the general brilliant life advice she offered as Aunt Sally in *The Sunday Times*. She wrote like the wisest, most knowledge-able person in the world, partly because of the enormous respect that she had for her correspondents, and the compassion with which she treated them.

She seemed to live and breathe the maxim 'Be kind, for everyone you meet is fighting a hard battle.' The word 'battle' has featured in many of the obituaries that have been printed after she took her life. The London *Evening Standard*, the *Week* and her old employer *The Times* led with her 'losing her battle' with depression. The *Mail* went for 'fight'.

As someone who struggles – sometimes desperately – with her own mental health, I'm not always sure that 'battle' is the right word for it, although I do feel as though I'm constantly sending my own tiny soldiers over the top and down into some bloody abyss. Perhaps the biggest case for 'battle' being a bad analogy is that by definition, a battle has an ending, with a clear winner and loser. How can some-one like Sally be a loser? This is a woman who, during her sixty years on earth, inspired, comforted, counselled and touched millions of readers. No matter how her life ended, surely she was a winner, someone responsible for many triumphs, both tiny and tremendous.

Whenever I write about my own anxiety, I tend to do so with

perspective and distance. The way we discuss mental health is such that we're happy to let people talk about it, as long as they seem out of the woods. On paper, it's possible to claim that I 'won' a 'battle' with anxiety about a year ago when I quit the job that was making me weep around the clock, and stumbled my way back to life, eventually finding myself able to breathe through my nose and leave the house without convincing myself that I'd return to find it burgled and burning down.

But the bastard is back. And I desperately want to find the words to explain how – in want of a more elegant and stylish expression – how shit it is to be an adult woman who feels as though her life depends on showing up, meeting deadlines and getting things done, and to suddenly be blindsided by the unshakable conviction that she's useless, friendless and that everyone sees straight through her. When I was trying to explain it to a friend, I likened it to being in a car where the brakes are broken, and you're speeding down a hill. You know you have to slam the breaks like your life depends on it, because it does. But nothing happens, and all you can do is notice that everything is speeding towards you, somehow in slow motion, just so you can really appreciate how awful it all is. I know how my body works and I know where the brakes are, but they're not doing anything right now. The medication, the meditation, the runs and walks and early nights just aren't working for me.

I can't wake up every morning thinking 'Oh good! Another day, another twenty-four-hour battle with my mental health!' because it's hard enough to get out of bed as it is, without the sense that I'm about to shuffle into the Pit of Sarlacc and attack a weaponised evil beast armed with nothing but a wooden lolly stick. I'm tired. Many of us are so tired, and we don't always have the energy to chase our demons away. A battle is just something else to lose, another place to fail. The fact that I've 'won' before doesn't help when the beast comes back – it just reminds me that even when I'm winning, I'm not good enough. Mental health isn't something to conquer, that can be sent cowering with a trail of winners in its wake. It's just a case of working with the bodies and minds that we have today, and sometimes daring to hope that tomorrow might be better.

One of my favourite novels, Lisa Jewell's *One Hit Wonder*, explores what happens after the suicide of Bea, the estranged big sister of protagonist Ana. The words from Bea's suicide note will always haunt me. 'Music doesn't move me anymore. Kind words and good friends and happy days don't move me. The thought of the future doesn't move me. There's no magic left in anything.' How can we force anyone to carry on when they're absolutely certain there's nothing left to hope for?

Suicide is heartbreaking for the people who have been left behind. It happens because the alternative feels simply impossible for those who have gone. It's not a solution we'd choose for anyone, but it discredits everything they have lived and experienced if we dismiss it as a battle lost.

Mind's Mental Health Awareness week is in May. In some ways it's helpful to try to respond to MH problems as we would to visible, physical illnesses. But I think it's time to stop talking about 'battles' and 'survivors'. We're all fighting, and it's hard, but life feels that much harder when we think that we'll only succeed if peace is a permanent state. Every day that doesn't feel like a struggle is worthy of celebration.

Is there ever an upside to anxiety?

RESEARCH SUGGESTS THOSE WITH ANXIETY HAVE
SHARPER MEMORIES, ARE MORE TRUSTWORTHY AND CAN
BE INDISPENSABLE IN A CRISIS. LIZZIE POOK, WHO EXPERIENCES
ANXIETY DAILY, FINDS COMFORT IN THE NEWS

BY LIZZIE POOK

We all know anxiety is a cruel mistress. We're aware that a panic attack can feel like a near-death experience; that being blighted by an endless cycle of sabotaging thoughts is debilitating and suffocating and terrifying all at the same time. But what if something good could come of anxiety? What if we could start to reframe the way we think about our nervous natures?

For years, anxiety sufferers have been strafed by studies that suggest we are lesser people. Social psychologists at the University of Iowa, for example, recently argued that anxiety makes us less able to feel empathy for others. Academic researchers from the University of Illinois believe it can have a negative impact on cognitive performance too. Well, call it science, but believe me – this sort of thinking is like a punch in the gut to those of us who already feel like we are failing in most aspects of our lives.

So when I stumbled across new research from the French Institute of Health and Medical Research, which suggests those with anxiety are actually better in crisis situations (because our brains are hyper-alert and poised to react to threats in lightning-fast time), I wanted to weep into my keyboard with relief. This was the first time I had read anything remotely positive about anxiety. The first time it wasn't presented as a life sentence, a sign of fragility or an unwieldy annoyance to be whispered about then hurled like a silent grenade swiftly out of sight.

I wasn't always an anxious person. As I child I had the kind of arrogant confidence that comes with being popular at school, good at sports and completely oblivious to the idea that something could ever happen to upend my perfect existence. Things changed. And I've negotiated anxiety for over a decade of my life now; often dancing with it at three o'clock in the morning, when I become certain my widowed mother – some 200 miles away in her bed – is suffering a heart attack. ('Who'll find her body in the morning?' I'll think in the small hours. 'I'd better ring the house phone in case she needs an ambulance.')

Questions like these have become my incessant internal dialogue; the same voice that likes to remind me that I can't do my job and that my friends would rather I wasn't around. The same voice that calls me a 'fat' or 'disgusting' on a regular basis. (I have the harshest of inner critics that takes advantage of the sense of shame I feel every day.)

I have felt for a long time that anxiety has changed me wholly as a person. That it has forced me to live as a decrepit shadow of my full potential. So when I read about these studies, it was like a small sort of revelation. Being anxious does not mean I am not a good, strong person. I had forgotten that.

There is plenty of research out there reinforcing the idea that anxiety has its upsides. Small-level studies carried out by PSL Research University in France, for example, found that those with anxiety are better at reading negative emotions in other people. Research from the University of California, Berkeley, suggests those with mild anxiety are seen as more trustworthy than others. Anxious people have also been proven to have better memories and one study, by researchers at King's College London, has even found that anxious adolescents are considerably less likely to be killed in an accident than their less anxious peers (well, that's a win).

Some of the world's most brilliant thinkers were anxiety sufferers too, including Charles Darwin, Emily Dickinson and Abraham Lincoln. Edvard Munch's iconic painting *The Scream* even came to him during a panic attack that played out as a vision of a blood-red sky – proof that us anxiety sufferers don't always have mush for brains.

Personally, I do believe my anxiety is part of what makes me a good person. As someone who feels vulnerable on a daily basis, I think it puts me in a better position to imagine another's pain. I also know it makes me kinder, less judgemental and more tactful with the emotions of other people, and I'm very sure it has lent facets to my personality – unpredictability, a creative streak and the tendency towards pantomime emotional extremes – that just wouldn't be there without it. I'd miss them if they were gone.

For today, this new research may just be a headline on a rolling news-feed, but for me – it's a reason to celebrate what I previously saw as my biggest flaw. Yes, anxiety can be messy and ugly and paralysing, but I refuse to be bowed by it. I will not feel guilty or selfish or ashamed because my brain is wired a particular way. I know I am not weak. I know that my mind is curious and strong. And if there is any glimmer, any shred of science that reinforces the idea that playing host to something so parasitic for all these years could potentially have bred something good in me – I'm sure as hell going to latch onto it with my clammy, anxious fingers and never let it go.

I had no idea what depression felt like, until suddenly, I did

LAST YEAR, ZOË BEATY BEGAN TO FEEL ABRUPTLY, IRRATIONALLY, UNREASONABLY SAD. NOW THAT SHE'S ON THE ROAD TO RECOVERY, SHE'S TRYING TO UNDERSTAND WHY

BY ZOË BEATY

Every evening, I leave the office and make my way to Green Park Tube station. I walk down the stairs, I follow the grey markings on the signs towards the Jubilee line, to get closer to home. It's a busy station. There are elbows and hushed, aggravated voices; and there are bodies – hundreds and hundreds of bodies, walking, rushing, pushing, desperate to get somewhere better. And among the thousands of bodies each day, and the tens of thousands each month and the millions each year that walk the same path through stations like Green Park, there are the hidden few, beside you on the escalator and lined up on the platform, who are desperate to get nowhere. Last night, as I walked through the tiled corridors, under the ugly lights in Green Park, one of those people died.

On a different evening, a few weeks ago, I left the office to make my way to Green Park Tube station. I walked down the stairs, I followed the grey markings on the signs towards the Jubilee line. Amid a smaller afternoon crowd, surrounded by bodies, I lined up my toes very precisely with the yellow line parallel to the edge of the platform. But when the Tube came, I couldn't get on. And I couldn't get on the next one, either, or the next one. Instead I stood there, watching the trains whoosh in and whoosh out like my thoughts, feeling quite terrified. The noise scared me. My own body scared me. The feeling of being so very removed from everyone around me – and the very normal scenario playing out in front of me – scared me. I wanted to opt out of being. I don't know how long I stood there for. It felt like an hour, maybe it was less. Finally, I looked down at the ground as another train pushed its way in, to see another two pairs of feet were stood either side of mine: two police officers.

I am grateful that they stood beside me and spoke to me. If they hadn't would I have jumped? Hopefully not. I was thinking about it an awful lot, and it certainly wasn't the first time I'd thought about it in the past few months. But the fucking annoying thing about wanting to die is that death is still terrifying. And it is not easy to die. Actually (and I have researched it thoroughly), it's more than likely that you'll fail. And so, in another quite comedic bout of self-pity, my own lack of self-worth has told me each time I've come close that I would probably fail at that too. When I learned that, last night, another person felt so incredibly hollowed out that they too stood where I had been, and that they didn't come back from it, it frightened me all over again.

Let's rewind. If I'd have read about an outwardly successful, privileged, safe, financially secure, healthy woman standing alone on a platform edge six months ago, I would have had thoughts amounting to approximately this: 'that's sad'; 'that person needs some therapy, I hope someone is helping'; 'she must be lonely, I am grateful I am not'. A small part of me would have thought of it not as hyperbole as such, but as a dramatically charged scene. Something slightly performed or unbelievable, only because I couldn't truly empathise with it. Despite having had mental health issues and cognitive behavioural therapy in the past, I couldn't read or listen or watch something like this and know the depths of that feeling that some of us, who have stood on that yellow line all over this city, can feel. Now it feels so big and so loud and so rooted and rotten inside me that I want to scream at myself: for not understanding before, and for not completely understanding now.

It was in July that I first felt a familiar uneasiness in the space just below my heart. It started as a small question mark; a morsel of doubt hovering at the end of each thought. In the middle of the summer, life was ostensibly good – I had a job I loved, wonderful friends and family, a boyfriend I admired, a fun and comfortable house to live in and a newly clean bill of health. I dismissed the feeling as a hairline fracture of the mind and assumed it would heal itself. Instead as the question mark grew larger the fracture became a fissure, big enough that I tumbled in.

The very clever thing about mental illness is that the symptoms are barely visible until, all at once, they become all you can see. Basically, at some point my inner voice started to change. The things I had been taking for granted – a functioning level of confidence, self-worth, self-respect, interests, independence – began to disintegrate without me realising. The question mark became largest when I tried to sleep, so I stopped sleeping. Predictably, the intrusive thoughts were afforded more power. I did my best to suppress them, to hush them up, but they broke out over my skin – a faint rash on the back of my neck and over my chest. I got a stomach ache and probed it like you would a bruise, to see how much pain was hiding inside. I felt like I could touch the anxiety rising and falling through my belly.

By August I felt ugly. By September I felt wholly inadequate. I'd never had a panic attack before, and didn't know that's what was happening when my chest started constricting in the toilets at work. It's weird, that stuff. The fear felt like sitting helplessly in the passenger seat of a speeding car, hurtling towards a wall but never quite hitting it. My heart beat ferociously for weeks and made me too full, and sick. Simple thoughts and assertions about myself were soon subject to a constant, complex, internal cross-examination. Of course I haven't read enough; of course I'm not smart enough; or interesting enough, or funny enough, or pretty enough. Sure, people say I'm doing OK in my career, but they don't mean it. Because, isn't it entirely feasible that they are lying, or worse, laughing at me? And isn't it plausible, then, that the friend who wants to go for a pint later pities me, and actually thinks I'm incredibly boring? And that the man who claims he once found me attractive is really just playing a very cruel game? And, and, and, and, and.

I want to write to tell you every small thing that happened, which felt so huge and consuming at the time, to expel it, or expose it: a self-awareness so acute that I could feel each of my pores prickling; unconquerable irrationality; the sudden and uncompromising inability to eat, or to sleep, or to write. Compulsions: the surging impulse to rip the skin clean off my face and the hair out from my head and to escape from my own body, or disrupt it somehow. The realisation that I was no longer who I was supposed to be, that I was barely a person at all, and the frightening acceptance that I might never feel happy or loved or worth anything again.

I want to write it all to you not for your sympathy or to make you look at me, but because, for the first time in six long, wordless months, I feel compelled to write, and because I am desperate to try and make you understand how it felt so incredibly isolating, so contained within me and only me, so utterly convincing and so fucking lonely. Though I know with renewed perspective that I was most certainly not, I felt like the only person on the planet to feel it. Now I want to pour out my heart and start again.

Does it sound pitiful, and self-indulgent? It does, doesn't it. But, fuck me, it does that to you. Depression comes out of the arse end of nowhere and not only takes away control – of who you are, of what you believe and what you see – but also the will to gain it back. And if it's tiring reading this pity-party on a page, it's because being sad and scared is fucking exhausting. Even more so because the fear is so present, but absolutely invisible – you don't know what it is frightening you, so you're rendered completely vulnerable to it. During weeks spent off work, barely moving from the furthest corner of the sofa, I thought, over and over, I am tired. I am tired of it, of trying to live, tired of trying and failing; I am tired of thinking and most of all I am tired of myself. I thought, I am aching. My body hurts. My jaw clenches so tightly that my face hurts. I ground my teeth so hard that I chipped one in anxiety.

Why now? Why did this happen? I can't answer the question, and I've learned that the many, many people who have felt like this or who still feel like this – one in five of us will experience severe depression in our lifetimes – can't either. In theory there may have been so-called 'triggers' – for seven months last year, and not for the first time, I watched nervously as doctors searched my body for multiple sclerosis; in March I watched someone very dear to me die in a hospital bed. A couple of other things happened, which I won't drag up here. My past happened. But all of it was simply unfortunate, inevitable things that happen in life. They made me worry, but they weren't half as bad as situations my friends deal with every day. And, anyway, I was absolutely fine – until I wasn't. Until I was suddenly, inexplicably, unreasonably sad.

It has changed me. I am – whether that is temporarily or permanently – different to how I was in July, when I took my first tumble. Things that are different include but are not exclusive to: I am more aware of my body; loud noises feel like they're suffocating me; often when people talk to me I can hear words but they appear in pencil, smudged with cheap rubber, or dissolving like they have been dipped in acid. The cogs in my mind are running at half-speed. My bones are dislocated and I don't know how to put them together again. I'm a stone and a half lighter. I can no longer watch a train pulling into a platform without placing my hand, firmly, on a solid wall to physically ground myself. I can barely read or write. I am single. I take a lot of Prozac and it makes my jaw clench and my head itch and my dreams insanely vivid and it also makes me feel like I might not die today.

It has changed me, but that's not always a bad thing. More things that are different now, compared to six months ago: I am more aware of looking after my body; music sounds more meaningful; I listen harder; I am trying harder; I talk to a therapist regularly; I am more accepting of my flaws; I am able, sometimes, to feel a deep gratitude that I am here and alive and laughing; I am single; I feel like I might not die today. I am making a point of telling people 'I have depression'. I want to try, like many others who I know have felt the same, to eradicate the humiliation of it all.

And I see mental health differently. Some days I think about conversations I've had with friends, when I've listened to them tell me they feel 'low', or alone, or scared, and feel the sharp sting of remorse that I couldn't hear them. Not wilfully, but ignorantly nonetheless, I couldn't really understand what they were saying at the time: I'd never been where they had. Most of my friends couldn't understand me, either. But the really good ones tried and, fuck me, did they help. Even when I was humiliated by my own disposition, even when I was awake for days. Even when, during one particularly frightening time, I reached a point that I genuinely wished I could swap lives with Mark out of *Peep Show* – a fate arguably worse than death. I knew things were bad then.

I don't know how or why – just as I don't know how or why depression happened to me – but now things are (slowly, gently) getting better. My peripheral vision is coming back, after months in blinkers. With the help of an endlessly understanding and patient team of colleagues, my sturdy, unmovable mum and stepdad, who helped every single day, and friends that have been roots in the ground, I've taken my first gasp of air after months of being submerged under very dark, very cold water. I'm still frightened – about where I have been and what lies ahead; I'm terrified of feeling so fucking broken again – and you still feel far away. But I'm nearing a conclusion. This isn't it. Soon.

If you are feeling depressed or suicidal, please call the Samaritans anytime, for free, from any phone, on 116 123.

You aren't alone, even if it feels that way. There are lots of NHS recommended support groups who want you to call if you're struggling with ill mental health.

Stop calling me a 'drama queen'

WOMEN'S MENTAL ILL-HEALTH IS STILL BEING REDUCED TO NOTHING MORE THAN 'HYSTERICAL DRAMA'. IT'S DANGEROUS AND IT HAS TO STOP

BY NATASHA DEVON

For seven years during my late teens and early twenties, I had a serious eating disorder. Diagnostic criteria aren't everything, but a specialist clinic gave my disorder a score of eighteen on a possible severity scare of twenty. By the end, I was barely functioning professionally, physically or socially. A couple of years into my recovery, I confided in a friend. 'All women go through a little bulimic phase,' she said. When I tried to impress upon her that it was more than that, she told me to stop being a 'drama queen'.

Accusations of exaggeration and attention-seeking are rife within mental-health conversations and they are most often directed at women. My campaign, the Mental Health Media Charter, asked our social media community where mental-health difficulties and misogyny intersect. We were flooded with responses from women who had been told that their mental illness was simply a facet of womanhood they weren't dealing with particularly well.

One respondent had her anxiety disorder dismissed as 'just a bit of PMT' by a former partner. This is infuriating not only from the point of view of misdiagnosis, but also because there is evidence to show hormonal fluctuations can make symptoms of mental illness more severe, particularly during adolescence, pregnancy and menopause.

In 2016, in response to a government-commissioned study that revealed that one in four young women was experiencing symptoms of depression or anxiety, *Daily Mail* columnist Sarah Vine wrote that asking a teenage girl if she's depressed is 'like asking a dog if it wants to go for a walk'. While her casual dismissal of what president of the Labour Campaign for Mental Health, Luciana Berger, called a 'crisis' was shocking, her views are far from unusual.

So, why the rush to silence female mental-health concerns? One answer is prevalence. Women are twice as likely to receive a diagnosis of anxiety or depression than men, which has led commentators to assume either that women suffer disproportionately or that psychological distress is part of the female experience.

What these people fail to recognise, however, is that there are equivalent patterns in male mental-health statistics. Men are three times more likely to need to seek help for drug and alcohol addiction and, as is widely publicised, far more likely to die by suicide – a man in the UK ends his own life every two hours.

Mental distress is part of life's tapestry, but while women are more likely to talk about it and seek medical advice, men are more likely to respond by self-medicating. Rightly, several campaigns and charities have focused their attentions on encouraging men to talk, but it seems that women are being punished for doing exactly that.

The second answer is good old-fashioned misogyny. While men are considered 'brave' for sharing intimate emotional battles, women are perceived as 'whinging'. Is it any wonder, then, that young women are self-harming in record numbers, perhaps a desperate attempt to manifest physically a pain which isn't properly acknowledged when they express it in words?

We're not 'drama queens', we're not 'crazy' ex-girlfriends and we're not 'hysterical'. Women suffering from poor mental health deserve better than those reductive, silencing labels. We deserve to be taken seriously.

The in-between of grief – when you have to remind yourself to cry

THIS IS CATHERINE GRAY'S FIRST CHRISTMAS AND NEW YEAR WITHOUT HER FATHER. AND SNATCHING MOMENTS TO REMEMBER HIM IS ESSENTIAL

BY CATHERINE GRAY

This year, the impossible happened. Somebody invincible died.

I'd always assumed my dad was invincible. I think we all subconsciously believe that about our parents, until the universe-altering moment when they are snatched from us. It's a moment that shakes the very foundations of your being. At the end of June, he was diagnosed with pneumonia and, at the end of July, he was taken by lung cancer aged just sixty-five.

In the first month, grief was a mugger. A mugger that snuck up, kicked my feet from under me and robbed me when I least expected it. It was triggered by the tiniest and most unexpected things. Reminders of Dad that plucked me from grocery shopping or yoga or whatever workaday task and plunged me into a place of absolute sorrow. The word 'eejit' (what he called me, often), the phrase 'skedaddle' (what he told me, often), a book by Graham Greene (his favourite author), swingball (he didn't believe in letting me win, ever), a Jack Russell with a black face (just like one of his dogs, Tod). I'd be walking down the street, thinking about fishcakes for dinner, and a caravan swinging past would transport me to that family holiday in Donegal circa 1992 and I'd find myself doubled over, having been punched in the stomach by loss.

I didn't have to consciously grieve – it just happened. But then that stopped. From month two onwards, I entered some sort of grief limbo. Whether it was the stress of organising his memorial (a political nightmare akin to a wedding, but with none of the fun, it turns out) or just my keep-your-shit-together Britishness that stuffed my grief down inside, who knows? But I entered a phase whereby I had to actively seek grief out.

Even on the day of his very touching memorial, six weeks after his death, I didn't cry. But the day after, I felt an irrepressible urge to do something. I went out for a run and my feet just took over, as if possessed. I went for a twelve kilometre run around Belfast, visiting each of the three houses he had lived at, and stood outside, under the safety cloak of night, racked with animalistic sobs. I followed my feet into a petrol station and bought the pink coconut buns he was so fond of scarfing (with zero impact on his daddy-long-legs frame) and inhaled two of them. I curled up in the sweet scent of the coconut and went to sleep serene.

I had made the grief happen.

A few days later, I felt the same sensation – the need to unpack. So, I went to Waterfoot beach and played 'Romeo And Juliet' by Dire Straits, toddler-wailing for a solid half hour, while a rainbow painted itself across the bay. The song transported me to being thirteen, simultaneously exhilarated and scared as my dad sped around the serpentine Antrim coastal roads, singing, 'When you gonna realise, it was just that the time was wrong?' at the top of his voice, while I rolled my teenage eyes and asked him to put 4 Non Blondes on already.

In-between grief is a shapeshifter. It shows up looking like work stress, irritation with a particular person or money worries. But now I know the key to unmasking its true form. Because when I'm snippy or sad or overwhelmed, I simply need to use one of the keys that unlock the shut-off room in my head that I 'don't have time for'. And the disguise the grief was wearing vanishes into a vapour. I wasn't any of those things – I was simply sad about my dad. Grief is something I have to consciously engage in. A mental-health to-do that I factor into my calendar, just like exercise and meditation. Otherwise the room becomes so full that I can't open the door.

I'm constantly cutting new grief keys. Framing a picture of a crazy-handsome nineteen-year-old him. Watching *In The Mood For Love*, the achingly beautiful Chinese film he played over and over.

Eating paper bags full of brandy balls, which you can only buy by the quarter in obscure Irish sweet shops. Reading his last email to me, which says: 'Going downhill so fast. Maybe gone soon. Love you so much. Have a great life.' (Thankfully, I made it out to the Philippines before he was actually gone and got to spend a week holding his hand.)

After I sit in the room for a while, I feel lighter, unburdened, clearer, more rational.

There is a positive flipside to losing a parent. As my dad's saying went: 'You're here for a good time, not for a long time.' It's unearthed a determination to grab life by the scruff of the neck. A steely resolve never to be cowed by my fear of 'What will people think?' (Dad didn't give a damn.) So, there's that.

Maybe I'll reach a stage, in a year or so, where I'll only visit the Dad room by choice, rather than need. It won't be a room of requirement any more – just somewhere I go to honour him. I don't know. I don't know what it will look like.

But I do know that room will always be there. And I wouldn't have it any other way. Grief is savage, but exquisite, too. After all, the reason you feel such depths of loss is because you reached such peaks of love. High, low. Up, down. You can't have one without the other.

So, I choose both.

The exhilarating joy of being utterly, unashamedly unhealthy

WE'RE TOLD THAT HEALTHINESS – EXERCISE, ABSTINENCE,
THERAPY – IS THE ROUTE TO HAPPINESS. ACTUALLY,
IT'S MORE COMPLICATED THAN THAT

BY ROISIN AGNEW

People reminiscing on the happiest times in their lives rarely begin their story with, 'There was this one time when I reduced my meat intake, came off the booze, started vaping, went to bed at 10pm every night and got to grips with my relationship with my mother. Man, that was amazing. Good times!' No. No one says that. Yet, somehow we've got to the stage where we equate happiness with healthiness all the time. When we see someone dieting, working out, dealing with their issues, reducing their vices, we show them affirmation on social media and validate them in real life, because we believe these things are synonymous with someone's happiness. All that unhealthy stuff was just a manifestation of their inner turmoil and misery, but now they're healthy and therefore happy, hurrah, Like! Maybe, to some extent, this is true. But how did we end up deciding that happiness is a by-product of healthiness? What about the lasting benefits of denial? How about the relief of suppressing painful thoughts and feelings? Or the regenerative power of short bouts of continual total insobriety? The sheer joy of eating every caloric obscenity in sight and the rebellion of gaining weight? Or the exhilaration of sleeping five hours in three days because of a powder a man in a sequin coat gave you?

I'm not minimising the gravity of the effects 'unhealthy' behaviour has on people with addictions or serious mental-health issues – that's a different subject. What I take issue with is how mainstream culture at large rewards and celebrates behaviour that we've acknowledged as healthy. We don't appreciate how our worst and least healthy behaviours often bring about our moments of greatest happiness.

Perhaps it's because you cannot market, brand and sell an unhealthy lifestyle today, while you can certainly market, brand and sell a healthy one – it's highly profitable and makes up the vast majority of my Instagram suggestions. Gone is the cool Marlboro man. Every advert for alcohol comes with a call for responsibility; ditto condoms. Menus in restaurants have the calories listed next to them. Because being healthy leads to better productivity – and better workers. You not showing up hungover to work is good for your employer. And, yeah, capitalism. So, at some stage, as a society we accepted that happiness has a correlation with healthiness. Yet I remain unpersuaded, mainly because my happiest moments have coincided with my least healthy moments and there are vices I am happy to admit I will never give up on.

I do not seek to advocate a life of unchecked hedonism, but I think there is a confusion between the pursuit of healthiness and the pursuit of happiness. You can be engaging in the former and be unwittingly distancing yourself further and further from the latter. In fact, often the effort to be healthy while being unhappy only serves to compound the fact that you're failing to achieve the end goal you desired.

Over the past six months, the pendulum of my health has swung both ways. Around Christmas, I checked my drinking, took up jogging, undertook cognitive behavioural therapy, reduced my smoking and my consumption of meat. It felt good. And then I moved to Lisbon. For the past three months, I've been consuming nothing but white bread and beer (I have a wheat intolerance), I often don't sleep at all, I haven't FaceTimed Trish, my lovely shrink, once, I've realised with little to no dismay that I'm back on almost a pack of cigarettes a day and I'm consuming a fair share of ungood substances. And, hand on heart, I have never been happier.

A piece of writing I return to again and again is Zadie Smith's essay *Joy*, in which she seeks to make the difficult distinction between pleasure and joy. She explains how she experiences pleasure daily in her meals, her children, in the purchase of a new dress. She goes on to describe how she thinks she's experienced joy only five or six times in life, three times through falling in love and twice through drugs. She recalls a night on ecstasy in Fabric in the nineties and how she didn't experience joy, but she 'was joy', describing it as an egoless feeling, a journey that suggested what joy might possibly be like: 'At the neural level, such experiences gave you a clue about what joy not-under-the-influence would feel like, Helped you learn to recognise joy, when it arrived.'

Arguably, unhealthy behaviour, or what we might call 'bad behaviour', is really the engagement in pleasures in the hope of obtaining eventual joy. It leads to happiness in some ways precisely because of the egoless feeling it allows for – a total lack of consideration for the self and the consequences of one's actions, the submission to bad habits and a collective unhinging. While it can be self-destructive, it isn't solely self-destructive. Unhealthy behaviour can be freeing and optimistic – it's driven by the idea that joy is obtainable in some nebulous way, perhaps not through this drink or this three-day bender, but somewhere close by. Healthy behaviour is the opposite. It's an exercise in ego – discovering what is lacking, what needs nourishing, what new goal can be achieved, what can be done to stave off the approaching doom. It can of course be a source of great happiness. It's just not the only one.

'Most people die of a sort of creeping common sense, and discover when it is too late that the only things one never regrets are one's mistakes,' Oscar Wilde writes in *The Picture Of Dorian Gray*. While Dorian isn't exactly the poster child for how unhealthy behaviour can lead to happiness, I still think the quote is a good one. Our unhealthy behaviour sometimes can signpost moments in life when we were most free, hopeful and, perhaps, joyful. And, for this reason, we should remember to celebrate it and allow for it.

Why are trans kids so unhappy? Blame grown-ups

HALF OF THE TRANS KIDS IN OUR SCHOOLS HAVE TRIED TO KILL THEMSELVES. IT'S URGENT THAT WE STAND UP TO THE BULLIES – EVEN THE ADULT ONES

BY JUNO DAWSON

Stonewall (a charity for which I'm a School Role Model) released a report on schools.

Let's start with the few promising green shoots sprouting up through a very murky compost: from the survey of 3,700 students, Stonewall found LGBTQ+ pupils are reporting fewer instances of bullying – from 55 per cent in 2012 to 45 per cent in 2017. Furthermore, fewer pupils report hearing homophobic language in school. So that's good.

But they are pretty much the only rays of light. The rest of the report is sobering – to say the least.

Perhaps the most worrying statistics of all are those concerning the rising number of trans and gender non-binary (NB) pupils in our schools. Eight out of ten young trans people have self-harmed and almost half have attempted suicide. Think about that for a second: half of the trans teens in our schools have tried to kill themselves.

The schools I visit (and, yes, the fact that they invite me suggests they are trans-friendly, I admit), in my capacity as a Stonewall Role Model and teen author, are trying to accommodate trans youth – in terms of bathrooms, changing spaces and school uniform. I almost always find teachers and librarians to be a heroic, supportive bunch. So what's the problem? Why are trans and NB youth so at risk of bullying and its associated mental-health issues?

(Let's do the disclaimer right up front: I DO NOT SPEAK FOR ALL TRANS PEOPLE, but here's my take. Warning – I'm mad as hell and I'm not holding back.)

The problem is not young trans people or the practicalities of schooling them in a safe environment. The problem is other people. Other people are arseholes. It's that simple. As the final pieces of my gender jigsaw puzzle clicked into place, I felt euphoric, not depressed. After many years of begrudgingly styling it out as a bloke, I could finally actualise the version of myself I'd always been in my head. That wasn't a cause for anxiety – it was a reason to celebrate. Alas, I was early to the party. And I'll say it again, other people can be ARSEHOLES. On a day-to-day basis, I get (best case) stared at, muttered about, called a 'tranny' on buses in BRIGHTON where you'd think Lil Jenny Flowercrown and Tommy Votes-Green would have dealt with it by now. I often wish I had sticky gold stars to hand out to people for successfully 'clocking' me and telling their girlfriends. Why were you staring in the first place, matey? Hmm?

I'm a big girl. I came out in my late twenties and I already had a rhino-thick hide from my previous incarnation as a feminine gay man. But if I was in a school, where kids can be shady AF on a good day, I honestly don't think I'd be able to hack it.

Worse still, young people live online now. There is literally no respite from insidious, transphobic white noise. You have Piers Morgan asking if he can identify as an elephant if trans people can identify as non-binary. You have Jenni Murray on *Woman's Hour* asking if trans women are 'real women', you have Germaine Greer calling us delusional and the *New Statesman* suggesting we're dangerous.

It's water torture, let me tell you. I'm from Bradford. I'm dead hard and even I find it gruelling. If I were fourteen years old, struggling with puberty, exam stress, shifting friendship dynamics and widespread ridicule, mockery, abuse and endless questioning, I have no doubt that I'd crack.

LGBTQ+ kids are not broken. They do not need fixing. They don't need to suppress themselves or keep their heads down lest they draw attention to who they really are. LGBTQ+ kids should be joining me and my friends in celebrating Pride (capital P) and pride (little p). LGBTQ+ youth are glorious and they going to save us from the dirge we're in socially and politically, I really believe that.

The problem is in the way trans and non-binary people are spoken to, spoken about and treated culturally. Until there is a broader shift in conversations in magazines, online, on television and in cinema, how – honestly – can we expect playground discourse to evolve beyond that of their so-called adult role models?

When it comes to suicide, awkward conversations can save lives

IT'S NOT EASY TO TALK ABOUT SUICIDE. BUT IF YOU KNOW SOMEONE WHO IS IN DESPAIR, TURN UP, BE A NUISANCE – AND ASK THEM ABOUT IT, NO MATTER HOW UNCOMFORTABLE YOU FEEL

BY POORNA BELL

Death attracts clichés like fruit flies to a banana, because they fill the gaps of awkwardness.

One of the things you hear most when people are trying to make sense of that most senseless of deaths – suicide – is 'they had so much to live for'. I heard it repeatedly when my husband, Rob, died by suicide in 2015.

After two prominent and public losses to suicide – Kate Spade and Anthony Bourdain – this phrase is being used over and over again, in the midst of articles listing their achievements and zest for life. In Bourdain's case, it's underpinned by an interview he did with *People* magazine, where he is quoted as saying: 'I also do feel I have things to live for.'

The problem with the 'they had so much to live for' phrase is that it is attempting to make a clumsy connection between suicide and the trappings of money and power in a person's life. In our narrow and simplistic either/or perspective on the world, too many of us believe that a person at risk of suicide is someone who is alone. Someone who has a sad, unloved existence and doesn't have friends or family to live for. There is often a default implication that they are somehow responsible for the pain they felt – when, in fact, it was clearly so overwhelming and not within their control that the only recourse was to take their own life. Too frequently, too many of us believe that other people or material things give you a reason for your existence.

Although male suicide is still ridiculously high and teen suicide is rising, most people don't need a reason for their existence. We simply exist. A person likely to kill themselves is doing so because of a pain separate to any and all love and success that exists in their lives. As many people who have attempted suicide and survived will tell you, it's not about a fixation with death – it's wanting the relentlessness to stop.

The reason these deaths take us by surprise is because we assumed by proxy of their success and social network that they wouldn't have a reason to feel despair or hopelessness. But, speaking from experience, if we don't expand our idea of what suicide is, we're isolating the very people we want to help.

There are different schools of thought on how you can help someone who is at risk of suicide. I can only speak as to what I've learnt from Rob passing away – and from me subsequently feeling at risk. The biggest problem is that a person at risk of suicide is unlikely to be able to tell you that they are at risk of suicide. We can tell them to ask for help, we can talk about the need to create a positive mental-health culture free of stigma, but it's not as simple as that.

The best way forward, I think, is a two-pronged approach of being non-judgemental and letting them know that you'll be there as support, so they can reach out if they need. But it's also actually being there as support.

We found out the hard way that there are lots of people who say 'anything you need' but aren't there. When your life is literally in your own two hands, you don't have the mental space to deal with someone needing to check their fucking calendar two weeks from Tuesday.

I don't mean to say that anyone is in any way responsible for another person's life, because when someone you love dies from suicide, you punish yourself well enough for what you perceive you didn't do. But, as a general rule of thumb, good suicide prevention means proactively checking in on a friend or a loved one if you think something isn't quite right with their behaviour. Then, engaging them in conversations about how they are doing, even if it feels awkward and uncomfortable for you. I remember when Rob told me about a suicide attempt he made back in 2013, when he was very depressed, and I completely emotionally and verbally shut down around it. I found the idea of him being dead so horrifying I didn't ask him questions about it – not how he got to that point or how he felt afterwards.

Not everyone who kills themselves is mentally ill, so if you have a friend who is going through a tough time but also seems to be pushing people away, make a nuisance of yourself and meet up with them. And if they do open up to you, ask them questions and try to get them to engage in services, whether that's charities such as Mind or CALM, or suicidal sanctuaries such as MayTree. Ask questions such as: have they gone to see their GP? Are they getting any kind of professional help beyond trying to pull themselves through it?

With suicide, restoring self-esteem and a sense of perspective is critical, so find out what they have in their lives that enables that. When I spoke to Natalie Howarth, who runs MayTree, she said that most people come in with their sense of self-worth completely flattened. Understand that it is perfectly possible for people to be two things – they could be a successful businesswoman and still have zero self-worth because of other circumstances in their lives. The chances are, it won't be any one thing, such as a broken relationship or money worries. It will be linked to something much vaster and deeper than that and, very often, it connects to bigger feelings of shame or an inability to see that things will be different.

I know that when it came to Rob, I was so naive about it. I, too, was fooled by the idea that he had a good job, me, our family, our dog, our house – a thousand reasons to live for. And yet he still felt so terrible that he was compelled to take his own life. I didn't ask him about the things that made life so unbearable, that made it necessary to leave in that moment.

And I think, if we are to support the people in our lives and understand the deaths of Kate Spade and Anthony Bourdain better, that is the real question we need to start asking.

Self-harm – and why it's time we paid attention to it

THOSE WHO SELF-HARM, PARTICULARLY WOMEN WHO SELF-HARM, ARE OFTEN WRITTEN OFF AS ATTENTION-SEEKERS. WE NEED TO ADDRESS THE PROBLEM WITH COMPASSION AND UNDERSTANDING

BY ROWAN HISAYO BUCHANAN

'Oh, no, that won't work,' my friend said. 'I have a meeting with my therapist then.' We were trying to make a lunch date. She is a friend, but not a particularly intimate one. She said the word 'therapist' as simply as she might've said 'dentist'. I've had many conversations like this. They're light and frank. At least, in the circle of my young city-based friends, a therapist is nothing to be ashamed of.

We don't talk about the scars. The thin white marks that appear in the summer when sleeves are shorter. I have several friends with such scars. They are people who care for pets, hold down jobs and move gently through the world. They don't refer to the marks and nor do I.

Once, someone I loved cut their fingers and touched my face with the blood-warm tips. They loved me back and in the heat of mania could find no other way to say it. We were both young. I didn't know what to do. I felt there was no one I could tell. Malaise or grief might be socially acceptable, blood was not. And so, I walked home, with blood crusting on my cheeks. I barely remember what we said to each other or how exactly the cut was made. But the silence of that walk remains with me. I stood alone in the pale light of a bathroom and slowly sponged off the dark flakes.

Almost a decade later, I still think about how the most frightening thing was not warm, red liquid, but the silence afterwards. We are both OK now, but I wonder how much easier it might've been if we'd felt less alone. Everything in the media seemed to say it was gothy. It was in some way self-indulgent. Worst of all, self-harm was attention-seeking.

The person I loved didn't want to be judged. And I didn't want to be judged for loving them. We didn't know how to ask for help.

Almost a decade later, and self-harm doesn't seem much easier to talk about. When I mentioned to a friend that I was going to write this article, he seemed worried. Was self-harm really something I wanted to be associated with? But I wanted to find out where this stigma comes from and how we might change it.

In a crowded London coffee shop, I looked around for Dr Sarah Chaney. It was the morning and the small space was filled with caffeine-seeking bodies. Chaney is a historian specialising in self-mutilation and psychiatry. Her book on the history of self-harm is called *Psyche On The Skin*. I knew her research interests, but I had no idea what she looked like.

Eventually, a woman with wavy hair and a wide smile caught my eye. 'Are you Rowan?'

At first, it felt a little awkward to be asking this stranger about something so unhappy and intimate. I couldn't help but think of the suited men one table over. Were they listening? What must they make of us? But soon I was absorbed by what I was learning. She explained that, for much of history, blood-letting was an accepted medical practice. It was only in the 19th century that medical literature began to describe self-injury as a problem.

In 1870, a British medical journal ran a series of articles on what they called 'motiveless malingerers'. These motiveless malingerers were women, often middle-class women, who injured themselves without any apparent reason. Usually, these women created artificial skin lesions or burned themselves with household substances. Psychoanalysts described it as motiveless-malingering, because they assumed that a man or a working-class woman injuring himself or herself would be shirking work. The psychoanalysts couldn't see a motive for these middle-class women. This was true even when the women provided the explanation. Chaney described a study in which a patient, 'said that she struggled to get by in the world, she'd been denied job opportunities that would have happened if she was a man'. Her psychoanalyst considered such a reason to be ridiculous and further proof that the woman was making up her miseries.

By the early 20th century, hysterical self-injury was treated as attention-seeking. Psychoanalysts felt it proved 'that women, all women, are naturally more deceptive than men'. The profile of the deceptive, self-harming woman seeped into studies in the 1960s and 1970s. At this time, studies on self-harm focused on 'delicate self-cutting', which was, again, associated with women. This image of the attention-seeking woman seeped into popular culture.

This prejudice from over one hundred years ago had wormed its way into my life. It was what kept me from trying to find help for one of the people I loved most. We were sure everyone would think it reflected poorly on our characters. And this concern is common.

It's not a topic most people feel comfortable talking about, so I reached out using the veil of the internet. I asked if anyone wanted to talk about their experience with self-harm. I was struck by the fact that, far from seeking attention, most responders wanted their names held back. W, a British novelist living in New Zealand, wrote, 'I would keep my self-harm absolutely private, with a deep shame and covering myself in layers of clothing or jewellery that covered up any marks.' W was so careful that even her partner was unaware of the harm for a while. 'Any mistaken idea that I was seeking attention was terrifying to me.' W didn't want attention. Instead, she longed for understanding and acceptance.

A Korean-American woman in her twenties, Z, complained that 'I feel like the misrepresentation made it really difficult to speak out about it . . . The media paints it as a teenage-girl thing where people just slash their wrists and wear heavy eye make-up. In reality, a lot of us cut elsewhere to hide it and, rather than attention-seeking, it's something that brings you deep shame.'

Those who wrote gave many reasons. L, a Chinese-British woman, wrote that, for a time, self-harm was the only way she could cope with the stress of having two autistic children. A man, whose struggle with self-harm is ongoing, explained that it began when he was fifteen. 'I was really depressed and it feels good to focus the hurt into something physical and concentrated instead of just a diffuse pain throughout my whole mind.'

I have received few correspondences so frank and personal as those I exchanges. I was so grateful that these individuals had given me their stories. But my responses felt weak. All I could say was, 'I'm so sorry you're going through that.' Or, 'It's wonderful that you're find thing things easier now.' They weren't the responses I'd need if I was in pain. So, I went out looking for hope and better answers.

Ian Noonan is head of the department of mental-health nursing at King's College London. He facilitates a group for young people dealing with self-harm, is running a research project studying adults who have succeeded in stopping self-harming and has worked in A&E assessing cases of self-harm.

Noonan is softly spoken. He's the sort of man you can imagine wanting to talk to if you were in pain. As soon as I sat down in his office, he offered me a cup of tea. Noonan explained that, increasingly, studies showing instances of self-harm are evenly split between men and women. Self-harm can be cutting. But it can, as in the case of one of Noonan's patients, be a young boy asking his friend to jump on his arm and break it. Often even medical professionals can fail to recognise instances of self-harm if the person hurting themselves doesn't fit a recognised stereotype.

Noonan described a couple he encountered in A&E. A young woman had been out drinking all day with her boyfriend. They argued. The woman smashed a bottle of Bacardi Breezer and cut herself. An ambulance was called and she was referred to Noonan for his mental-health expertise. She explained that she'd cut herself because she was drunk and in a rage. She smashed the bottle, initially thinking she might cut her boyfriend. She'd realised she couldn't do that. But the angry energy had to go somewhere and so she cut herself. At the end of their session, she asked Noonan if he was going to see her boyfriend. Noonan was surprised and asked why. The woman explained that after the ambulance had been called, her boyfriend wanted to travel with her, but had been stopped. He punched through the ambulance window and cut his hand badly. He had to see plastic surgeons. But no one referred him to Noonan, because the A&E view was that that was just how drunk men behaved. 'But functionally,' Noonan said, 'I don't see how they're different. They're both expressing anger, in a way that involved breaking glass and injuring themselves.' It was only because the young woman told Noonan that the young man received therapeutic attention

We may not recognise self-harm in 'the boy with the broken arm, the boy with the re-infected wound, the man who punched a window . . . if you go to the pub and drink thirteen pints over the course of the evening, you fall off the bus, hurt yourself and spend the night in A&E covered in your own vomit – you're a lad.' Yet, this behaviour can serve the same function as something like cutting, which we more easily recognise.

The stereotype of self-harm as a teenage-girl issue doesn't work very well for women, either. In Noonan's words, 'As soon as you label it as part of a different group, that labelling prevents you seeing what the person's asking for.' This can mean that women, like Z, find it harder to seek help.

I asked what he thought of the idea of self-harm as attention-seeking. He paused before saying, 'I've never understood this idea of attention-seeking as being in and of itself a bad thing. My thought is always, 'What is it that you want me to attend to?' None of the patients he'd dealt with in his work framed self-harm as a way to get attention. However, it could, on occasion, draw attention that was sorely needed.

Even well-intentioned professionals can enter a sour relationship with the patient – I'm trying to heal you. You're trying to hurt yourself. In fact, the professional should be addressing the issue that has led the patient to self-harm.

One patient self-harmed to escape a violent partner. She locked herself in the bathroom to escape him. She knew he didn't want her to die. So, she opened the medicine cabinet and overdosed. He stopped trying to hurt her and called an ambulance. At least in the hospital she was safe for a moment. 'Thank God that she sought that attention. It saved her life,' Noonan said. Although it took her a while to be able to articulate the abuse, Noonan said she wasn't hiding anything. It was just that it wasn't something she was able to express at first. In her case, the threat was coming from the outside – her partner. Even when the threat is internal, depression or stress, Noonan emphasises that the best way to understand self-harm is to look at the problem the patient is using self-harm to address.

There are many strategies for approaching that greater psychological pain, more than can be covered here. But Noonan is working with a choice-based treatment. The idea of stopping can set patients up to fail. Self-harm is, as he says, a coping mechanism. Deciding to give up a coping mechanism can be stressful or upsetting in itself. This can lead to an increased desire to self-harm. Noonan tries to move self-harm lower down the list of coping mechanisms. He suggests that the sufferer consider another coping mechanism first. For example: talking to a friend, smashing a watermelon, punching a cushion or yelling.

He tries to discover what the self-harm helps with. If the answer is a negative emotion, stress, for example, Noonan asks patients what for them is the opposite of that emotion. For one patient the opposite of stress might be calm. For another it might be hope. Noonan would then ask, when was the last time you felt hopeful? They might respond – painting or working with clay or exercising. He'd then encourage them to try engaging in that activity before resorting to self-harm.

In all his strategies, Noonan emphasises the importance of acknowledging that people self-harm for a reason. There is some deeper problem that needs help, attention and understanding. This receptive approach is one I think we can all consider. When we discover that a family member or friend or acquaintance self-harms, our first response can be to choose to listen.

The day I went to see Noonan, the light was low and clear. It was a winter brightness that has been with me for so many years. Red double-deckers tooled by on the street below. It was a day like so many others. In his office, there were no futuristic brain scanners or mind-reading devices. Yet, our conversation felt fresh and radical. His approach was so kind and so pragmatic. As I thought about the events of all those years ago, I wished I'd had someone like Noonan in my life. Stepping out in to the sun, I felt comforted to know that people like him are working on changing the way we talk about self-harm.

Those who self-harm aren't the only ones accused of doing something upsetting for attention. It's a charge that has been thrown at feminists for decades. Women who were trying to get attention – not for themselves, but for a major societal problem. Whether in the context of mental health or social justice, to say a person is doing it for attention is a way to dismiss the underlying issue. Often those being denied a hearing are those who need it most.

Attention comes from the verb attend, which originates from the Latin *tendere* – to stretch. To attend is therefore to stretch your mind towards something. When we ask for attention, we are asking to be stretched towards. It doesn't seem an unreasonable thing to want. Can we try a little harder to stretch towards each other?

Let's start offering our attention. It may make all the difference.

Money

MARISA BATE | BRIDGET MINAMORE
LYNN ENRIGHT | DAISY BUCHANAN
YOMI ADEGOKE | POORNA BELL

The reality of being a thirtysomething

SHOULD I FREEZE MY EGGS? WILL I EVER BUY A HOUSE? WE'RE ASKING THE WRONG QUESTIONS

BY MARISA BATE

'Welcome to the club,' our very own Lauren Laverne smiled at me when I turned thirty. For this was when life was about to start properly, no? That's what I had long believed. The anxiety and chaos of my twenties would just be a hazy memory, left behind with overdraft fees and the morning-after pill, replaced by navy cashmere and a promotion and a stable relationship and a house and maybe a dog. I would morph from Calamity Jane into a confident go-getter making Big Life Plans, like falling in love, buying a house, having kids that I can call Dusty and Shelby, who I'll read bedtime stories to featuring Gloria Steinem. See? Big Life Plans.

I had modelled this life on two women. One was my friend Jess. She's seven years older than me and has always had her shit firmly together, normally in black leather Mulberry that had one of those special pockets for a laptop. For most of her thirties, I've watched her in awe as she's worked hard and played hard (seeing her rip her jeans while doing the splits in a busy London pub remains a life highlight and one of the few moments she didn't seem firmly in control). And she had her own flat. I lived nearby and had to look for mice while she called me, standing on a chair, genuinely petrified. But it was all hers. Now she's married, has two beautiful little girls and she's the breadwinner of her family.

The other was Rachel Green. Yes, I still harbour a dream of life in New York and learning to like bowls of black coffee and falling in love with my best friend and all the other clichés I doubt I'll ever shake. Rachel was the poster girl for whatever fuck-up you make in your twenties (i.e. almost marrying a dentist called Barry), by the time you got to your thirties it would all be A-OK. Cue job at Ralph

Lauren, house, baby and realising the man of your dreams is just across the hall.

Because this is the narrative we've been led to believe we can have. Not just by glossy American sitcoms either, but by real life. I've seen it with my own eyes. I've seen Jess do it. My mum did it. From the post-war baby boomers, being able to own a house and have a baby has been far more than a possibility – it's been a likelihood. (Of course, this is a narrative mostly of the white middle classes, for whom social mobility and access to jobs and housing has been an easier and more expected route. While I whine, I'm very aware of the Focus E15 Mothers, who continue to fight for their homes, that the government has capped social housing and the country's budget has hit the poorest, hardest. Even dreaming of emulating Rachel Green is sugar-coated in privilege.)

But, for someone like me and for many people in this country, we've been led to believe that certain things are an inevitability: go to university, get a good job. Work hard, save for a house. Meet someone, have a baby.

The papers confirm what the thirtysomethings on the ground already know: that's not how things work anymore. A report from the Yorkshire Building Society found that 49 per cent of people in their thirties doubt they will *ever* own a property. And this is truer nowhere than in London. Recent research found that the average Londoner would need a 266 per cent pay rise to buy a place. Either we all have to get shit-hot at negotiating or embrace renting.

Another study claimed the number of women freezing their eggs had soared, from less than 100 in 2001 to over 800 last year. Experts warn this costly producer has no guarantees, but still women – the majority of whom are in their thirties – are paying up to £10k for the treatment.

Why? Well, because – to my mind, at least – it's one way of tackling the reality of the situation we've found ourselves in. It's a response to the moment we realise we are not, and never will be, Rachel Green, and not just because of her impossibly good hair game. If we can't afford a house, can we really afford a baby? And this web of tangled dead ends only gets more depressing when we throw in careers. Good job? Still can't afford to have house. Good job? Can you really afford to take time out to have a baby? A new report found that half all of working mothers' careers had been negatively impacted by having children.

URGH. It's enough to start mumbling that you never wanted a career/house/baby anyway. And, actually, let's just be continental and chic and rent till we're a hundred because, that way, we're free of all the trappings of a patriarchal society and perhaps we could just start a revolution. Perhaps.

But perhaps we do need some sort of drastic overhaul – realign our dreams and goal posts and personal markers of success? Maybe, post the 2008 recession, the biggest financial collapse since the Great Depression, those of us in our thirties are the first fallout generation. In the debris of a broken banking system, is this the reality of the repercussions? Perhaps we simply can't have what people once had. A corrupt and unregulated housing market means we can't own homes. Women being allowed, in some instances, to thrive in the workplace means we might not have a baby. Waiting to get the job and house in order before you have a kid? Maybe it will be too late.

I don't mean to be a doom-monger. I am in this boat, renting as a single person, without savings, without a pension and without hope – on some days. But, as the dust settles on this new outlook for women like me, maybe it's an opportunity to take a long hard look to figure out what we really want. If you wrote down a list, what would the top three things be? And do we only want these things because that's just how things have always been? What if things could be different? Perhaps let's start asking different questions. Not 'Should I freeze my eggs?' or 'Will I ever buy a house?' Perhaps, instead, we should ask, 'How do we have a healthy, protected renting culture? How do we protect against maternity discrimination better? How do we help women who want to have a baby if, funnily enough, the dream man isn't across the hall?'

I'm still delighted to be in Club Thirty. I don't have a house or a baby, but there is definitely more cashmere and less chaos – and that's not a bad place to start.

Does how I make my money define what kind of adult I am?

BRIDGET MINAMORE MAKES HER LIVING AS A FREELANCE
WRITER WHEREAS HER MOTHER WORKED CLEANING OFFICES AT
NIGHT. DOES SHE HAVE A RESPONSIBILITY TO EARN MORE
MONEY THAN SHE DOES, SHE WONDERS

BY BRIDGET MINAMORE

I started feeling like an adult when I began spending like one. I've never spent my money on clothes – despite my penchant for over-priced trainers and oversized jewellery, I've never been a massive shopper – but instead, I spend my money on life. On nice food and theatre tickets, on gigs and proper bedsheets, but also on rent and bills. While, as a writer, I've never been anything close to rich (or even well paid), I spend my money on things that I enjoy because I can, and I recognise what a huge privilege this is. For lots of people – people like most of my own family – this is a privilege they have never had. As I've grown up, I've found myself coming to terms with my money-related privileges, and these thoughts are perhaps what make me feel like an adult more than anything else.

Despite how easy I find it spending money on myself, money has never been something I've enjoyed thinking about. Like my working-class immigrant parents before me, I think about it a lot. I dream about money. I worry about money. I cry about money, and laugh about money, and love and hate and obsess about the money I have and the money I don't. For someone who doesn't earn anything close to a high wage, I feel like I think about money far more than I should. Perhaps this is just the way the world works. Those of us without much money, or those of us who grew up without it, know its value and so devote much of our time to thoughts of gold coins and crumpled blue paper. I know I have. And like all freelancers know, keeping an eye on money matters isn't a choice. It's a necessity.

My money-related worries are also linked to thoughts of my family. My parents drilled the importance of money into my brain but if I'm honest, it's not exactly their money talk that has helped me to grow up. Morphing into your parents is one of the big markers of adulthood, but for me, my journey was more about realising how different I am to the people who raised me. While I might worry about money like my parents did, and while I also don't earn very much like them too, there's one main difference: in lots of ways, I chose the life I lead.

I choose to be a freelance writer because there's nothing else I can do that would make me as happy as I am with my life – and I am happy with my work, in spite of the endlessly delayed invoices and the constant hustling. Whenever I begin moaning about my work, I can't help but remember how lucky I really am. Choice when it comes to career, or work, or even a salary, is something that my parents simply never had. My mum and dad had me to feed and clothe, bills to pay and large families back in Ghana that needed money sent to them on a regular basis, so they worked the best-paid jobs they could get. There wasn't any time to consider if their work was their calling.

I have a very different relationship to money compared to my parents because we earn our money differently, and we work in very different fields too. My understanding of this, and the fact I subsequently made the decision to do what I do (despite the risk I'd be broke and hustling forever), was a hard choice to stick to. In lots of ways it feels like a choice only an adult could make – albeit a privileged one. Now, I often feel doubly guilty when I think about money and my family: on one hand, I wonder how selfish it is to have a precarious job that could leave me in a position where I can never afford to support my parents. On the other hand, I feel guilty about earning more than what my mum would have earned cleaning offices late at night, a job that is definitely much harder than typing on a laptop. When I grew up, I began to recognise that my money was not just about me.

Money makes me feel like a 'real' adult, in the best and worst possible way. I'm in my late twenties, at an age where I'm more aware than ever of the options in front of me, and the knowledge that lots of these choices – having kids, travelling, changing career, finding somewhere permanent to live – are expensive. Underneath all this is the fact that I'm not the only person who's growing older: my parents are, too. I'm an only child, and I have a feeling a big part of my growing money anxieties revolve around the fact I know at some point, I'll be the only person who has any real responsibility towards my pensioner parents. A few years ago, when I could spend three figures of my student loan on a frivolous night out, caring for my parents in their old age was something I had never even considered. Today? It's something I think about with every passing day, and something I share with a lot of adults all over the world.

We're finally talking about money more openly. Now we need to get brutal about it

THE PAY GAP ISN'T A MISTAKE; THE PAY GAP IS PART OF THE WAY WOMEN ARE CONSISTENTLY UNDERMINED. LET ELLEN POMPEO LEAD THE CHARGE FOR CHANGE

BY LYNN ENRIGHT

During the final hour of my hen party weekend, when a few of us were standing in a small regional airport, hungover and deflated and broke, about to board a flight and after that get on a train and after that another train and then go to bed for approximately five hours before getting up for work, we looked over at my sixty-one-year-old mother, who was glowing with an almost giddy energy. 'What's your secret, how do you stay so perky?' my friend shouted over to her as she went to leave the airport, our goodbyes having already been said. She turned her head and gave us a smile revealing her perfect white teeth. 'My pension!' she said. 'Make sure you have a good pension.' With that she was gone. And the mood within our hungover cluster turned sourer. Because if anything can make four thirtysomething private-sector-working women feel worse at the end of an expensive and boozy weekend, it's the mention of pensions. None of us in that group – of project managers and social workers and journalists – had a pension. And we had no real sense of how to get one.

We had thought my mother was going to say something easy like magnesium supplements. We could have handled magnesium supplements. But instead she was suggesting that her trim figure, her indefatigable spirit, her cheery disposition was down to the fact that she had worked hard in a public-sector job for thirty-five years or so before retiring on a generous pension.

As a piece of generation-to-generation advice, it felt brutal, a cruel baby boomer joke but hey, the truth hurts. And it feels like we are living in a new era of financial honesty. With the housing market broken and wages stagnant, the once-standard path of job-mortgage-retirement is no longer a possibility for many, and so it's particularly interesting to read or talk about how much people earn and how much they spend and save. A recent *Refinery 29* Money Diary outlining a hapless twenty-six-year-old's financial woes got people talking on social media. I found her reckless pursuit of experiences – of joy, of life, of fun – in the face of a paltry £14k-a-year salary endearing and almost commendable, but many others thought she was 'irresponsible' and an 'idiot'.

For women, this new openness about financial matters is particularly important. Because while our twenty-six-year-old (anti-)heroine is spending hundreds of pounds she doesn't have on cocaine and Deliveroo, the gender pay gap remains stubbornly wide. It's around 9 per cent for full-time work generally, but much worse in lots of particularly lucrative industries – and a newly published report from the Office of National Statistics has destroyed the notion that the gap exists because women naturally choose or somehow prefer to do less well-remunerated work. Straightforward discrimination probably plays a part, the figures show.

For anyone who followed the BBC pay gap story, this won't be a surprise. Carrie Gracie's case was clear: as the BBC's China correspondent she was paid less than the Middle East correspondent and the US correspondent. Why? Because she is a woman.

What the BBC pay gap fallout has shown, though, is that transparency doesn't necessarily end the discrimination. Knowing the clear, embarrassing, shameful details of the pay gap isn't enough to stop pay discrimination. The pay gap isn't a mistake; the pay gap is part of the way women are consistently undermined. Just listen to how the BBC's John Humphrys and Jon Sopel discuss the gender pay gap, listen to how they make light of a colleague and a major economic injustice. (No, seriously, if you haven't listened to this already, do it now, it's really quite something.)

So transparency is a help, and learning to talk about money more frankly is necessary, but it's not enough. The way women talk about money has to change if we are going to close the pay gap. Enter Ellen Pompeo.

In a piece published in the *Hollywood Reporter*, Pompeo gave women everywhere a masterclass in asking for what they are worth. Her honesty is striking; her tone is ferocious. She is a woman who will fight for the salary she deserves (more than $20m a year, apparently). If Ellen Pompeo worked at the BBC, she would train her sights on John Humphrys, and she'd probably win.

Pompeo acknowledges that being a woman from an Irish-Catholic background is bit of a double whammy in terms of feeling guilty or squeamish about asking or a pay rise but throughout the article, there is a glorious brashness that we're just not used to seeing. Speaking about how women are routinely screwed over in Hollywood she says: 'I'm not necessarily perceived as successful . . . but a twenty-four-year-old actress with a few big movies is, even though she's probably being paid shit – certainly less than her male co-star and probably with no backend. And they're going to pimp her out until she's thirty-three or thirty-four and then she's out like yesterday's trash, and then what does she have to take care of herself? These poor girls have no real money, and the studio is making a fortune and parading them like ponies on a red carpet. I mean, Faye Dunaway is driving a fuckin' Prius today. Now, there's nothing wrong with a Prius, but my point is, she had no financial power. If we're going to invoke change, that has to be part of it.'

It's the kind of statement that makes four hungover pensionless women look even more pathetic. And it's the kind of statement that reminds us that transparency is good, getting advice from your mum about a pension plan is good, but when it comes to closing the pay gap and paying women what they deserve, employers respond to pressure and ultimatums and bloody determination. So that's better. The obliteration of the pay gap will involve a battle; Ellen Pompeo can lead the way.

I'm economically infertile, and I've made peace with that

FOR DAISY BUCHANAN AND MANY WOMEN LIKE HER, HAVING A CHILD SEEMS ALMOST IMPOSSIBLE. BUT IT DOESN'T FEEL DEVASTATING, AND IT CERTAINLY DOESN'T MAKE HER SELFISH

BY DAISY BUCHANAN

A couple of weeks ago, just after the Queen's birthday, my granny turned ninety. She might be the most inspirational woman I know. She worked through World War Two and lived in several different cities. She was a member of Mensa: 'But then they lowered the IQ requirement and all sorts of people kept getting in – it was awful, darling!' She was a guest on *Woman's Hour* several times. She's better travelled than me, almost getting busted in Dubai en route to Melbourne. ('Anything to declare, ma'am?' 'Only the crack in my arse!') She's an amazing woman. She's also raised six children: four uncles, my auntie and godmother and my mum.

Granny's children have given her eighteen grandchildren. We're now all aged between twenty-two and thirty-five. We were all in attendance at her recent birthday party but, between us, we only managed to produce a single extra guest for her – she has just one great-grandchild. What's going on?

In the US and the UK, the teen birth rate has plummeted to a record low. This is obviously something to celebrate, although there's a suspicion that the usual culprits – sexting and smartphones – are to blame. First-time mothers are getting older and, in Auckland, it's thought that expensive housing is lowering the birth rate. New Zealand's president is suggesting that fertility is taught in schools, to 'raise awareness' of the fact that it declines with age. In the UK, the chairman of the British Fertility Society is suggesting that eleven-year-olds are taught about their 'speeding' biological clock.

Such scaremongering makes me furious. I'm pretty sure that most of us know our bodies and biology well enough to realise that it is much harder to have children once we're past our thirties. But I also suspect that increasing numbers of us are looking at our lives, our tiny flats, our overdrafts, and thinking, 'Well, perhaps it's for the best that I don't bother.'

When I was twenty-five, I thought that meeting the perfect part-ner was the biggest obstacle between babies and me. At thirty-one, I now realise there's much more to worry about. I appreciate that having children is a life-changing decision which means making some major sacrifices – but I don't think I even have enough to sac-rifice to do it. Thinking about it is like playing an unsolvable game of Sudoku. If we had a baby, we'd need more space. We can't afford to rent anywhere bigger in London, so we'd need to move away. But we have jobs that are in London and we can't afford to feed or clothe the baby without the income those jobs provide. When working, we'd need to pay for childcare, which, if you're earning an average UK salary, seems to leave you with about a fiver of take-home pay. This is all before the baby needs wild luxuries, like a school uniform and Calpol.

Some people can look at the problem and see love as the solution. Their love for their imaginary baby is infinite, elastic, electric! If needs be, they will feed their family with foraged acorns! They will gather the rushes to weave the Moses basket! They don't care if their next holiday isn't until 2047 – in fact, if they wait until then, trips to the Caribbean will probably be incredibly cheap because everyone will be spending their vacation on the Moon. They will not have proved their worth as humans until they have cleaned ten metric tonnes of poo from a perfect baby bottom.

I've given it some thought and I am not one of those people.

I've been poor. I've been desperately frightened of every brown envelope and unknown-number phonecall. I've stayed awake at night for what feels like months and years, wondering what my future holds, but certain that it probably isn't good, as I struggled to make day-to-day financial plans, feeling frightened by the sheer impossibility of knowing how I'll be surviving in a year's time. I've been so anxious that I've woken up crying in the night, had panic attacks on trains, in toilets, at motorway service stations. It has taken me the whole of my twenties to work through this state of practical and emotional terror, and feel as though I've finally come out on the other side. My ducks are, if not in a row, in some kind of visible formation. Now that I've got here, I don't know how I'd cope with a baby. I might do brilliantly – but the odds aren't good.

When you're a youngish newlywed, people like to ask you when you're going to have kids. Not if, but when. As you explain that you're thinking probably never, they look at you as though you're either very stupid, or the sort of cold, calculating bitch that might have a handbag made from human skin. There's a barely challenged, lazy assumption that deciding not to reproduce is selfish.

'What if you change your mind – and it's too late?!' is my favourite response, as if it's better to bring a tiny human into the world, and desperately struggle to look after it, than it is to remain child-free and experience an occasional pang during *One Born Every Minute*. But my friends aren't doing it either. Some of them have vague plans to try 'in about a year' – that year stretching across an infinite, time-bending horizon. Others drunkenly clutch my hands at dinner parties and murmur, 'I keep thinking about it, and I just don't want to! Does that make me selfish? Is that awful? Am I awful?' Anecdotally, our reasons are very similar – after ten years of trying, we finally have a savings account, some seniority at work and a partner we love spending time with, and we know that, if we were to have babies, we'd spend the rest of our lives going back the way we came, unable to catch up with where we are right now.

In a parallel universe, I'd love to have children – in fact, I might have them already if housing was affordable, if parental leave and childcare were seen by everyone as responsibilities to be shared by both parents, and if I didn't have to be a banker or a lottery winner in order to give my hypothetical children the things I grew up with, like occasional holidays by the sea and a garden to run around in. But I'm not solely responsible for the declining birth rate and I suspect that, in the next few decades, the government will have to deal with the serious consequences of rendering a whole generation of twenty- and thirtysomethings economically infertile.

However, I think a declining birth rate is a sign of real progress for women. The more control we have over pregnancy, the more we have over our bodies and our choices. I'm almost grateful for the global issues that have made me think incredibly carefully about whether or not I'm capable of raising a child. Sometimes I'm sad that I probably won't have children, but I'm also happy about the freedom that choice will bring, and excited about the presence I might have in the lives of other young people as a mentor, auntie or friend. They say it takes a village, and not being a mother won't prevent me from embracing my responsibilities as a villager. Ultimately, I've tried to make a sensible, considered decision that's best for me and best for society. I don't understand how that makes me 'selfish'.

Pensions might be scary, but they could be women's most powerful weapon

WHEN THE FUTURE LOOKS SO UNCLEAR,
WE SHOULD REMEMBER THAT ECONOMIC
INDEPENDENCE IS A WOMAN'S FIRST DEFENCE

BY MARISA BATE

It is rather fitting that next to me in the cafe where I'm sat writing about women and pensions is a group of white-haired women in their seventies and eighties. They're shooting the breeze over pots of tea. 'Edna is so devil-may-care!' says one opposite the other, with metallic purple nails holding a flip phone. Like a slightly more mature Carrie and co, minus the cocktails, they burst into a round of giggles as one announces she's off to find out if she's for 'the scrap heap'.

It's hard to know what being a pensioner will look like by the time I get there. And I try not to think about it too much, if I'm honest. We know we'll all be living longer, although we're not actually getting any healthier, warn the experts. We know we have a social-welfare infrastructure that is buckling as we speak, let alone in forty or fifty years. We know, in part thanks to the work of the Jo Cox Commission, that we're lonelier than ever. And if you couple this with the economic climate, the picture is as bleak as a Monday morning in January. Millennials can't afford to save, they can't invest in assets like property that could double up as financial security and personal debt is mounting. And just to add insult to injury, the pension gender gap is widening. Women are retiring on average with 40 per cent less than men, according to the Department for Work and Pensions (DWP), which shouldn't be that surprising – we're still paid less and take more part-time, lower-skilled roles. Looking at my mum and trying to have what she has – the baby boomer with the civil-servant pension and a house – feels as achievable as owning a condo in Malibu.

I have never been very good at saving. Mostly because my career began post-2008, I work in the media and I've always lived in London – a perfect recipe for life in an overdraft. But, in recent years, I've really started to regret this. Once, someone bought me a copy of *Ms.* magazine from the seventies. On the back of the issue, the magazine was advertising its own savings scheme because, as Gloria Steinem advocated, a woman's first defence is economic independence. Yet, this evaded me. I've always got by on my own, but I've only ever considered 'getting by' at that moment in time – that week, that rent payment, that electricity bill. There hasn't been the financially ability nor the long-term outlook (maybe personal, maybe my Insta-generation) to think about 'getting by' in The Future. I'm currently putting a teeny-tiny amount into a savings account, but that's more of a rent safety net than a retirement property in northern Italy. In 2016 – warning, you may need to sit down – the *FT* published one economist's forecast that suggested you'd need to save £800 a month, for forty years, to have a pension of £30,000.

I don't think I'm alone in my contradictory worrying about pensions yet refusing to look at the issue head-on. A spokesman for the DWP told me that a quarter of women 'don't understand their pension information', and one in ten 'actively avoids checking their pension pot'. I asked my friends how they feel. Jamie, thirty, who works in fashion, told me: 'I've never had a personal pension and, to be honest, have totally ignored the whole thing until I turned thirty and suddenly realised that unless I want to work for the rest of my life, I better sort something.' Remi, a project manager, told me a similar thing: 'Last month, I made the effort to actually address the amount of money I was putting into my pension because, finally, at thirty-four, I've realised that I'm going to have no money when I'm old and I'm terrified.' Other friends, however, have been more savvy. 'I just always knew it was smart,' thirty-two-year-old Hannah, who works in the arts, told me. 'I think because my parents were always teachers and always paid in. And they now have a comfortable life as a result.' Amelia, who lives in Birmingham and works as a graphic designer, told me she puts £200 a month into her pension – and the government gives her a tax break on it. Both Jamie and Remi nod to lack of education about why they haven't saved more. 'We were never given any info,' says Remi. 'An ad on TV with a cuddly big monster telling us that we will have to opt out, instead of in, isn't enough.'

And they have a point. We know that, traditionally, maths and economics have been subjects for boys, with girls and female students increasingly discouraged from the topics as they've got older (the number of females studying these subjects falls off with alarming regularity). This isn't an issue of 'poor helpless women not having a maths brain' – this is a form of cultural and educational sexism that has divorced women from knowledge about money as a method of power. And, for Hannah, it's changing the way she lives now: 'I'm less convinced now about our generation's hopes for a healthy pension, which is why I'm trying to make the most of life now.'

The DWP encourages women, in particular, to remember National Insurance credits if you take time out of work to look after children, as well as remembering to chase up pensions perhaps forgotten with old jobs. But I wonder if the gender pension gap can only be closed if there is a cultural shift, too. Girls and young women have been discouraged from studying economics, but encouraged to marry men who will probably earn more than them and therefore buy the house or have the big pension. Economic stability has historically fallen to men. In our modernising world, we mustn't leave pensions in the 20th century with traditional gender roles. We must take responsibility – not consciously, or subconsciously, assume that a man, somewhere along the line, will save us.

Of course, it can feel helpless. Why save for something that won't be enough in the end, anyway? I think our 'retirement' will look so different from our parents' there's little point trying to emulate it. Maybe we will work and rent for longer, but maybe that's OK. Economic independence is the best any woman can hope for today, for so many reasons; now, and when planning for the future – particularly one that seems so unclear.

Are women really 'worried' about out-earning men?

AN ARTICLE ON THE DIFFICULTIES FACED BY WOMEN EARNING MORE THAN THEIR MALE PARTNERS HAS RESURFACED AND BEEN RUBBISHED BY READERS. BUT THE DATA DOESN'T LIE

BY YOMI ADEGOKE

There are three undeniable truths of article-sharing on Twitter: a) the exact same handful of articles continues to resurface every so often; b) readers will almost only ever respond to the intentionally provocative title; and c) when they do, they will quote-tweet it with the exact same sassy responses as the last time this happened, with perhaps increased levels of snark.

An oft-discussed article on millenial women earning more than their male partners has risen from the dead and, with it, the inevitable disparaging choruses of 'can't relate'. According to the piece, based on a report by writer Ashley C Ford, in 2015 38 per cent of American wives earned more than their husbands in the US, which, in some cases, negatively affected couples.

The overwhelming and entrenched ideas that men are providers and women caregivers means that, when the roles are reversed, couples were reportedly left struggling to cope. As Ford puts it, 'these messages trickle down with almost unavoidable emotional and psychological consequence', which usually conclude in men feeling emasculated and women feeling guilty. Alongside these feelings, some women reported feeling anxious about the situation and resentful toward their significant other.

'Unlike the traditional trajectory of men who earn more, or are sole financial providers, most of these millennial women either believe out-earning their partners is temporary, or lament the idea that it may not be,' Ford wrote.

Lots of lucky people on the internet found themselves unable to relate to Ford's report or, more realistically, unable to relate to the snappy headline they are more likely to have actually read, which summarised the write-up as 'Millennial women are "worried", "ashamed" of out-earning boyfriends and husbands'.

'This is honestly so laughable,' one user posted. 'We are a team. If I make more than my SO [significant other] then we high five and move on.'

'If a man is making me feel worried and ashamed for my successes because he feels "emasculated" instead of cheering me on and having my back, he sure as hell ain't ever gonna be MY man,' chimed in another.

'I do not know one woman who is worried about this,' concluded another. Several others added anecdotes about their own positive personal set-ups, where they were either earning more than their male partner or were a male partner earning less. Which is all well and good, but sadly doesn't negate the fact that there are women who have found themselves more financially fortunate and, thus, less fortunate when it comes to relationship struggles. 'I just want to say that whether you agree with these women or not . . . this is what they said,' Ford tweeted in response to the continued write-offs.

The worries highlighted in the piece are not by any means rare – rather, they are backed up by statistical evidence that show for all it isn't simply plain sailing. The report outlined that, on average, women are still generally paid less than men and are more likely on average to do more of the housework, meaning the burden for female breadwinners is not always simply financial – sometimes they are doubling up on responsibility as opposed to swapping places. More notably, The University of Chicago Booth School of Business found that often in these types of relationships, dissatisfaction increased and could lead to divorce. While this shouldn't be the case, it doesn't mean it isn't for some.

'I'm surprised to see unanimous derision for this,' a Twitter user said. 'Because they don't know anyone openly admitting this, people assume it doesn't exist.'

She has a point – we are embarrassed enough discussing money as it is, let alone the complicated set of feelings that can come with outearning a man in a patriarchal society, from both parties. As millenials, a generation characterised by liberalism and progression, we especially may feel like we have evolved past being tied down by such archaic and arbitrary rules around money. It might sound like a silly issue, but it remains an issue enough that, as Ford points out, when you Google 'I make more money than my boyfriend', the results usually dredge up problem-solving articles that posit a woman earning more than her husband as a hurdle to overcome. We can only ensure it isn't seen as an issue if we discuss why it is seen as one – and brushing off these difficult conversations doesn't mean they aren't taking place in whispers elsewhere.

It's time women kickstarted an honest conversation about money

WHEN IT COMES TO MONEY, WOMEN HAVE GOT TO START BLOWING THEIR OWN TRUMPETS

BY POORNA BELL

Male friends are an important sounding board because they provide a different perspective on almost every aspect of life. The most striking of which is around money and career. In my experience, they are direct and honest about the amount that they earn, in a way that myself and my female friends are not able to be.

Maybe it's easy for them to be so confident about money because, after all, they belong to the gender being paid more simply by virtue of having a Y chromosome. But, putting the patriarchy aside for one moment, there have been significant conversations recently that are prompting a new sense of empowerment for women, by women, around money.

The biggest game-changer was undeniably Section 78 – legislation written into the Equality Act 2010, which was implemented in 2017 and, in 2018, meant companies with more than 250 employees had to publish their gender pay gap data. This rendered an unprecedented level of transparency because, where pay had once been this shadowy thing of whispers, there it was in black and white: eight out of ten companies in the UK pay men more and now we knew exactly which companies these were.

In no way should women being empowered around pay detract from the fact that companies have an urgent responsibility to close the gender pay gap. It's not up to women to fix a problem caused and perpetuated by men. But what is becoming increasingly obvious is that we have to kickstart a new conversation around a woman's right to be ambitious – and their desire to be paid well.

One of the most visible markers for change is the entertainment industry, where bold and big statements are being made. *Poldark* actress Eleanor Tomlinson this week called for pay equality with male lead Aidan Turner while, last month, actress Claire Foy received £200,000 in backdated pay from her lead role in *The Crown*, when it was revealed she was paid less than co-star Matt Smith.

In a piece that went viral, American author Jessica Knoll summed it up perfectly in a piece she wrote for *The New York Times* called I Want To Be Rich And I'm Not Sorry. It prompted a lot of conversation around money and women: why are we so uncomfortable about it?

Knoll remarks that one of the biggest problems is that women who say they want to be paid well are viewed as being obnoxious and that she herself has struggled with her ambition being viewed as bossy. Men don't care if the same accusations are levelled at them; if anything, being motivated by money is seen as a marker for success.

The fact is that the gender pay gap is not just going to be closed by companies doing the right thing. If that was the case, we wouldn't have a gender pay gap. There would be an equal number of women to men on boards and in decision-making positions of power.

Undeniably, we have to acknowledge that because women have been mostly conditioned to serve and nurture rather than provide and be forthright, we see domestic success as having higher value than economic success. Men don't and, for evidence, just take a look at the world order.

So, what needs to change?

Sam Smethers, CEO of The Fawcett Society, says that unequal pay thrives on secrecy. That means owning the fact that you are on a good salary because you do a good job and being transparent around it helps to empower other women.

'There are lots of low-paid women who can't fight the battle,' she says, 'so you have to fight the battle for them.'

Highly paid women may baulk at the idea of revealing what they earn – as would men. And understandably so – Knoll notes that women get punished when they exhibit the same ambitions as men: women are 'rich bitches'; there is no male equivalent.

Author and journalist Laura Jane Williams, who recently ran her first event Superlatively Rude Live, made a point of saying on Twitter that she had paid people who spoke at her event, and on time.

I asked Williams about why she tweeted that message and she said: 'Because the more women talk about money . . . the more women will talk about money. A woman earning her own money in an unapologetic way is a political act. We've gotta do it like men do it.'

But why do women find it so hard to be open about their money and ambition in the first place?

Danielle Newnham, co-founder of F equals, a female fashion brand and empowering women's platform, says: 'It stems from a more reserved view on discussing achievements and success, which I have found to be true based on several hundred interviews I have done with both male and female founders.

'Historically, wealth was not seen the same way for men versus women due to social norms. Women were expected to stay home to raise a family and not even allowed to handle money. So, our success back then was measured by how well we performed as mothers, whereas for men it was measured by how much they earned, what house they had and what car they drove.'

Williams says: 'We want to be liked, so we don't want to risk pissing people off by asking for "too much". It's another way of staying small, so it is so uncomfortable when we step outside of this – but like Hilary Rushford (Dean Street Society), says, it's better to be profitable than popular.'

I can certainly relate and have been terrible at bringing up pay either in negotiations or whether someone asks me to do work for free. As a result, I always under-charge or agree to do the free work because I'm worried, if I don't, I won't be the person picked for the job, despite being the most qualified.

A big part of that is imposter syndrome, which generally is thought to affect women in particular – where you deem yourself unworthy for a job (despite being fully capable of doing it) and are petrified you'll be found out. It's internalised bias and is fuelled when you are competing with men. A huge gulf is then created because not only are women not charging what they are worth, a rigged system means that even when men royally fuck up in the workplace, they still somehow get promoted – or, as Michelle Obama said recently about the practice, 'fail up'.

However, while we might not be able to stop men from failing up overnight, we can control the narrative around what we charge. Natalie Campbell, award-winning entrepreneur and co-founder of A Very Good Company, says, 'Women consistently charge low and when we charge the equivalent of what a man charges, people are confused by it. We need to ask how much people are charging and be transparent about it. No one is scared of talking about money when you have to produce the work, so we need to get over that.'

Susan Sheehan, founder of Back Yourself Mentoring and a former CFO and COO, says that learning about your company's financial performance, and researching the salary for your industry and role, is critical. 'I was speaking to a COO of a tech company recently and he said he had been interviewing for engineers and the women were asking for £10–£15k less than he was willing to pay. Afterwards, he spoke to one of them and she hadn't researched the market before going out to job search. We need to do what is within our control before we enter these conversations.'

As women, we also have to be aware of what we're asking other women to do, and whether we would accept it for ourselves. Again, it's not our job to fix pay disparity for ourselves, but we can start with good practices within our own gender.

A good starting point is to not make other women feel like shit in pay negotiations. 'There has been more than one occasion where I've been asked to name my fee and been met with a sharp intake of breath,' author Daisy Buchanan said. 'Perhaps it's all in my head, but I'd rather someone be upfront and say, "Sorry, our budget is x," than make a value judgement on the way I value myself.'

We also need to remember that, while women struggle as a gender to get paid fairly, women of colour face a double whammy of gender and racial bias. The Fawcett Society raised concerns about ethnic minority women being left behind in the conversation, finding black African women experiencing the largest full-time gender pay gap at 19.6 per cent, and Pakistani and Bangladeshi women having the biggest overall pay gap at an eye-watering 26 per cent.

Leyya Sattar, co-founder of The Other Box, an organisation that celebrates and supports people of colour in the creative industries, says: 'As women of colour, getting your foot in the door in the first place is difficult, but when you find yourself in the position, you're generally offered lower salaries compared with your white counter-parts and culturally made to feel like you should be grateful for the role in the first place.

'There needs to be transparency within organisations to allow women, but more so women of colour to feel confident to be able to have these conversations so they feel comfortable and confident to have the discussions about being paid equally. Institutional sexism and racism still exist and women of colour are exposed to this on a daily basis, which can be exhausting to navigate, as well as perform-ing well in your job. Other candidates don't have to deal with these micro-aggressions and exhaustion.'

The uncomfortable truth is that some women need to acknow-ledge their blind spots and get on board with supporting women in the fullest sense, whether that's offering to pay properly or champion pay rises for direct reports. Or, considering that the number of female freelancers has been steadily rising due to a number of reasons includ-ing flexible working required for childcare, damn well paying them a decent rate.

Newnham has had first-hand experience, saying, 'I would natur-ally hope that women in positions of power would lead this change, but that is not always the case. I know many examples where women have treated other women on their team poorly and paid them less than they were due.

'Perhaps the lack of women in powerful positions makes the environment more competitive between women, but regardless female empowerment is a mindset – and they should ask themselves daily how they can empower more women, whether at work or in their community.'

The fact is most people – and I include myself in this – have a dream scenario in which your boss notices the hard work you've put in and hands you a wodge of cash just for being brilliant.

But, to me, this is almost akin to that other fairytale that has pushed back women's liberation for decades: expecting a knight in shining armour to come and rescue you, rather than you rescuing yourself. If we wouldn't accept this in our personal life, then we definitely shouldn't accept it in our work life.

Since doing the research for this article, I've applied some of the advice and techniques in a number of ways. I've pushed back gently on rates and have been elated when the person on the other side has increased them. I've also said no to doing free work and have then been told they'd 'try and find budget'. Both of these are things I never would've dreamed of doing for fear of losing the work, but instead I've augmented my own value.

We've got to put aside our sheepishness and awkwardness and not undercut what we are really worth, based on what we think someone will accept. Men will never do this. And we're worth exactly the same as they are.

Life lessons

LAUREN LAVERNE | SOPHIE HEAWOOD
DOLLY ALDERTON | VIV GROSKOP
JAVARIA AKBAR | ROBYN WILDER

10 best things about being a British woman

A NEW STUDY FOUND THAT BRITISH WOMEN HAVE THE SECOND-LOWEST LIFE EXPECTANCY IN EUROPE. BUT AS TROUBLING AS THAT NEWS MAY BE, THERE ARE LOTS OF REASONS WHY IT'S BRILLIANT TO BE BRIT

BY LAUREN LAVERNE

The World Health Organization have revealed that British women are among the unhealthiest in Europe. This news was greeted by British women with a mixture of fake surprise and no defensiveness whatso-ever. For example, nobody commented, 'GOD, WORLD HEALTH ORGANIZATION. WE KNOW, OK. WHAT ARE YOU, OUR MUM?' before stomping upstairs to listen to loud grunge music, while crying into a pillow, even if they felt like it. No. British women faced the facts head on, with polite equanimity and maturity, for that is how we roll.

You see, even though we have the second-worst life expectancy in fifteen European countries, because we eat, drink and smoke to excess, and don't do enough exercise (I KNOW! I'M SHOCKED, TOO!) there are many, many great things – like having the good manners to take bad news on the chin – about being a British woman.

So, while I acknowledge the importance and gravity of our situation health-wise (I'm typing this on an exercise bike), in the interests of balance I thought I'd highlight a few of the great things about being a woman in the UK. We might not live the longest, but we know how to live well. Here's why.

(1)

WE ARE POLITE

British courteousness may be a cliché, but it's rooted in reality. However, our manners aren't just adorable, they're fascinating. They are a language in themselves, one which – I believe – women speak best of all. For example, the phrase 'I'm sorry' can mean anything from 'I apologise' to 'You appear to have just bumped into me' and even 'You are incorrect and unbearable, now shut your face while I explain why'.

(2)

TIGHTS

Oh God, tights. A good enough reason to live in this country even if you hate everything else. The only thing Danny Boyle's London 2012 opening ceremony was missing was a section where hundreds of women skipped around the stadium singing the praises of opaques, and the fact that, thanks to our terrible weather, we can wear them for nine months of the year. An accessory-cum-security blanket, opaques make everything you wear look better, turn bum-grazing hemlines into a doable proposition and provide a daily opportunity to yank them up to your bra and pretend you're a cat burglar before you put anything else on.

(3)

FOOD

OK, so we eat too much of it, but who can blame us when it's so bloody delicious? British food was once a laughing stock; these days, it's the best in the world. Just like Britons themselves, our food is a glorious mishmash of global and cultural influences. Given an unlimited budget and a pair of sufficiently elasticated trousers, a lady could travel to any reasonably sized British city and eat herself around the world over the course of eighty days or so, like a greedier Phileas Fogg.

4

PUBS

No matter how stylish and excellent HBO box sets make America look, I always feel sorry for the cast when they end up in an American bar. Even *Mad Men* can't make them seem appealing. Pubs, on the other hand, are heaven. A great pub is a cross between your nan's comfy house and a really good nightclub, multiplied by a great restaurant, minus people being knobby about the food. In the summer, their gardens are beer-splashed, fairy-lit LOL dells; in the winter, they light cosy fires and make daytime alcohol consumption socially acceptable. My local pub is loud enough to feel buzzy, but quiet enough to have a conversation, offers great food, occasional non-obligatory dancing, a wall of Kinks fan art (long story) and (on Tuesdays) table magic. For a thirtysomething woman like me who is equally apt to be seized by the need to dance as she is to have a little sit down and a chat, there is no better place.

5

OUR JOKES/IRONY/SCEPTICISM

I'm not claiming that these are unique to us. A while back, Eddie Izzard travelled to over thirty countries doing stand-up in different languages and claimed there was no difference in what people laugh at. All the same, I do think there's a particular British outlook that we're lucky to have. It's a certain, gentle kind of scepticism. An arched eyebrow at things that are too loud, too bossy, too earnest, too much . . . it's satire that punches upwards, towards power. There is a row of portraits of former PMs lining the stairs at 10 Downing Street but, next door at number 11, the chancellor of the exchequer has a row of newspaper cartoons of his predecessors, dating back several centuries. George Orwell wrote that fascism didn't take in Britain because people would laugh at the goose step, and one of the interesting things about zealots of every stripe is their lack of humour. Our keen sense of the absurd is a firewall that protects us from their mindset.

6

STAYING IN

'Go to Miami/Marrakech/Ibiza,' people tell you, 'the evenings are warm and lovely, and everyone just lives outside, hanging out and socialising. It's amazing!' And it is. It's just not as amazing as staying in. There is nothing so delicious as the torpor of a plan-less, obligation-free Sunday afternoon, or as sweet as a lazy weekend. There is no outfit more pleasing than fresh pyjamas after a hectic day. Contentment lies just the right side of a rainy window, especially at a particular time of year. British women are more engaged with the world than ever, which makes it even sweeter to spend time in The Nest.

7

OUR MANY WONDERFUL NERDS

In other parts of the world, nerds are looked down upon, considered strange or comical. Not so in Britain. Here, nerds are heroes. In fact, citizens who are merely conventionally physically attractive often have to spend part of the year in other countries, where their Route 1 attributes can be of some sort of benefit. People often say that British actors find work in America because the money is so much better and the weather is amazing, but this isn't true. In actual fact, Idris Elba, Tom Hardy and Daniel Craig are simply too handsome to remain in the UK full-time. This is bittersweet, especially for nerds cursed with pointless good looks (like Professor Brian Cox), but, for the rest of us, it makes this country a more interesting place to live, one where ideas matter, and where our national treasures include Richard Ayoade, Jarvis Cocker, Caitlin Moran and JK Rowling.

8

IT'S OK TO HAVE SHIT HAIR

Obviously, my colleagues and I all have excellent hair. This hair is more of a metonym – a figurative expression of a broader idea (which may include hair). For the most part, Britons don't expect one another to look perfect. Whatever judgements we might make on the strength of our appearances, median grooming levels are much lower than in, for example, Los Angeles, where, as I understand it, it is obligatory to have a full body wax, blow-dry what's left and then bleach one's anus before heading out of the door each morning, to eat a meal known as 'brunch' in which other foods pretend to be bread. This might explain why hobbies like stamp collecting, rambling and Top Trumps are less popular on America's West Coast than they are here. People simply don't have the time.

9
BRITISH STYLE

In an age where it sometimes seems the blogosphere is contouring itself into one homogenous aesthetic blob, it's important to applaud quirks, kinks and subversive style statements of all kinds and, despite internet monoculture, there are still plenty of them to be found here. There is an iconoclasm about British style that makes it special. It's about the pull between tradition and rebellion, between history and cutting-edge street style. It is epitomised in the fashion industry by designers like Vivienne Westwood, Alexander McQueen and Christopher Kane, but worn best by British women themselves.

10
WE WORK TO LIVE

I'm incredibly lucky (and perhaps unusual) in that I love my work, but I believe that I am typical of my countrywomen in one respect: no matter how much I love my job, I know there's more to life. It's considered bad manners and poor conversation to ask people what they do (though personally I'll take small talk about work over traffic or weather). This is because Britons know that the 5–9 counts just as much as the 9–5. As a radio DJ, I am privileged to accompany thousands of listeners each morning of the working week, so I know from their constant feedback that the nation's mood shifts palpably over the course of the working week, reaching a giddy zenith on Friday. Even people who are incredibly committed to their jobs can't wait for the weekend. Perhaps this is why we tend to overdo it when wine o'clock arrives, as the WHO points out.

So, while I'll be taking their findings on board and striving to live as healthily as possible, I'll also remember that the most important thing is not how long we live, but how we live in the first place.

Unmoored, floating – my forties were met with existential panic

YOU'RE SUPPOSED TO ENJOY TURNING FORTY – SO, WHAT HAPPENS WHEN YOU WAKE UP, REALISING YOUR LIFE ISN'T EXACTLY WHAT YOU EXPECTED IT TO BE?

BY SOPHIE HEAWOOD

The thing about turning forty is that you're supposed to enjoy it. Aside from all the jokes about what an old git you're turning into, soon to lose your looks and your marbles, there is a sense of it being a celebration of the last gasp of youth. In our culture, fortieth birthday parties are bigger and boozier than the others – more interesting than thirtieths, more significant than fiftieths. A hearty swansong for the part of your life that you are ready, if reluctantly, to leave behind. Yet, as I approach forty-two, I can finally admit that I found entering my forties terrifying. Cold sweat in the night, waking up in a panic for months, paranoid like never before, terrifying.

So, it is with great relief I note that the legendary fashion designer Barbara Hulanicki, now aged eighty-one, told the press that turning forty was the lowest point of her life. Even though she had already set up Biba and already enjoyed years of success as a fashion pioneer in London's Swinging Sixties, she was lost. 'I locked myself in a bedroom,' she told the *Observer*, 'and howled.' I don't know the full details of why she howled, or how many moons she howled through, but it's bloody reassuring to hear that someone who has also turned fifty, sixty, seventy AND eighty still agrees that forty was the pits. 'It was the worst age milestone,' she confirmed. 'You feel that that's the end.'

Of course, I haven't met those other decades yet, so may discover that my fortieth was a mere walk in the park without a Zimmer frame – but I doubt it. Because I experienced it as a sort of exit poll on my life, when I had to take my deepest-ever breath, look around and see what I had done with my time here on earth. And despite being a fairly cheerful person who has travelled a lot, had some career success and lives with a lovely, healthy daughter, I didn't exactly like what I found.

The ageing in itself didn't bother me – I'd never worried about wrinkles or stuff like that. (Of course, that turned out to be because I'd never had any – easy mistake to make if you're blessed with a big round babyface like mine.) And the celebrations were good – I held a lovely party with a best friend who was also turning forty, got my hair done and went out singing. And panicking. And sweating. And singing again. And realised that all the friends who'd said it would be fine and they loved turning forty were friends who'd had the requisite number of children, and were now settled with the partner they wanted, in the home they wanted.

If those are the things that you always presumed you'd have sussed out by the age of forty, unlocked like levels on a video game, then it's quite an existential shock to wake up one day and discover that, while you have indeed found yourself on the Age Forty level, you haven't acquired the shields, the weapons and the tools. Skidding around on your own weightlessness. Unmoored, floating, a little afraid of gravity. It can almost feel like grief. Particularly when it comes to fertility.

If you're a woman, you know that there's still a chance you could have a baby, or a second baby, in your forties, but there's a tough road ahead if you've staked your entire life around that chance. I'm lucky – I had a baby at thirty-five. But accepting that – along with all the other things she's missed out on – my daughter will probably never get a sibling has been hard.

Then there's realising that I've been a wayward freelancer too long and I'll never get to work in a newspaper office, never get to work on a team in the magazines I dreamed of as a teenager. I know this might sound faintly ridiculous or just negative thinking, because I could apply for those jobs if I wanted, but the whole point of turning forty is that you get realistic and say, 'You know what? I won't. I just won't. I'll stay here, writing freelance on my own, because that is what I do.' A person can't live forty years without any of their cards getting marked. I just don't believe in eternal reinvention, as it goes. As for all the lessons I have learnt from my hugely successful and loving relationships – oh God, no. I really tried! But no.

Perhaps the most humbling bit about turning forty is realising that all your life you have mistaken your personality for moods. Those moods – that's you, that is. All you!

I am not here to doom-monger. I am here to say, 'Listen up, people younger than me, who expect their future to be a certain way – look at the life you're living right this minute, because if what you want at forty is something totally different, then where is the link? Things lead to things, and then to other things. The person you turn out to be is not an entire coincidence, and not everything in life is down to luck or chance. So, put your drink down and take a good look around. And then take heart from the old saying that I have discovered to be true, as I've gradually relaxed into this decade and learnt to count my blessings: the first forty years of childhood are always the hardest.'

8 ways to tackle the life crisis you think you're having

NEW RESEARCH HAS FOUND THAT OVER HALF OF US
THINK WE'RE EXPERIENCING A LIFE CRISIS. FROM
WASHING SHEETS TO LISTENING TO PATTI SMITH,
DOLLY ALDERTON HAS GOT SOME VERY USEFUL ADVICE

BY DOLLY ALDERTON

It came as no surprise to me to read that almost half of the British public are going through a life crisis. The majority of the last decade of my life has been spent in the state of a life crisis – either about to have one, in the middle of one or coming out the other side.

'WHY' is the crux of their general theme – 'Why am I still in my overdraft?', 'Why have I been single for four years?', 'Why did I spend all that money on drinks for that table of people I hardly know?', 'Why do I always have to prove to people at dinner parties that I know every word to the *Fresh Prince of Bel* Air rap? Why? WHY?'

And over the years, I've found there are some ways of avoiding them; some simple to put into practice, some a little harder. But I've found even doing just one will make difference.

①

MARVEL AT SOMETHING MASSIVE

A personal crisis is more often than not an inward collapse of identity or confidence. One of the most healing things you can do is get out of your head, let yourself be distracted by something mind-blowing and get some perspective. Go for a walk on a rugged coastline, go stare at big trees in Kew Gardens. Go to the British Museum, look at the mummies and try to get your head round how many humans have roamed the earth with broken hearts and dreams and managed to carry on. You have a part to play in the universe, but it is only very, very small. And take comfort in that. The implosion is in yourself, not at the earth's core. You're a speck of dust in the air; you're singular plankton in the sea. Float accordingly.

(2)

DON'T LIE

If you're not careful, so much of your life can be spent performing; be it pretending there are two people in the flat when you're on the phone to the takeaway place ordering two pad thais and eight spring rolls or faking an orgasm so your one night stand doesn't feel let down. These lies, however big or small, engender shame and make you feel closer to a crisis.

Admit them – admit that sometimes after you come home from a dinner with friends who earn much more money than you, you buy a birthday cake from Marks & Spencer and you eat it in bed under the covers. Admit you have been having an online relationship with a Texan man called Travis you met in a chat room for two years. Admit you only wash your bed sheets once a month. If you admit it, you'll probably change it. 'You're as sick as your secrets,' is what you're told in AA. Lift the lies you tell from your life and you'll start feeling lighter.

(3)

DON'T WASH YOUR BED SHEETS ONCE A MONTH

Come on, dude. Once a fortnight, minimum. Once a week is better. Wash them once a week and also be one of those nutters who irons them too. I PROMISE you it will make you feel better. Self-care is one of the most wonderful things you can learn and it's nearly impossible to have a crisis when your house is clean and tidy, you're stomping around on eight hours' sleep and your body is crammed with fresh air and poached eggs on toast.

It's the small things that make you feel invincible – not the huge lifestyle upheavals. You don't have to be the woman who only consumes green juice three days a week or owns cashmere knickers to feel like everything's together. Finding peace and routine happens in the habitual. I once heard Lena Dunham say in an interview that the way you know you're being healthy is if you have developed habits you'd be proud of people knowing about. So wash your damn sheets once a week and have a shower every day.

4

GO OUTSIDE

It's a boring and obvious point to make but everything is clearer once you've gone for a walk. Go out of your way to spend as much time as possible outside. Walk to work if you can – even if it takes an hour. That's probably as long as your commute would be door-to-door; you save money, your waistline and you can listen to nearly two episodes of *Desert Island Discs*.

5

LOG OFF SOCIAL MEDIA

You're a product of what you ingest. Read a Bill Bryson book, listen to a Patti Smith album, watch a Mike Leigh film. If you take in big thoughts and clever voices, you'll cultivate big thoughts and a clever voice. Don't cram your brain with an endless stream of photos of girls you don't know in workout clothing doing peace signs then wonder why your head feels so fuzzy and lethargic.

And don't be embarrassed if you have to be strict with yourself. There was a long period when I was wasting so much time on social media, I had to ask my flatmate to change all my passwords so I could have a monitored five minutes in the morning and five minutes at night, like a conjugal visit. God, I got a lot of work done.

6

HELP OTHER PEOPLE

It has long been a central rule of American therapy that you can't help others until you yourself are completely happy. Well, I'm calling bullshit on this idea. I think one of the best ways to stay balanced and fulfilled is to look after other people. I don't mean putting on apron and volunteering at a soup kitchen every night – although it's great if you want to do that – I mean buying a *Big Issue*; sending your friend soup and dumplings to work when she's having a bad day; offering to carry an elderly woman's Tesco shop back to her house. Taking a Saturday out to help your little brother move into his new dingy flat he's so excited about even though it smells of chicken jalfrezi. It's really simple – stay connected to other people and you'll stay connected to yourself.

⑦

STOP GETTING DRUNK ALL THE TIME

One of the hardest pulls in life is the one between being Keith Richards or being married in Tunbridge Wells. The answer to this particular conundrum: you can be somewhere in the middle. You can have a few drinks. Hell, you might even get drunk on the odd Saturday night. But getting pissed three times a week will have an effect on your mental health. Trust me – I've put the hours in on this line of research.

Think of it this way: there's a chain of events. Three drinks at the pub = in bed by 12 = up for work at 8 feeling a bit floppy. Six drinks at the pub = onto the next pub = another few drinks = going back to someone's house = more booze = embarrassing confession = an expensive taxi at 5am = being late for work = eating rubbish food all day = crying on your sofa = thinking about selling all your belongings and going to an ashram because you obviously are having a life crisis. You're not having a life crisis, my friend. You're having a serotonin crisis. Stop at three drinks and get the bus home next time.

⑧

YOU DO YOU

Above all else, the best way to avoid a life crisis is to put your blinkers on. And this bit is the really hard bit. Work out what you want – it might be your own business, it might be to save up money to travel the world, it might be a husband and a couple of babies – and every day keep focused on those goals and let them inform your decisions. Do not let yourself get distracted and down when you hear about other people's journeys. Don't convince yourself at your friend's baby shower that all you've ever wanted is a baby. Don't read an interview with a stage actress and suddenly panic that you never gave musical theatre a go and now it's too late to ever be big on Broadway. Stay focused on your path and you might just learn to enjoy it, crisis-free.

What happens if you replace 'sorry' with 'thank you'?

IT MIGHT SOUND LIKE JUST *ANOTHER* BULLSHIT IDEA – BUT VIV GROSKOP ARGUES IT'S A TECHNIQUE THAT COULD MAKE YOU LESS ANXIOUS AND INSECURE

BY VIV GROSKOP

What would happen if every time we felt like saying, 'Sorry,' we said, 'Thank you,' instead? This is an idea I came across on a hippy Buddhist website and it really works. You gotta love the Buddhists. (No, you really have to love the Buddhists. That is the first rule of karma.) Basically, instead of saying, 'Sorry I'm late,' you say, 'Thanks so much for waiting for me.' Instead of saying, 'Sorry – I'm not making any sense', say, 'Thanks so much for listening.' Instead of saying, 'Sorry I've been rubbish at keeping in touch,' say, 'Thank you for being such a great friend.'

Woo-woo bullshit? Or useful? Well, this idea first appealed to me because I am always researching ways that I can help myself stop apologising. But this in itself has become a controversial subject of late. Some quote the line taken by ex-Google exec Ellen Petry Leanse – that women sound 'like children' when they apologise because, in that moment, they cede power to the other person. A study by the University of Waterloo in Ontario, Canada, concluded that women apologise a lot because they are 'more likely than men to conclude that their behaviour is objectionable'.

On the other hand, though, there's a school of thought that this analysis is in itself demeaning to women; that it's just another way of getting women to question their behaviour and find it – yet again – at fault. After all, apologies (and being able to admit to potentially objectionable behaviour) grease the wheels of social interaction. They show you care and you're not a selfish cow. Why should we stop apologising? Why should we feel bad about saying sorry? Why can't we just say whatever we want and not have to think about it?

Jessica Grose, editor of Lenny, has argued that the way women speak has been 'subject to increased and unwarranted scrutiny'. Similarly, the feminist linguist Debbie Cameron says there is little scientific evidence that women say 'just' or 'sorry' more than men (although you can also find plenty of studies that argue the opposite). Cameron's take is this: 'Women, please understand: it's not you that's undermining yourself by using powerless language; it's the bullshitters who are undermining you with their constant incitement to anxiety, insecurity and self-censorship.'

OK, I get it. It's complicated. But I know for a fact that I do over-apologise when I don't need to and I feel pointlessly guilty about things and I would like to fix this. Replacing 'sorry' with 'thank you' makes sense to me. It actually makes me feel less anxious and inse-cure and self-censored. And I also like the way this technique takes the focus off you and puts it on to the other person.

So, you're late. You feel bad. You wish you had been on time. But it's not all about you, is it? Put it on to the other person (in a good way). They waited patiently. They took the trouble to get there on time. They've done a nice thing. The 'thank you' they deserve is more important and more productive than your self-pitying 'sorry'. It's actually a way of thinking more about other people – not less. Well done, Buddhists!

There's something so much more generous and positive about acknowledging someone else's feelings instead of being focused on your own deficiencies all the time. On that, at least, we can all agree, whether or not you think women are constantly being beaten over the head with ideas about how to 'improve' themselves. So, I won't apologise for making this issue a bit more complicated than maybe we would like it to be. Instead, I'll say this: 'Thank you for understanding that this stuff is sometimes nuanced.' See? Thank you is so much better than sorry. Namaste.

Who do you want to be when you grow up?

APPROACHING FORTY, LAUREN LAVERNE IS STARTING TO CONSIDER WHAT SORT OF OLDER PERSON SHE WOULD LIKE TO BE. GRACE JONES ISN'T A BAD PLACE TO START

BY LAUREN LAVERNE

What kind of older person are you going to be? I ask because it's an important question and I'm worried you might not have thought about it. I hadn't until recently but, with my children growing up – both at school now; no babies in the house – there is a sense of life moving on, with the invisible, terrifying speed of an enormous river. If I am lucky, I will get there and (judging by the way decades seem to be evaporating) sooner than I think.

The problem is that you can't embrace something and be at war with it at the same time and, in our culture, ageing is something you fight. Do I want to do this? Almost-forty seems to be a good time to decide. I'm more or less at the summit, the top of the hill between youth and age. For the first time, I can see both clearly. I understand my twenty-one-year-old self much better than I did when I actually was her. Growing up was so confusing – a tumultuous mixture of luck (good and bad) and happenstance. I don't want to grow old in the same way. There's no knowing what life will bring, of course, but I'm a planner. I need to know the direction I'd like to go in, even if things end up taking a different course. I want to live with intention and purpose. I look at women older than me who are at war with themselves and it scares me. How do I not become them?

I need alternatives. So, I'm collecting role models – awesome older women from every walk of life. There's Grace Jones (sixty-seven, with a 'fucks given' score so low it's actually now less than zero. Grace is in the minus fucks). She shocked the *Daily Mail* by flashing photographers at her New York book signing. Probably best for their coronary health that they didn't meet her the same night as me. She arrived for our interview in tears and a floor-length mink, and proceeded to regale the crew with an un-broadcastable tale involving herself, Andy Warhol and the film *Love Story*, before mounting a stuffed polar bear and biting our handsome director on the nipple. As I say, role model. I'm a music lover and, as such, I'm incredibly grateful that so many of the women who inspired me as a teenager are still at it, showing all of us a new way to be fifty, sixty, seventy . . . Madonna, Siouxsie Sioux, Deborah Harry, Patti Smith, Kim Gordon, Pauline Black, Chrissie Hynde, Viv Albertine, Neneh Cherry – they are all superheroes: as smart, cool, vital and creative as ever. Not all of my heroes are famous. There's Other Grace, the 104-year-old street artist who made the news for 'yarn bombing' her home town of Selkirk recently. My mam (who really should run the world), my late gran and my great-auntie Bertha, from whom I inherited an evil sense of humour, good legs and a love of capes.

A straw poll of *The Pool* offices reveals that I'm not alone in looking up to older women who live life on their own terms. It turns out our team are making lists of their own. Yoko Ono, Iris Apfel, Meryl Streep, Marina Abramovic, polka dot-obsessed artist Yayoi Kusama, Gloria Steinem, Barbara Hulanicki, Anjelica Huston, Baroness Trumpington and the Many Mothers motorcycle gang from *Mad Max: Fury Road* (both on film and in real life – apparently, they did all their own stunts) are just a few of the heroes whose names came up when I asked. They're all completely different, but there is a common thread: they are women who live life on their own terms. They live fearlessly and bravely. They might not all be loud, but they are strong. They stand out in a world where older women are expected to blend in, to disappear. On our list there is a dearth of beige, a paucity of shrinking violets. Instead, it is bursting with ideas, colour, life.

So often, when women talk about ageing, we really mean how we look – but the process is also about who we become. It's about how we live. To be optimistic, to face the future with open eyes, heart and mind, and without clinging to the past – those are my goals. I can see the person I might get to be one day in the distance. The path between us isn't completely clear, but I'm not too worried about that – there are some incredible women ahead, paving the way. I'm ready for the journey; what about you – are you coming?

How to make a new start without the pressure of a new start

FEELING READY FOR A CHANGE, BUT UNSURE OF THE DIRECTION? YOU NEED SOME 'CHRYSALIS TIME'

BY VIV GROSKOP

Because September means back to school, it always reminds me of a fresh start, crunchy leaves and the sense of something new and exciting on the horizon. Unfortunately, being a parent, it also now means spending £83 in WHSmith on stuff miniature people don't really need and will have lost by Halloween. But, setting that aside, the great thing about when 'back to school' rolls around when you're an adult is that it doesn't have to mean actually doing anything anymore. Instead, it can mean hibernating. Or what you might call 'chrysalis time'.

This is an expression I picked up from the US coach Tara Mohr, author of *Playing Big*. (Yes, I know I mention her a lot. That's because she is the best.) 'Chrysalis time' is an incubation period for a new idea or a new direction. It might even be the start of a total reinvention.

It's that feeling you get when you know that something's not quite right in your life, but you also know that you're ready to change it. If only you knew what you needed to change and what you wanted it to change into . . . It's a new start without the pressure of a new start.

I love this idea. We give ourselves so much stress with goals and targets and to-do lists, and we schedule things and put a date and a time on when we want them to happen by. This has become a disease of modern life. Plan, achieve, plan, achieve. I had a letter on Dear Viv recently where the correspondent was obsessed by the fact that she 'should have been further on in life' than she was. I felt like whispering: 'Slow down. You're right where you need to be.'

Chrysalis time is the solution to this. It's an acknowledgement of the fact that we don't always know what our next incarnation is going to be or even whether we need another incarnation or just an ever-so-slightly tweaked version of the person we are now. When we come out of the chrysalis, we might be a butterfly. Or we might still be a scrawny pupa insect with a slightly better haircut. (Sorry, I didn't do biology. Pupa, right?) The fact is, we need some downtime.

Instead of screaming, 'I have no idea what I'm doing with my life,' you can just think to yourself: 'I think I might be having some chrysalis time right now. I'll wake up when I'm good and ready.' If one of those weird beasties was trapped inside its chrysalis, you wouldn't shout at it to come out sooner or try and pry it out of its pod early, would you? So why do that to yourself? Instead, take some time out to rest, give yourself a break, let some ideas germinate and give yourself some breathing space.

Tara Mohr thinks of it as a time when you only have the tiniest vision of what's coming next. Maybe you can see 5 per cent of the picture. 95 per cent is missing. That is a scary lot of stuff to have missing. But there's no point in stressing out about it. Just focus on the 5 per cent you can see – articulate it, sit with it, think about it. Who needs to go back to school when you can go back to your cocoon? Don't expect me to bust out of it before the spring.

Ramadan mornings – and the power and promise that exists just before sunrise

JAVARIA AKBAR IS RISING EARLY – TO PRAY AND
TO FEED HER BABY. IT'S REMINDING HER OF
HOW IMPORTANT AN EMPTY HOUR IS

BY JAVARIA AKBAR

I've been waking up before sunrise for the past week, thanks to the combination of two very special things: a breastfeeding five-month-old (who has a sumo-wrestler-style diet regimen) and the start of Ramadan, the holy month where Muslims get up very early to eat breakfast in the dark and fast until sunset.

I'm not fasting this year, because I'm still nursing my sumo-baby, but I have been trying to wake up for a special morning prayer called Tahajjud that's offered before sunrise. In previous Ramadans, I'd go straight back to sleep afterwards, but, this year, my son has made it particularly hard to return to bed because he thinks 4am is his designated playtime.

And, while watching the sunrise and listening to spring's buoyant birdsong, I've once again been reminded that early mornings are imbued with a distinctive magic that is perfect for managing the mind and clarifying life's fog of worries.

For me, it's the stillness of the hour before dawn that I love, where the darkness feels like a friend, a companion that gently carries me into the first moments of the day. The fresh, featherlight air is waiting to be filled with whatever I wish to fill it with. There's no effort to remember what's on my to-do list, because nothing needs doing right now. Instead, I have time – the time to listen to my internal voice and to tend to my mind. Because it's only in the silence, in the quiet time, that we can hear the forgotten tone of our own voice, the one that's been forcefully hushed by the previous day's relentless racket of bills and business and bodies and babies. Here, we are free to break down. And free to rise up. Nobody is watching in these stop-gap moments, and no one is asking or expecting anything from us.

At dawn, everything is pared back and slowed down for me. Harsh noises, responsibilities and pinging mobiles are replaced with the gentle sounds of a boiling kettle and a cooing baby. I can have a cup of tea and do nothing (or everything). I can get a head start on the day without the usual rush. I have planning time, like the first ten minutes of an exam, when you're supposed to outline the structure of your essay and think about what you want to include. I feel cosseted by the earth and I have the time to consider my place in it and ask myself a simple question that often gets lost amid the day's duties: who do I want to be?

This was a question I once posed to a group of university students during a lecture on journalism. First, I told them about freelancing and pitching, how to handle criticism and payment rates. But then I reminded them that while they figured out what they wanted to be, to never lose sight of who they wanted to be. To remember that their work should be a practical extension of their internal character, because it's only when the mind meets matter, when a thought turns into a deed, that it becomes palpable and real. If there's a mismatch between the person that you want to be and the person you are inadvertently becoming, that tiny discrepancy will grow and the real you will be swallowed up into the aperture. That dissonance is what makes our minds turn into overwhelming jungles, instead of established gardens.

The thing is we often forget about all that. We don't tend to our minds because there's too much stuff to deal with first. Too much news, too much heartache, too much misfortune, too much to do. We're startled awake by foghorn alarm clocks, we dash into the shower after checking social media, we stuff breakfast into our mouths while prepping lunch boxes and finding lost PE kits, and we run for the bus while our shoes rub on to yesterday's blisters. We have lots of things to do and we do them at the cost of forgetting who we are.

Isn't it time to pause for thought? And isn't the morning the best place to do it? That's what Ramadan is for me. It's pressing the reset button, taking a breather, regrouping and reconnecting with the personal (and, in my case, with a higher power). It's allowing yourself to feel like you're a miniscule part of a big, beautiful universe, while simultaneously realising that little old you matters – that you are one in a million and the million is in you.

Lots of us feel lost in our jumbled minds. Lots of us are bungling our way through love and life tangled in anxieties and fears, but we can rise together with the dawn. As the sun rises, we can rise. The magic of the morning will help us to muster the courage.

When it comes to motherhood, career and, well, life, I'm a late bloomer

THERE WERE CAREER U-TURNS IN HER TWENTIES AND MAJOR BREAK-UPS IN HER THIRTIES. BUT STARTING LATE HAS ITS ADVANTAGES

BY ROBYN WILDER

How old do you feel? I look at my neon trainers and inept home balayage, and tentatively place myself at twenty-nine. I mean, I haven't perfected winged eyeliner, I enjoy music that can only be described as 'industrial robot disco', and I've yet to grasp the full practical implications of Brexit. On the other hand, I'm married with a family and a career, and I've just bought a house. I'm a mix of adult responsibilities, youthful exuberance and millennial concern. Twenty-nine fits me perfectly.

Except, the thing is, I'm forty-one. Forty-bloody-one. I know I'm forty-one, because firstly, maths; secondly I clearly remember watching Charles marry Diana on TV and thirdly because on my forty-first birthday I rang my best friend and sobbed, 'I'm already fucking forty, and now there's a fucking ONE on top of it.' My best friend, sitting primly in the London flat she rents with her cat, replied: 'Well, I'm thirty-seven,' and I don't think either of us felt any better.

This wasn't what I expected forty-one to look like. On the rare occasions when I've envisaged my forties (I mean, why would you?), they involved sharp tailoring, slightly boring murmured dinner party conversations, and the owning of 'objets'. They certainly didn't involve me clawing my way through early motherhood while trying to navigate a freelance career, my own faulty mental health and never-ending personal debt. In jeggings.

And yet here I am – first baby at thirty-eight, career at thirty-five, family home-owner at forty-one. I have hit every milestone around a decade later than my contemporaries, and for a while this caused me a great deal of shame. Throughout my thirties I hemmed, hawed and outright lied about my age for fear of judgement. At the same time, if I ever met a twentysomething with an established career, relation-ship, family – or even mobile phone contract – I'd want to run shrieking from the room at the thought of such responsibility. I just didn't feel ready. I didn't feel old enough. And I began to think I never would.

The truth is, I've never really known what I wanted to do, so I've spent my life so far figuring out what I didn't. I had a late start thanks to a nervous breakdown at twenty-one and its subsequent four-year recovery, and after that I tried being a professional musician, which wasn't for me in the end. Nor was a career in theatre tech. Or being a web editor. Or managing web editors. Or being a technology jour-nalist. Or, in fact, being in a childfree relationship. All these things are perfectly fine states of being, and I thought I had wanted them, but had then spent the duration constantly doubting myself.

When I figured that last one out, I had already been in the rela-tionship for ten years and was nudging my mid-thirties. We broke up, I moved from north London to south London (which somehow seemed more dramatic than breaking up), and I pretty much assumed my life was over.

But just two years later I found myself waiting in a midwife's office, stroking my newly swollen belly, surrounded by women around my age. And, for the first time, I really wanted something. I really wanted to be there, facing that enormous permanent responsibility. I was approaching forty and never before, except when I was saying my wedding vows, and sometimes when writing, had I felt this want so clearly.

So now I just go where the want takes me. So far it's taken me to writing and parenting, and out of London to Kent, where I can just about afford to do both of those things. Thanks to my inveterate prevarication I think I'll always come late to things – *Game of Thrones* and Sufjan Stevens, for example – but being so far behind the herd has its advantages. Firstly, when you have no peers left you don't have to worry about keeping up with them. Secondly, there's a whole new generation of peers coming up behind you, and you can learn a lot from them.

So here I am. Forty-one. Actually forty-one. I have some stuff I want, and I'm figuring the rest out. Which, now I think of it, is a hell of a lot better than being twenty-nine and freaking out about falling behind.

Keep on learning for as long as you live

LEARNING AND STUDYING AREN'T ACTIVITIES TO CONFINE TO YOUTH

BY LAUREN LAVERNE

'Back to school.' As a child, the phrase struck terror into my bones, signifying as it invariably did a trip to BHS and the purchase of stiff, navy blue polyester vestments in which my temporarily liberated summer limbs would soon be permanently, itchily encased. Now that the shoe is on the other foot and I am a parent, I feel quite different. The kids are back at school and I'm actually pretty jealous, as it goes.

In Britain, we tend to think of study as the pursuit of the young. 'Student', in most contexts, is shorthand for youthful idealism and immaturity. It's a notion that seems tricky to shift, even though the last forty years have seen higher education opening up to 'mature' students (soberingly, for statistical purposes, this means anyone over twenty-one). According to the NUS, back in 1980 only 10 per cent of graduate and diploma students were mature. By 2012, the figure was closer to 30 per cent.

I'm all for young people studying, obviously. I just wonder why we assume it's a life stage that ends with full-blown adulthood, and whether we expect too much understanding from people who have so little experience of the world. We hand teenagers *Romeo and Juliet* and *The Grapes of Wrath* at the very moment they need them least, when they are (or should be) beautiful, hopeful, loved, cared for and blissfully ignorant of what an absolute bitch life can be. Let's face it, most could get by quite well on a listicle's worth of WhatsApp hacks and the ability to operate a microwave – and why shouldn't they? There's a lot to be said for the simple life and plenty of time for experience to scuff you up a bit and make you realise it's time to become interesting.

The older you get, however, the more you need to know. Especially if you already have 'an education' – the more you have, the better you appreciate how little that is. If the wind is in your sails, you will have acquired more responsibilities and privileges as you age, along with the ability to effect change in other people's lives and perhaps even the world at large. This obviously requires greater comprehension about the way things work. It also necessitates empathy, because you will have so many people's feelings to consider – perhaps even the responsibility for the happiness of your children. You will need to know more about the problems other people have survived and how they overcame them, because you will experience pain, loss, frailty and failure with increasing frequency. Now is the time to appreciate Steinbeck.

Yet, too often, we think of study as the pursuit of the young, and of education as something that you earn, count and then keep. We treat learning like money, but it isn't. It's more like gardening, running or record collecting. It is endless, but (weirdly) that's fine. For some reason, the pleasure of the thing is in the pursuit, often packed inside its most difficult aspects – which is something else that makes me think study is better suited to older people. The slow burn, the long haul, the systematic striving and partial, incremental success . . . this is not the stuff of youth, but of adulthood.

I hope this doesn't sound depressing, because it isn't. Quite the reverse, in fact. Action For Happiness (whose patron is no less an authority on the subject than the Dalai Lama) cites 'learning something new' as one of their ten keys to happier living. It doesn't have to be anything as formal as a qualification. It's a question of stretching yourself and expanding your horizons in small ways. I once knew a man who swore that the secret of long life was to be learning something new, always. The last time I saw him, he was about to turn fifty and had just taken up the bagpipes (this was not connected with the fact that I haven't seen him since, I promise). It seems that there is an increasing body of evidence that agrees with the piper's idea – though not quite in the way he meant it. Learning new things is one way to make life seem longer. Scientists studying 'brain time' have been looking into the way our brains perceive the passing of time and it appears that the key to slowing time down, to stop the sensation that life is passing you by in a blur, is to step outside of your daily routine and try new things. This, the theory goes, is why the school summer holidays seemed endless back when you were a kid, but your commute to work can disappear without you even noticing it has happened. Your brain is only bothering to log the new stuff.

My formal education topped out at A-level, but I'd love to continue it one day. For now, I'm happy to remain incurably curious. I'm told it can be an annoying trait to live with, but it keeps me productive. It worked for Michelangelo, too, apparently. His work as an artist, architect, poet and engineer had already begun to change the course of Western thought when he died, three weeks before his eighty-ninth birthday. His last words? 'Ancora imparo.' I am still learning. Me too, man. Me, too.

Parenting

CATHY RENTZENBRINK | STEPHANIE MERRITT
ANON | ROBYN WILDER
JOHANNA THOMAS-CORR | VIC PARSONS
JUDE ROGERS | ZOË BEATY
LAUREN LAVERNE | LAURIE FRANKEL

There is no such thing as a smug mother, we're all terrified and struggling

BEFORE SHE HAD HER SON, CATHY RENTZENBRINK BELIEVED IN THE MYTH OF THE SMUG MOTHER. NOW SHE KNOWS THE TRUTH: EVERY NEW MUM IS PROTECTING HERSELF AND HER BABY BY ONLY TELLING HALF THE STORY

BY CATHY RENTZENBRINK

I didn't want children until I was thirty-five. Then, after years of getting annoyed when people told me I'd change my mind, I changed my mind. It was a sudden thing. Luckily the man I lived with, to whom I had made childlessness a condition of our relationship, was happy to change his mind too. We were off.

I knew nothing about children or babies, but one thing I was sure of was that I was never going to be one of those mothers, the smug types who push you out of the way so they can get their enormous buggies on to the Tube and hand out dirty looks to anyone who swears or smokes anywhere near their little bundle. I was going to be something else entirely. Hassle-free. How hard could it be? All you need is love, after all. I'd heard talk of sleep deprivation, but I was used to staying up for days drinking and snatching a bit of kip on the move, so I thought I'd cope well with any sleepless nights.

I bought some folic acid tablets, stopped getting drunk for half of every month and, eventually, gave birth to a healthy baby boy after a botched induction and a horrific labour that ended in an emergency caesarean. I was so swollen up with drugs by the time they sliced my child out of me that my feet looked like pig's trotters for a good week afterwards. I didn't much care. The only important thing was my baby and keeping him alive. He was so beautiful. I loved every single eyelash, every tiny toenail. The fact that my body was knackered – back problems, carpal tunnel syndrome in both wrists – only bothered me because it made it trickier to cater to his needs. I was a cocktail of love and fear made in fairly equal measures with a good dash of sleep deprivation – a big deal, as it turned out – and a side order of being convinced I was doing everything wrong.

I had sworn that having a baby wouldn't change me or affect my friendships but when my friends came round to hand over pretty outfits and tell me about promotions and new or misbehaving lovers, it wasn't that I didn't care but I could hardly hear them over the noise of my own internal chatter: 'I haven't had any sleep and I don't know how to keep this little thing alive and I'm scared I'm going completely nuts and I haven't had any sleep and I don't know how to keep this little thing alive . . .'

And, of course, I didn't say any of that out loud, because you can't, you don't.

What I was trying to get to grips was what I now think is the paradox of motherhood. You would give up your life without question for this little thing – gleefully and happily take a bullet – while, all at the same time, you'd do almost anything for someone you trust to just take him away for a couple of hours so you can try to remember who you are.

Six years later my little baby is very much a boy and I am still a – slightly calmer – cocktail of love and fear. If I gave in to my yearnings to keep him safe, I would wall him up in his bedroom and lie down in front of the door like a human draught excluder to block incoming dangers. I don't, of course. I know that would be bad for both of us. And it's only half the story. I also like escaping from the self I am with him. I love being out in the world, where I have an identity other than Mummy. Because looking after a small child is often boring. Mind-bendingly, brain-zappingly dull. And the tantrums. In the year he was three, I went from thinking that anyone who hit a child was a monster to being genuinely surprised that more people aren't in prison. I didn't hit him, but there were days when I longed to, when I had to put myself in another room and cry hot, angry tears as I tried to calm down.

What I continue to puzzle over all the time is why all of this came as such a shock to me and why women don't tell the truth about the darker side of motherhood. Social media amplifies the dishonesty, or, rather, the selective truth-telling. Countless times I've posted a picture of my son looking cute on Facebook and later that weekend, possibly even just one hour later, I've been sobbing with despair at what a useless mother I am. Of course I don't share that. Both feelings are genuine, but only one gets out into the world.

So why the secrecy? I've distilled it down to five main reasons:

①

'IT'S ONLY ME'

I now think that lots of mothers of small children feel some kind of combination of pointless/angry/feeble/insane/bored a lot of the time but I used to think it was only me and it was a shameful secret that needed to be kept under wraps so no one would come and take my baby away.

②

INGRATITUDE

I have a beautiful healthy child and am in comparatively fortunate circumstances. I loathe the thought of complaining about my trials when other mothers are fleeing combat zones, or in refugee camps, or having to go to food banks, or can't afford Calpol or are dealing with any sort of health problem. It fills me with horror and loathing that I might moan on about Lego all over the floor to someone who has had three miscarriages or has just learnt that their sixth round of IVF has failed.

③

TEMPTING FATE

Every time I say anything that acknowledges that being a mother is anything other than an uncomplicated joy, I immediately imagine that my son is falling off the climbing frame as I speak. I picture him spinning through the air, landing on the tarmac. I hear the smash and I know that not only will he be dead but it will be my fault, and everyone will say, 'Well, I guess it's a shame her son died but she didn't really like him very much anyway and was always banging on about how hard being a mother is . . .'

THE UNTHINKABLE HAPPENS

I have never dared write any of this down in my diary in case my son is abducted and the police read my grumbles and decide that I've done away with him myself. This matters not because I will care about being arrested and unjustly convicted, but because the time they spend suspecting me will stop them looking for him.

5

THE FEAR

The fear that I will fall under a bus the day after being honest and that my last words about my child were anything other than a song of love.

So that's why mothers look smug. We're only telling the good half of the story because we're terrified of the pitfalls and consequences of honesty.

I no longer think smug mothers exist. I remember the first time I was getting on the Tube with my son in his pram. Various bits of my body leaked. I was exhausted from getting out of the flat and down the stairs at the Tube station. As the train drew in, I stared at the gap, terrified I'd get a pram wheel stuck in it, that his tiny body would catapult out and be crushed. I didn't want get on the train at all. Wasn't it too dangerous? Didn't they sometimes crash? I summoned all my courage, ignored the pain in both my wrists and lifted the pram up over the gap. We were on. I looked up and saw a woman stare at me. I realised I'd pushed by her. She thought I was a smug mother and had no idea how broken and frightened and responsible I felt, and I thought of all those times I'd been cross at what I perceived as maternal smugness when what I'd been witnessing was fear.

We need to lower our expectations around mothers. Now when I see a woman with a baby, I give her the benefit of the doubt and accept that for the moment she has been ambushed by her biology.

Every bit of her is doing what she can to keep a tiny life alive. We just need to be kind and let her get on with it.

PS If I do fall under a bus tomorrow, I'm relying on you all to tell my little dude that he was the great joy of my life and I've no idea why I ever spent time on anything other than gazing at his beautiful eyelashes.

The damage done by demonising single mothers

BRINGING UP A CHILD ALONE. WORKING HARD AS THE SOLE BREADWINNER. SINGLE MOTHERS HAVE IT HARD ENOUGH, WITHOUT BEING STIGMATISED BY THE PRESS AND THE GOVERNMENT

BY STEPHANIE MERRITT

If you were a victim of the TalkTalk hacking, I'd like to apologise. Technically, it wasn't my doing, but as you'll no doubt be aware by now, the hacker was a fifteen-year-old boy raised by a single mother – the most important fact about him, to judge by the *Daily Mail's* headline – and since most of the lawlessness and delinquency in our crumbling society is the fault of us single mothers, I thought I'd better get my apology in early, just in case. After all, I have a teenage son too so, according to the right-wing press, it's only a matter of time before he steals something from you. Sorry about that.

Iain Duncan Smith, the government's self-appointed Witchfinder General when it comes to the evils of single mothers, is often to be found trumpeting statistics about the high crime rate and poor life chances of children who grow up in lone-parent families. In a speech after the 2010 election, he claimed that the soaring crime rate caused by the 'collapse of marriage' was costing the country £100 billion a year.

Children of single parents were nine times more likely to become young offenders, and more than twice as likely to live in poverty. His answer to this spiralling moral crisis back then was to encourage an increase in 'stable families' by offering marriage tax breaks and further stigmatising single mothers. Not, apparently, to alleviate the poverty or improve the educational chances of those children growing up in one-parent households. Because you can do what you like with statistics, but it always amazed me that it never occurred to IDS or the *Daily Mail* that it might be poverty and lack of opportunity that crush children's chances, not necessarily the parenting.

It's the relentless demonising that makes me spit nails, though. According to the charity Gingerbread, lone-parent families (of which 91 per cent are mothers) make up a quarter of all families in the UK with dependent children. Of those, less than 2 per cent are teenagers; 64.4 per cent are in work. But, just as certain elements of the media choose to present all benefit claimants as work-shy yobs faking illness and scamming the system, so they also like to paint single mothers as Vicky from *Little Britain* – irresponsible slappers buying knock-off designer clothes on state handouts while our feral children terrorise the neighbours, because it's an easy way of judging our morality as women. I've cried tears of anger and frustration watching TV debates about marriage tax breaks, as politicians talk relentlessly about the importance of rewarding the people who 'do the right thing' – by which he means getting sensibly married and buying a house *before* having children.

It was the smug piety of the phrase that made me despair, the lack of compassion it implied. I could point you to a number of single mothers, myself and my friends, who work their arses off day after day to 'do the right thing' – which is to give their children the best possible upbringing with the resources they have. Women who are bravely doing their best, earning a living, rushing home to read bedtime stories, endlessly juggling, worrying that both our work and our children are being short-changed, because when you're the principal carer and the sole breadwinner, you always feel it's never enough. And all the time you're conscious that your children and your parenting are being judged by different standards from your coupled-up peers.

I don't know anything about the mother of the teenage hacker, but I'd be willing to bet she's tried to 'do the right thing' most of the time in bringing up her son. Most parents do, single or otherwise. Not all of us manage to organise our lives according to a nice neat plan. Many of us find ourselves trying to make the best of a bad decision or unforeseen circumstances at one time or another, and the demonising makes it so much harder. After all, as Tony Parsons pointed out in his novel *Man and Boy* (and I promise this is the first and last time I'll look to Tony Parsons for inspirational quotes): 'The single parent is the one who stayed.'

Controlling parents and the damage they wreak on their children

A NEW STUDY SAYS ADULTS WHO WERE CONTROLLED BY THEIR PARENTS ARE MORE LIKELY TO HAVE POOR MENTAL HEALTH

BY ANON

I read with sad recognition the details of a new study, published in the *Journal of Positive Psychology*, which claims that children raised by overly controlling parents face a lifetime of mental health problems. Researchers found that people whose parents failed to respond to their needs or encouraged dependence on them scored lower in surveys of happiness and wellbeing throughout their lives.

Dr Mai Stafford, the lead author of the study, said 'Parents give us a stable base from which to explore the world, while warmth and responsiveness has been shown to promote social and emotional development. By contrast, psychological control can limit a child's independence and leave them less able to regulate their own behaviour.'

Although I have never been in any doubt that my parents loved me, both of them in their own ways sought to exercise psychological control over me, and I have borne the scars ever since.

My father was brought up in boarding schools where he learnt strict self-control. He was afraid of feelings, would physically leave the room if I expressed strong emotion, would ignore or punish me when I was frightened. I learned that my disruptive emotions were not welcome in our home and began to repress them from an early age.

My mother meanwhile was raised with a history of trauma. She was abandoned by her own parents and subsequently lost a brother to suicide. She was terrified that if she did not present a perfect front to the world, she would be abandoned again, so everything had to be flawless: her behaviour, her appearance, our home and me.

Many of her anxieties revolved around food and the fear that I might get too fat or too thin. She weighed me daily, cut up my food for me and spoon-fed me well into my primary school years. One of my earliest memories is of stealing and hiding food; I still have a tendency to starve myself when under intense stress.

My mother also believed that the world was a dangerous place, foreseeing disaster around every corner, from the fear that I would be run over every time I crossed the road to the risk that I would be kidnapped and murdered if I travelled alone. I became afraid to leave her side, but knew that I must not voice my fears: my father would be angry with me, and my mother worry that my negativity might make me unlovable.

Throughout my childhood and well into adulthood, I followed a pattern of emotional self-control to the point of numbness, interspersed with intense spells of anxiety, panic attacks, anger and shame, when the feelings I have been repressing could no longer be held back. It was impossible to form healthy relationships as I was either too claustrophobic or too needy. In my early thirties, my anxiety became so overwhelming that I eventually had to be hospitalised. I still remember the relief when I entered the hospital: finally, I was in a place where my feelings would be heard. Equally, however, I was aware of the disturbing attraction of being in an institution: that once again somebody else would look after me the way that my mother used to. But the therapy I received there helped me to open the doors to my emotions, to let go of control and begin to voice and act on my needs.

Now aged forty, I am about to move in with a partner for the first time and I ask myself whether I can allow myself to depend on him without losing myself again. In the mirror of our relationship I see my learned helplessness, my tendency to expect him to do everything for us, my terror of expressing my feelings and risking rejection. But I'm excited by the opportunity to learn and grow together, to live as independent yet interdependent equals. I am not only the result of my upbringing; I have moved on, and have more strength than I ever could have dreamed of as a child.

Dr Stafford says that the study is not seeking to blame parents, and nor do I blame mine. Despite everything, it has always been clear to me that they had my best interests at heart. There was no malice, no cruelty, just two people, imperfectly raised themselves, who were taught the wrong lessons and passed them on to me. All that I can do is to learn from their mistakes and, by letting go of their control, finally take healthy control of my own life.

I'm reaching new lows, juggling a toddler and a newborn

ROBYN WILDER HAS LONG BEEN A FAN OF CRAP PARENTING. BUT SHE'S PLUMBING NEW DEPTHS IN THESE EARLY DAYS OF HAVING A SECOND CHILD

BY ROBYN WILDER

Last week, my husband came home late from work one night and walked in on a scene straight out of a horror film. Before him, a creepy trail of abandoned baby paraphernalia. Above him, an unearthly wailing. And all around him, beeping robot toys and something on the walls that might have been blood*. Gingerly, he climbed the stairs and entered the darkness of our toddler's bedroom to find, huddled on the bed, not a banshee or a possessed doll, but me, our toddler and our newborn, all of us red-faced, shrieking and inconsolable. And me with breast milk flowing freely down my dress, too.

Honestly, props to my husband for not turning on his heel and starting a new life in Argentina.

The evening had started decently enough – I wasn't too fazed by the prospect of solo parenting. Our newborn tends to sleep through the day, have a period of fussy wakefulness just when we're about to sit down to dinner, then dozes again after our son's gone to bed – so I just figured that if I delayed everything by an hour we'd be just peachy.

Reader, we were not peachy. The baby would not go to sleep. He wouldn't sleep, and he wouldn't go to sleep, and he wouldn't sleep again. He suctioned on to my boob at 4pm, then screamed bloody murder every time I tried to put him down. My C-section wound is healing wonkily and I'm not allowed to wear a baby carrier, so all I could do was frantically click around the kids' section of Netflix while the sky darkened outside and my toddler made polite noises about dinner.

My toddler was good as gold. He did not complain when dinner was eventually served alongside a baby tantrum at 9pm, and bathtime was serenaded by baby screams. But eventually, when he couldn't cuddle up to me at storytime because the baby was thrashing on my lap, he lost it. 'Mummy!' he screamed, throwing his arms around my neck. 'I'm your baby, too, Mummy!' Which is when I broke down, too. And when my husband came home.

'You know,' my husband whispered later that night, like some sort of bastard. 'I'm going away again next week, remember.'

Last night was that night, and my only objective was to prevent the Unearthly Wailing. Let my son eat his spaghetti bolognese on the sofa, with his fingers, while I tended to his baby brother. I congratulated him as he ground some beef into a cushion. I cooed when he hid his spaghetti under the ottoman. I gave him Iced Gems and lollipops when he asked for them, simply because it meant he wouldn't complain. Finally, when his gaze was getting too long and the shadows under his eyes too deep, I took him upstairs and began the bedtime ritual – pointedly ignoring the newborn, who was shrieking, heart-broken but safe, in his rocker downstairs.

I've written before about how, as a parent, you need to let go of perfectionism. Unless you're very lucky, have staff or are psychotically Type A, your house won't always be a spotless monochrome wonder-land, your parenting won't be straight out of Enid Blyton and you won't always feel sane. Embrace low-standard parenting, I have always advised, and don't sweat the small stuff.

But now I have two kids – two kids in the neediest phases of their lives I'm having to lower my standards even further. When I'm solo parenting, it's not enough to embrace 'crap parenting', in order to survive I have to fully enter the world of Bad Parenting. I have to neglect each of my kids in turn just to get through the night.

That's what I did last night. On one hand, I'm not proud. On the other hand, everyone was asleep by 11pm and – most importantly – I didn't end up in tears. Out of all the parenting styles I have tried to adopt – attachment, permissive, authoritarian – I have to say that Bad Parenting has been the most effective.

* But was actually chilli con carne

Are you an unpaid emotional labourer at home, and at work?

WOMEN BUY THE BIRTHDAY CARDS. THEY ARRANGE THE GET-TOGETHERS. THEY REMEMBER THE NAMES OF THE CHILDREN'S FRIENDS

BY JOHANNA THOMAS-CORR

If you mention the term 'emotional labour' to a man, it often provokes a strange reaction. A look of forlorn disbelief crosses their features, followed by indignation, facial twitching and a barely audible mutter that might be translated as: 'What fresh feminist hell is this?' My otherwise very progressive husband seemed to crash like an over-loaded PC when I brought it up the other day, having read a frenzied Metafilter thread on the subject.

Mention it to a woman, especially (though not exclusively) those with children, and there's often a slow instinctive nod, as if to say: 'This is what I've been talking about all these years. Finally, it has a name!' My friend Amelia immediately came up with a definition I find it hard to improve: 'Emotional labour means the time and energy spent on things considered by society to have no real value but which are in fact essential toward functional relationships and a functional society. Traditionally, a burden placed on or taken by women.'

So while emotional labour sounds like a PR strategy for a new touchy-feely Jeremy Corbyn, it actually refers to the 'affirmation, for-bearance, consultation, pacifying, guidance, tutorial and weathering abuse that [women] spend energy on every single day,' as writer Jess Zimmerman put it. The term was coined in 1983 by the sociologist Arlie Hochschild but is increasingly coming back into vogue as the new frontier of feminism. You know the sort of thing. Organising all the family get-togethers. Consoling your boyfriend's mate after his break-up. (Reminding your boyfriend that his mate has had a break-up.) Fielding all communications that pertain to your child's welfare, education, playdates, etc. Generally feeling like you're the emotional CEO (or more likely PA) at home, but also in the workplace.

And while I can hear the collective 'b-b-b-b-but!' coming from men of my generation – who are often proactive fathers, keen cooks and conscientious partners who occasionally even quote Lena Dunham at you – I feel these are battle lines worth drawing.

I've been an emotional labourer so long, it's hard to untangle what I'm naturally inclined to do from what's imposed upon me. It often starts quite innocuously: 'You're so much better at this than I am . . .' Which is exactly how so many women end up doing men's emotional work for them. It peaks in the run-up to Christmas, where it almost always falls to women to co-ordinate arrangements, intuit how to make everyone happy and suffer the shopping-bag lacerations that result. Throughout my teens, I did all of my brother's present shopping for him – he just handed over the money. The first year he managed it himself, he called me triumphantly to describe how many gifts he had 'actioned', only then realising it was an actual thing that took time and care.

Emotional labour exists at work too. When I was a desk editor at a male-dominated newspaper, I was always the one to organise leaving presents and charity collections. In a later position, I experimented with withdrawing from these tasks and felt hugely liberated. But it was clear that my female colleagues were picking up the slack.

Back at home, when I see my husband – also a writer – go off on a creative flight of fancy, I envy how free he is from anxieties pertaining to nieces' birthdays and nursery timetables and his good friend with a long-term illness who he must remember to call. All of these can absorb a woman's headspace and stifle her creativity. Just because she is 'good at these things' doesn't mean they don't take up a frankly impertinent amount of her time.

Of course, it's a hard case to make without sounding martyrish – and my husband has a whole suite of burdens that I'm only half aware of. He does all the driving, defragments the hard drive, handles anything bin-related and is actually making me a butternut squash salad right now, even as I chronicle his shortcomings. In any relationship there is a negotiated give and take.

But even within these new domestic settlements, I feel there's still an undervaluing of what women provide. My mother – a proper old-school Greenham Common feminist – speaks of my husband's butternut exploits in the most heroic terms, but doesn't recognise that my actively giving a damn about people's feelings – and all the phone calls and Tube dashes this entails – is even a job at all.

A friend believes that we won't win the battle in our lifetimes. 'But our daughters will win it,' she says. 'And our sons will understand the meaning of emotional labour.' But until then, we're not helpless. We can withdraw our time and energy. We could even call a National Emotional Labour Strike. Maybe the only the way of finding out the significance is to say fuck it – and see what results. We might surprise ourselves.

My dad is an LGBTQ+ ally and a hero. This is my thank you to him

VIC PARSONS SAYS THANK YOU TO THEIR DAD FOR HIS UNWAVERING LOVE AND SUPPORT

BY VIC PARSONS

The last member of my close family who I came out to was my dad, Tim. In my mind, a middle-aged, middle-class, straight white man who worked in the City and had a *Times* subscription was the most likely to reject me for being a lesbian. This was back in the summer of 2011 and I was too scared to tell him for months. When I did come out to him, it wasn't planned. He asked which of my friends I was going on an upcoming holiday to Amsterdam with. I couldn't lie. I took a deep breath, looked around the Starbucks we were sat in and said, 'Actually, I'm going with my girlfriend.'

There was a small pause and then he said, 'OK.' He asked if I was bisexual or a lesbian. He asked if he could meet her; he said he would like to. Then it was time for him to go back to work.

The changes were small, at first. Along with the political articles we had always emailed each other, he began sending pieces that covered LGBTQ+ issues and asking my opinion. On the phone, he would ask after my girlfriend. After he met her, he sent me a message saying how lovely it was to see me so happy.

Fast forward seven years and he has a rainbow flag on his desk at work and wears rainbow laces in his trainers. He's a member of his work's LGBT & Allies group. When his employer ran an event with Stonewall two years ago, to offer practical advice to parents with LGBTQ+ children, I sat in a crowded boardroom, watching as my dad stood up to share his experience. He talked about what it was like, when first I and then my sister came out as gay, and how he tried to support us. He said he was proud of us both – so proud – and he started to cry. The previous speaker had talked about being thrown out of home at sixteen for coming out as gay, and my dad, still emotional, said he didn't understand how a parent could do that.

I am telling this story now because it's Father's Day this weekend and I want to publicly thank my dad for being such a hero. I want to acknowledge how much his support means to me and how much happier and safer I feel because of it. I want to say it out loud because it's important to say thank you, and mean it, and it's important to celebrate positive parent allies. So many people aren't afforded the privilege of having someone like my dad in their lives – I know too many people who recall horror stories of how their relationship with their dads changed or even dissipated once they came out.

For me, thankfully, it wasn't like that – my dad can't imagine rejecting your children for their sexuality or gender identity. But lots of parents do. Almost a quarter of young homeless people are LGBTQ+ and over two-thirds of them are homeless because they have been rejected by their families. Last year alone, more than 10,000 young LGBTQ+ people were made homeless – just for being who they are.

For black and ethnic minority (BAME) LGBTQ+ young people, the situation is even worse. Of the homeless sixteen to twenty-five-year-olds who identified as LGBTQ+ in 2010, three-quarters were BAME. Many of these young LGBTQ+ people cited religious homophobia as a reason for their homelessness. And then there are those who couldn't come out to their families for this reason.

June Eric-Udorie wrote an article for *The Pool* in which she revealed that she severed ties with her parents to come out. 'I knew that being open about my bisexuality was not a possibility for me,' she wrote, 'especially with my fiercely Pentecostal, homophobic parents.' There are too many young queer people who have to hide their sexuality or gender identity from their parents.

I am extremely lucky to have my dad. He read up on how to support his gay kids and he's gently shown his interest in this part of my identity over the years: have I experienced discrimination (which he was very concerned about), what was it like for me at school, how did I work out I was gay. He's told me about times when he's stood up to his friends for making homophobic jokes; when he's called out gay couples for making derogatory remarks about lesbians at weddings he's attended. He was fiercely tender towards me when I had my heart broken by my now-ex girlfriend.

It's not that complicated to be a supportive parent like my dad and it shouldn't be rare. You can mention gay, lesbian and trans people in conversation and be inclusive in your language – don't let straight and cis be the default assumption. Show that it's an open topic and not something to be kept quiet. Look up words and concepts to do with queer identities – like non-binary or pansexual – that you may not be familiar with and talk about them with your children. Talk positively about LGBTQ+ people who appear in films or real life. Make it clear that you'll love your children no matter how they identify – even if they're straight and cisgendered (not trans).

I came out for a second time earlier this year, as non-binary (a person who doesn't identify as exclusively male or female). Apart from my sister, who'd known all along, my dad was the first person in my family I told. I wasn't scared this time. I already knew that he was going to make me feel loved when I told him. He told me about a non-binary colleague at work who, as far as my dad knows, is only out to him. He asked questions that meant I felt heard, rather than doubted.

A few weeks later, I saw him for dinner before he went on holiday and he asked my advice on his holiday reading list. Given that, usually, he strictly reads autobiographies of politicians or cricketers, I was a bit confused – until he showed me on his Kindle. He'd downloaded *How to Understand Your Gender*, a guide to trans and non-binary identities, to read by the pool.

And then, when I went down to his house to look after his cat while he was away, he'd downloaded the US show *Billions* for me – it's the first time a non-binary actor has played a non-binary character on TV and he'd downloaded the episodes from when they first appear. Of course, he'd already watched it.

We need to change the way we treat mothers who keep their own name

WOMEN ARE ASKED WHO THEIR OWN DAUGHTERS
ARE AT BORDER CONTROL; SOMETHING MUST GIVE

BY JUDE ROGERS

The first time I heard about it, I couldn't believe it. A good friend, travelling alone with her kids, had been interrogated harshly at border control about whether her children were hers. I kept thinking about what this scene would look like to a child: a stranger in a uniform, accosting your mum, questioning her role in your life, her care over you. I'm not saying this would lead to deep, lifetime repercussions for their little mind, but what does the nature of that exchange tell us about the way we treat mothers? Mothers who've decided, very reasonably, to keep the name with which they were born?

An MP has revealed this had happened to her. Tulip Siddiq was stopped before boarding a Eurostar on her way home from holiday to be asked who her daughter was. 'I was really surprised by the question and he repeated it,' she explained – she was juggling a pushchair, a toddler and God knows what else at the time. Siddiq's husband was elsewhere in the terminal, she added, and the couple's young daughter, crying for her 'mama' throughout, looks more like him. Marriage, birth certificates and more documents were demanded, driving Siddiq to tears. All because the border guard kept asking 'why we don't have the same name'.

There is a blindingly obvious answer to this, but no matter – Siddiq was even told to leave her eighteen-month-old with the border agents to go and find her husband. 'I got married aged thirty, I lived my life, I had a reputation under my maiden name,' she went on, which saddened me a lot – we still live in a world where women like her, just like me, still get asked to justify this choice. What she said next spoke volumes, too. 'I don't want my daughter to have to go through that kind of questioning as she grows older, because it won't happen with her father, only with me.' The sound you're hearing is the heads of nails being hammered.

I'm not ignoring the reason the Home Office gave for this encounter, which comes from a place of absolute care for a child – the practice of trafficking children is notoriously difficult to police. I also bet being a border guard is not particularly delightful. Imagine that pressure to keep the queue moving, deal with harried travellers, keep a cool head. But the campaign Siddiq has launched to get both parents' surnames on passports helps them, too – it wouldn't require a change of legislation and it would make their jobs a lot easier. Additionally, surely some basic training on being more humane would help? It would also stop guards getting into situations, like one another female friend went through a few years ago, with her son, at an airport. The border guard said directly to the child, 'Point to your mum.' The child replied, amazingly, 'It's rude to point.'

Be it funny or not, this rudeness needs to get sorted sooner rather than later. According to a 2013 survey by Facebook of their 33 million UK users, women are increasingly keeping their own names; 38 per cent of women in their twenties were keeping theirs after marriage, up from 26 per cent of women in their thirties.

In my wholly unscientific real-life experience, many of my friends in this cohort have children with their husband's surname, too, and I know this warrants broader questions, and ones I'm not immune to (my son has both mine and my husband's surnames, although mine is a middle name of sorts, which sits uncomfortably on my shoulders, despite it being a decision I made).

Nevertheless, I also have many friends who have changed their names after marriage and – surprise, surprise – I still bloody love them. Choosing what we call ourselves is our decision alone. We shouldn't be treated harshly if those decisions differ. After all, whatever our names, we're still the same people.

These women have made legal history as the first best friends to be co-parents

AND RAISING A CHILD WITH A BEST FRIEND OVER THE UNCERTAINTY OF ROMANCE COULD BE BRILLIANT FOR WOMEN

BY ZOË BEATY

When I was a child, I told my mum I wanted to be just like her. Not a nurse or a Fleetwood Mac fanatic. Not a brilliant baker or even such an enthusiastic dancer. But I did want to be a mum – and a single mum at that. At the time, we lived alone and, since mum worked full-time, I was constantly around her friends. Her best friend, a raucously funny extrovert with stories for every occasion, did everything with us, including going on holiday. We laughed so much as a three that I wondered why anyone would want to get married or have a boyfriend, when being best friends was so much fun. Mum laughed when I told her my hypothesis. 'I don't think that's how it works, darling,' she said.

But what if it was how it works? What if best friends could be families, even in the eyes of the law? What if there was another option when it comes to being a parent, aside from being in a romantic relationship or on your own?

Two best friends in Canada have just become the first parents to do exactly that. They are not romantically involved with each other, but have been parenting together since their son, Elaan, was born seven years ago. Now, in a legal first, they have just been made 'co-mommas' (to use their words). They are the first friends to be recognised as a parenting partnership in the eyes of the law, with both of their names registered as 'mothers' to Elaan.

Their situation is unique in many ways. Natasha Bakht, now forty-four, decided to have a child using a sperm donor in her thirties – and, knowing she too eventually wanted to have children, Lynda Collins, her best friend, offered to be her birth partner. 'I thought it would be just an amazing life experience to see someone be born,' she told CBC News in an interview.

But there were complications during the birth and, at just six months, doctors discovered that Elaan would suffer a lifetime of disability, after discovering that portions of his brain were dead. He was left with spastic quadriplegia – meaning he cannot use any of his limbs – and he also has asthma epilepsy, visual problems and an inability to speak.

As a result, his care could be – and still is – demanding. Collins moved in with her pal and her son to help. They started to share responsibilities and attended medical appointments as a three. Theirs became a friendship bound like no other and a solid foundation for a family.

When Collins thought about having a child of her own, she realised that she already had one in Elaan, and that it made sense for her to adopt him and become his second parent. Which is what they set about to do. Now, after a two-year battle, they share legal, financial and medical responsibility for Elaan. And they're a little beacon of hope in a pretty miserable time.

They are a truly modern family – an example of how 'traditional' set-ups are quickly falling out of the zeitgeist as society evolves. And doesn't it make perfect sense? 'Relationships come and go,' goes the saying, 'but friends are the ones who stick around.'

A new set-up could provide a sense of stability for a child, allow single mothers (the majority of single parents are women) greater access to work and a relief from financial difficulties. And, as friends always do, be a source of unquestioning support to one another, with none of the complications or expectations of romance. Maybe I was on to something.

My kids have taught me how to be on holiday

TAKING TIME OUT OF HER BUSY LIFE WAS A LUXURY THAT
LAUREN LAVERNE ONCE COULDN'T ENVISION. THEN SHE
DISCOVERED THE JOY OF THE TRADITIONAL FAMILY HOLIDAY

BY LAUREN LAVERNE

There is a long-running joke in our family that, when it comes to holidays, we are cursed. I say 'joke'. It isn't a joke, actually. We really were cursed – if not in the supernatural sense then certainly from a statistical perspective. Every time we went anywhere, something went wrong.

I don't just mean rain. It always rained. This was more than that. Like the force-nine gale on the ferry to France. I remember trying to pretend I wasn't there, vomiting my way through Michelle Pfeiffer and Al Pacino's *Frankie and Johnny* in the cinema room as the ship descended vertical waves – the screen where the floor should have been. Then there was the coach trip up a German mountain, with a driver who kept falling asleep (presumably due to lack of oxygen) as the bus rounded terrifying, hairpin bends and the overflowing Portaloo divested its contents into the alley between the seats. The time we got lost in the actual Caves of Altamira. Worst of all was being struck by lightning. That happened on a chairlift in Austria. We were sightseeing rather than skiing, so we hung there for over an hour, wearing shorts and T-shirts in a hailstorm. Golfball-sized lumps of ice pinged off our pasty thighs as the shorted cables fizzed and buckled. We contemplated the increasing likelihood of death until the mountain rescue came and got us down. My dad – believing his aesthetic hubris had angered the Alpine Gods – never exposed his legs again.

We stopped going away-away after that. Then, in my early twenties, I met Mr Laverne. His dad worked in the hospitality industry so he'd grown up travelling. Not the kinds of holidays I was used to, which invariably involved an uncomfortable journey, followed by a cultural experience (if you think I'm exaggerating, I'm happy to tell you about the time we slept in a goatherd's attic before watching the Oberammergau Passion Play). Mr Laverne's family holidays were the cheese to our chalk. Specifically a smooth, uncomplicated brie. They stayed in hotels, ate in restaurants, played golf, went to the beach. They got tans. Wore linen. Unfathomable, alien activities which I regarded with a mix of envy and suspicion.

Many of my friends spent their twenties backpacking. Not me. I'd started broadcasting, and, while I travelled for work, I rarely did so for pleasure. I got married at twenty-seven and two days afterwards flew to Miami, not on honeymoon but to shoot a TV interview. I was back in London behind my radio mic within twenty-four hours. I worked harder than ever as my career began to take off and my two sons arrived. Things were always busy and – because I am freelance – unpredictable. We became expert staycationers, taking short breaks in the UK as and when time allowed. Then a few years ago something changed. I got sick with a bad case of stress-related shingles (ON MY FACE <—I mean wtf). I hadn't slept properly for half a decade, or taken a significant break since my sons were born. They meanwhile were at school and nursery, so we were no longer able to pack up and head off for a few days here and there. My career was in a place where I no longer felt taking two weeks off would be akin to resigning. Mr Laverne persuaded me that we should book [*torch under chin, scary voice*] a conventional family holiday.

I was nervous. Partly because I didn't have great associations with holidays, partly because I wanted to believe I was above jejune phrases like 'half-board family-friendly getaway', and also because I believed I was cursed. Mr Laverne, on the other hand, was delighted. He bought a new waterproof camera and a selection of 'Balearic' shirts, plus inflatables for the kids. I eyed them with suspicion as I loaded up my Kindle with a selection of difficult books.

Honestly, our first few trips were not unmitigated successes. I never got to read any of the books, at least not until I realised that 'self-catering' just means spending your holiday cleaning a kitchen that isn't actually yours. There was a bout of flu and a forty-degree fever. A villa full of terrifying art (sample piece: a massive depiction of Satan, made entirely of string) and a deep, freezing-cold, sheer-drop pool – not great for a two-year-old. An emergency landing at Gatwick followed by a night-long wait on the tarmac . . . But we kept trying, and in the process I realised a few things.

I am not cursed. I may never be a natural traveller, and will probably always be a little sceptical about tourism, but here's the thing – my kids aren't. They bloody love it. They love getting up in the middle of the night to catch a plane, arguing over who will push the airport trolley, sharing the window seat. They love hotels – the mysterious bed mints, making messy, mile-high sundaes at the buffet, kids' discos featuring confusing Euro trance and giant, foam cartoon characters they have no frame of reference for. They love breaks with friends – their gang spending the entire day at the beach or in the pool, staying up later than they ever have and being allowed to flake out still laughing, covered in sun cream and a fine dusting of sand.

My kids have taught me how to be on holiday. I won't say I'm an expert at doing nothing (full disclosure: I'm writing this on holiday) but their amazement at every aspect of the experience is infectious. People who extoll mindfulness say that a lot of it has to do with noticing what's right in front of you at any given moment. When we're away from home that's what they do. We all do. I love learning about the history and culture of the places we visit (old habits) but mostly I watch them learn things. With each new experience (seeing a volcano! Learning to dive! Feeding a sea lion!) they seem to grow in front of my eyes and I am at once unbelievably happy and completely desperate to slow everything down. It's only when you take a break that you realise Ferris Bueller really was an expert at taking time off. Life moves pretty fast. If you don't stop and look around once in a while you could miss it.

How do grandparents respond when their grandson becomes a granddaughter?

WRITER LAURIE FRANKEL IS BRINGING UP A
TRANSGENDER CHILD. AND, AT FIRST, SHE WONDERED:
COULD HER PARENTS EVER UNDERSTAND?

BY LAURIE FRANKEL

My paternal grandmother and I were very close. She was intelligent, curious, a dedicated self-taught student and a wide, smart reader. The margins of her many books are crammed with notes. She kept journals full of questions and ideas. She read Shakespeare for fun.

She had to, because she got married as soon as she graduated from high school, never went to university, never dreamed of going to university, never imagined there was any reason she should, never even contemplated having a career. Girls didn't study, didn't go to university, didn't get jobs. Girls got married and had babies. That's what it meant to be a girl.

Like me, she wasn't especially fashionable or concerned about what was in vogue. She had little use for fancy dress or coiffed hair or polished outfits. She dressed comfortably and modestly and always warmly, even though she spent the last decade of her life with her apartment thermostat set to thirty degrees. But she died at age ninety-two without ever having worn a pair of trousers.

She loved me unconditionally and was impressed by even my least impressive accomplishments, but she was alarmed by my jeans. She was alarmed when I joined the swim team, in the first place because who knew what germs lurked in swimming pools, but in the second because girls did not participate in sports. She was proud of me when I went off to university and then graduate school and then into the workforce, but I think it was a little bit like I went off into space. When I got engaged and told her I was keeping my last name – which, after all, was her last name as well – she rolled her eyes and said, 'Oh, you're one of those.'

For people lucky enough to live into old age, gender norms change hugely over the course of their lives. My grandmother would have thrived at university, but it was never even on the table for her. She never considered wearing anything but a skirt because women did not do so when she was growing up. That they then started to did not remotely tempt her to take up the practice herself. These norms are sown early and planted deep. Nice girls, normal girls did not wear trousers or ride bikes or leave home and family to study literature and philosophy. She had neither the need nor the ability to question this, even as she watched it change around her, change among her own.

One mere generation later, my parents dressed me in tiny, adorable baby jeans. They had me in swim lessons before I was a year old. They actually worried when I came home clean from nursery school. 'Why won't she get dirty?' they asked the teachers. 'How can we help her have fun and fit in?'

So, when my little boy became obsessed with dolls and pushing them around the neighbourhood in a pram, I wasn't worried about him, and I also wasn't worried about what my mom and dad would think. What it meant to be a boy and what it meant to be a girl had changed so much from their parents to their being parents. When he asked only for Barbies for his birthday, when he begged to have his toenails painted, when he cut his camp T-shirts into bras, no one was concerned. When he spent the summer before first grade playing dress-up in a floor-length sparkly green gown, my parents were OK with that, too.

It wasn't until he wanted – needed – to wear a skirt to the first day of first grade that they panicked. My dad's advice was to just say no. My mom was unable to tell me the only thing I wanted to hear: that it would be OK. She wasn't convinced it would be. As the dresses went from sometimes to all the time, from play to every day, from home to school, from optional to imperative, as the pronouns went from male to female and stayed there, as the name changed, as my son became my daughter, we all saw that this was a different thing than accepting a girl in trousers or a boy who liked to play with dolls.

One of the things that comes up all the time in the discussion group I'm in with other parents of transgender kids is how to tell the grandparents.

On the one hand, grandparents are dispensers of cookies, extra layers and unconditional love. It's so much less complicated to be grandparents than parents. It's so much easier to love little people you get to give back at the end of the day when they get cranky, to care hugely but without all the weight of responsibility for every decision and all behaviours, to be close but with enough distance to see what's really going on with clear perspective and gentle openness.

On the other hand, their adult children worry, grandparents are old. Or, they're old-fashioned. They're set in their ways. They've never heard of transgender kids. They still haven't accepted 'the gays'. They don't know anything about non-binary identities or cultural determinism. They already have trouble remembering names or keeping track of who's who. Their kids worry they'll never get it. Their kids worry that confusion and fear and loathing will override that unconditional love and lead them to reject their own grandchildren.

My family is lucky in that there is nothing – nothing – that would result in my parents rejecting my child. I never doubted they would understand and be supportive. But that didn't mean they didn't have questions, don't still have concerns or don't always get the pronouns right.

Their fears are the same as my grandmother's were. She didn't worry that because I wore trousers rather than skirts there was something inherently wrong with me. She worried that because I wore trousers rather than skirts no one would love me, that I would find myself rejected by society and my community for breaking social norms and traditions and expectations, that I would be weird and therefore unhappy. My parents' concerns boil down to the same: that their granddaughter will fail to fit in and find friends, will be bullied or relegated to the side-lines of her community, that she'll be weird and therefore unhappy. That she will find no one to love her but us.

I have the same fears of course, but I am enormously heartened that they have them as well, not because they validate mine, but because they invalidate mine. My grandmother's worries were perfectly understandable, but also perfectly absurd because they were worries from another world. By the time I went off to university, fear that a girl would be rejected for doing so, never mind for wearing trousers to class, was silly. My hope for my child – and, frankly, all our children – is that, by the time she goes off to university, the fear that she'll be rejected for being gender non-conforming will seem just as absurd. The world is changing. And she is changing the world. That is as it should be.

On the one hand, so much has changed since my grandmother was a child, when being gay was still illegal, when spousal rape was not illegal because there was no such thing, when being a girl instead of a boy narrowed life to the confines of your home, when being a boy who realised he was a girl meant, simply, misery or suicide. It's not that I'm not grateful to be living in a world of such expanded freedom and openness and tolerance. It's that it's not enough.

Because, on the other hand, we are living in a time of closing off and dragging down, where the people who would curtail and rollback our freedoms are winning, the ones who are threatened by gay people heading families or women heading states, who see equality for all as a punishment for themselves, who imagine that reducing the suffering of others increases their own, who are frightened by difference and angered by change.

And here, maybe, hope comes from being led by the grandparents. They have seen more than we have. They have seen bigotry and oppression and fear-mongering and hate and intolerance and even evil rise and then get taken down again. They have seen that history is long, that progress is often invisible while it's happening, that the steps back are painful but smaller than the ones forward, that when we get smacked down, we land in the crouch that launches us someplace even further ahead.

The more parents of trans children I meet, the more I discover this: the grandparents tend to surprise their kids more than anyone else in their lives. The grandparents who they think couldn't possibly understand are often the people most ready to embrace their grandchildren, whoever they turn out to be. They are often more ready than anyone to love uncomplicatedly and no matter what. They have seen a lot in their long lives and are therefore fazed by less than we imagine. They've witnessed great change, weathered it, spearheaded it sometimes. Often, and in many ways, their perspective, their faith in us and ours, and their love are wider and more agile than anyone's.

Style

LAURA CRAIK | SALI HUGHES | TOBI OREDEIN
MARISA BATE | KUBA SHAND-BAPTISTE
LAUREN BRAVO | EMMA BEDDINGTON
DAISY BUCHANAN | JUNO DAWSON
ANA KINSELLA

The Hollywood tax on not being size zero

AT THE GOLDEN GLOBES, ACTRESS BRYCE DALLAS HOWARD
REVEALED THAT SHE'D BOUGHT HER OWN DRESS. WHY? IT'S ALL
DOWN TO HOLLYWOOD'S SIZEIST STANDARDS

BY LAURA CRAIK

Stop all the clocks, cut off the telephone – though not before you've tweeted/Facebooked your amazement. I have seismic news. You probably won't believe it. But here goes. A real, live celebrity – one who lives in Hollywood 'n' everything, and has an agent and is a bona fide actress; not just someone off a reality TV show who once made a fitness video then got fat again – has gone into a shop and bought herself a dress to wear to an awards ceremony. I know! With actual money! Or maybe a credit card: I wasn't there, so cannot vouch for the specific method of payment, but a financial transaction was made which depleted said celebrity's bank account and increased the coffers of the store in question. Told you it was seismic!

That the actress in question, Bryce Dallas Howard, bought her own gown to wear to an event as prominent as The Golden Globes is surprising in a world of freeloaders who, as we all know, don't merely get to borrow dresses with four- and five-figure price tags, but are actively courted by designers to choose theirs. Dress the right star in the right gown, and the free publicity is priceless, far exceeding the cost of the dress. Little wonder designers fall over themselves to kit out that coterie of A-listers whom they know will grace the newspapers/magazines/websites that matter in the days and weeks after the event.

But if Bryce buying a gown is surprising, it isn't half as surprising as the reason why. Interviewed by Giuliana Rancic on the red carpet, she said of the floor-length, midnight blue $4,800 (£3,495) Jenny Packham gown that she 'just picked it up at Neiman's' adding that 'I like having lots of options for a size six, as opposed to maybe one option, so I always go to department stores for this kind of stuff.'

Yes, you read that correctly. The thirty-four-year-old actress is a size six – a UK ten – but may as well be a beached whale by the draconian standards of the fashion industry, where sample sizes are routinely a size zero or two, and if you don't fit into them, tough tittie. Judging from her choice of words – reading between the lines, at least – it doesn't matter if you're a beautiful, talented actress, and a presenter at one of the most high-profile, well-regarded awards ceremonies of the year: unless you slim down to near-skeletal proportions, you'll have to buy your gown off the peg.

The bad news? That we still live in an age where a size six celebrity is considered anomalous. The good news? Bryce's heroic venture into 'Neiman's' (Neiman Marcus, a US department store roughly the equivalent of Harvey Nichols) has turned her into a heroine overnight. Twitter has been awash with praise ('Bryce for president!') and memes of her clutching a lightsabre abound. Which is nice, even if 'celebrity buys own dress for awards ceremony' isn't exactly without precedent. In 2014, Hayden Panettiere spent over $10,000 on a Tom Ford gown to wear to the Oscars, after reportedly being turned down to borrow one because Ford was already dressing another actress that night.

Like Panettiere before her, savvy Bryce has raised her profile more adroitly than she ever could have hoped to simply by donning a size zero, hot-off-the-catwalk couture gown borrowed by her stylist. For anyone who hasn't yet got the memo: being best-dressed is all very well, but when it comes to your acting career, being relatable will get you further. And in the crazy world of Hollywood, nothing says 'relatable' more than going into a shop and purchasing something off the peg just like a 'normal' woman. Forget 'asymmetric' and 'burnt orange' – don't be surprised if the biggest trend this awards season is 'buying your own dress.'

I'm just a girl, standing in front of a high-street shop, asking it to dress her

THE BRITISH HIGH STREET NEEDS TO REALISE THAT MOST WOMEN OVER THIRTY-FIVE DON'T WANT 'COLD SHOULDER' DRESSES OR MIDRIFF-BARING TOPS

BY SALI HUGHES

Dear British high-street retailers,

I am a forty-two-year-old woman with an upcoming awards ceremony, three weddings (one my own), several important work engagements, a holiday in the unreliable British climate and some pottering about, doing bugger all. I have spent weeks browsing your wares, both online and in your bricks-and-mortar stores. My question for you is this: where, in the past five years, have all the clothes gone?

Let's begin with sleeves, for these cast a shadow over my entire shopping experience. Despite your apparent belief that my life is one long high-school prom, I would always like to cover my arms, at least to just beyond the elbow. I would not like capped sleeves to highlight the fact that I've lifted one kettlebell in my life, nor a bandeau top that precludes me from wearing a bra. I don't want to pick up any more nice-seeming dresses, only to find the entire back of it missing. I am literally always going to be wearing a sturdy underwire, whatever strip of wide elastic you so optimistically sew in to replace it. Like most women over thirty-five, who have either breastfed babies or done way too much reckless jiggling at underground raves (I know you're shocked), I like my boobs firmly encased, not increasing my dress size by two and covering my belly like a stab vest.

Ah, bellies. Mine is not taut or flat, and I'm mostly OK about it. What I'm not OK about is your obsession with tops that finish exactly around its middle which, when teamed with your persistently low-rise jeans, expose my protruding midriff for the first time since

Madonna went nuclear and I cut up my Aertex hockey blouse. I'd like, ideally, a T-shirt or jumper to reach my hips, skimming breezily across my stomach as if to say, 'Nothing to see here,' ideally with enough fabric to ruche so no one is quite sure where excess flesh ends and surplus cotton begins.

I say 'cotton', because you are quite mistaken in thinking that I'd like fabrics I can't safely pass a naked flame in. I want natural, soft cloth that stays the same size in a dryer, doesn't need dry-cleaning, can be put on a radiator without emerging as tactile as a Ryvita and still looks good on someone who hasn't ironed since the nineties. And my larger-sized friends would like their fabrics to be the same as mine, not sourced for three pence a yard from the cash-and-carry, and certainly not emblazoned with mimsy butterflies or garish Aztec prints, like pelmets from a static caravan circa 1992. When you do give them something more modern, they'd appreciate your not assuming any body confidence they do possess should manifest in dressing like a dancer at Spearmint Rhino. They're not freaks, ashamed, dowdy or inherently bubbly, kickass and outrageous. Please stop presuming that fat automatically equals tall with massive knockers, and thin equals short with a flat chest. Large women's lives and desires are the same as those of thin women. All of us want normal, nice, fashionable but unfaddy clothes with a little design flourish here and there, which make our respective bodies look their best.

Although, while we're at it, I'm a size eight (except in Topshop, where I'm a size ten, Gap, where I'm a size two, M&S, where I'm a six, and Whistles, where I'm at least three different sizes – do please all meet up for coffee and chat) and also feel strongly disinclined to show as much flesh as the teenage models on ASOS. Contrary to your sales blurbs, for many of us 'bodycon' is less an irresistible selling point, more a helpful signal that we will spend our evenings draped in a coat, unable to nibble more than an olive. Likewise, many of us haven't shared your love of tight-waisted skating dresses since puberty, think 'cold-shoulder' detailing makes us look a bit mad and we're not sure we'll ever be old enough for bias-cut linen. What would better tempt us is a whole department of 'eating dresses' – flattering frocks, neat at the shoulders, sleeves and neck, but with enough fabric around the middle to invisibly accommodate a bottle of red and more than nineteen calories.

Not that thirty- and fortysomething women are all about the socialising. We have busy jobs to do, families to care for, schedules to manage and bills to pay. Instead of 'occasionwear' seemingly aimed at black-tie beach parties we've neither hosted nor been invited to ever, how about a plain dress that, with a quick slick of red lipstick and black liner or a fancier shoe, can be worn straight out to drinks from a boring work meeting? Speaking of shoes, our taste didn't vanish with our flexible foot tendons. We like the bright colours, quality leather, femininity and high-design spec of stilettos, even though many of us would like to be able to run from a mugger after dark. Do put a little more effort into brogues, Oxfords, ballet flats and slides – in fact, go mad. Our feet are where we're up for anything – studs, neons, jewels, bonkers prints – safe in the knowledge that they'll fit almost everyone and inject some fun and personality into our outfits without going full top-to-toe Su Pollard.

So, once-beloved high-street retailers lamenting your declining profits, do consider putting into production this failsafe shopping list of garments that practically every woman over thirty-five, from size six to twenty-six, would buy tomorrow: a flattering sweatshirt dress available in several colours for school runs, evenings with close friends, dog walking and trips to the supermarket; one perfect tunic dress like those made by Goat and Victoria Beckham, only for less than a monthly mortgage repayment, which can be worn to any wedding, funeral or party, depending on accessories; a fancier, more fitted midi dress in a vintage print; a soft, navy, Paddington-style duffle coat with a hood; pockets on everything; sucky-in tights in different lengths as well as widths, that don't make us bloat and ache as though we've just flown long-haul; long-length T-shirts and sweatshirts that don't shrink, twist or bag; slim-fit, washable cardigans that finish mid-hip and have buttons spaced close enough to avoid gape; straight-leg (not prohibitively skinny or mortifyingly boot-cut) jeans with a waist that reaches the navel and judiciously placed patch-pockets to flatter our arses; some jumpers that go in and out as our bodies do, and have a deep-enough V-neck to stop our tits looking massive and saggy; a couple of A-line skirts that hit the knee; a *Mad Men*-style pencil skirt with a sturdy control panel across the belly.

I am a forty-two-year-old woman who is wondering where all the clothes have gone. My friends are all similarly perplexed. We are all in charge of our household budgets, all have some money, all love fashion and all want to look nice. So why, struggling high-street retailers, so frequently bleating about your misfortune, do you so persistently ignore us? The lucrative answer to many of your problems is standing right in front of you, desperately searching for sleeves.

Excluded by the wedding industry, black brides turn to Instagram

DISHEARTENED AT THE LACK OF REPRESENTATION OF WOMEN OF COLOUR IN BRIDAL MAGAZINES AND WEBSITES, BRIDE-TO-BE TOBI OREDEIN IS USING SOCIAL MEDIA FOR BRIDAL INSPIRATION

BY TOBI OREDEIN

This year, I was asked two very important questions. In January, my best friend got engaged and she asked – or, rather, she told me via WhatsApp – if I would be her maid of honour. Then, in March, after a romantic meal and walk through London, my boyfriend of six years got down on one knee and asked me to marry him. So, I resigned myself to the idea that a lot of my spare time would be spent looking at endless wedding imagery, flicking through digital and print versions of bridal magazines, and visiting wedding suppliers to make both big days as close to perfection as possible. And, the more I looked at bridal magazines and websites, the more I started to see that the brides featured in these publications all had one thing in common: they were all white. Looking through those bridal magazines, I felt overwhelmed because I never knew there were so many shades of 'white' when it came to dresses. I also was confused at the lack of models and real-life brides with a trace of melanin in their complexions.

At first, I second-guessed myself and thought maybe I wasn't looking at the right websites, or maybe I picked up a rare issue of a bridal magazine that had missed the memo that women of all races get married. But I spoke to my best friend, who is also black, and she shared the same feelings of irritation upon not seeing images of women of colour across wedding titles and in the brochures of wedding vendors. And, while feeling frustrated that I never saw anyone that bore my resemblance looking beautiful in a picture-perfect wedding dress, it was a familiar feeling.

It was that familiar feeling of looking at a range of pictures that feature beautiful women and not seeing myself represented. It was how I felt as a child when I would watch princess movies and read princess stories. It was how I felt as a teenager when I would read magazines only to see teenage girls who looked nothing like me. It is how I feel as an adult when I look at most fashion and beauty shoots; it is that feeling of being invisible. And I feel invisible every single time I look at anything wedding-related.

This erasure of black women when it comes to positioning womanhood in a celebratory or beautiful manner is all too common in society. But there's something particularly pernicious about the erasure of women of colour in the wedding industry, as it ties into the dangerous narrative that black women are undesirable. That marriage, which is unfortunately still seen by some as the highest achievement for women, is only reserved for white women.

After feeling deflated, reading numerous beauty features advising brides-to-be on the 'essential steps to getting a perfect tan for your wedding day' and not seeing a single article on how to style my afro on my big day, I turned to social media.

I started with Instagram and was overcome with joy when I stumbled across the American multicultural wedding account Munaluchi Bride – seeing black couples basking in the love of their wedding day. I found my make-up artist for my wedding on London-based multi-ethnic wedding account Crème De La Bride. I spend hours scrolling through a Nigerian Instagram account called Bella Naija, in awe of the lavish and glamorous weddings my fellow Nigerians create to mark their union. (There are countless more, including Afro Bride). And I spend even longer swiping through Pinterest and pinning hundreds of photos of natural hairstyles to my 'wedding-hair inspiration' board.

Through social media, I haven't just been able to decide which table centrepieces and colour schemes we will have for our big day. Instagram and Pinterest accounts that feature black brides have allowed me to have the full bridal experience; these social media accounts have allowed me to get lost in the sea of wedding inspiration without having to think twice, because my skin tone doesn't match the bride on my screen. Until the wedding industry catches up, that's where we black brides will be – celebrating our love and spending our money.

The woman who gave two fingers to looking like a Disney Princess at the Oscars

JENNY BEAVAN, WE SALUTE YOU

BY MARISA BATE

The Oscars. That strange time of the year when the world stops turning on its axis, and the sun seems to only shine on West Hollywood where the most famous sit in big dresses in a big room and give each other small gold statues. Glamorous? Maybe. Strange? Absolutely.

Yet the awards aren't just a celebration of great talent (congrats Brie Larson) or compelling, important films (yes, *Spotlight* was 100 per cent the worthy winner), it has become about the frocks. Or, in other words, what women are wearing. (Can anyone name who made DiCaprio's suit? No, didn't think so).

And much like the gold statues handed out to directors and actors and producers, beautiful women stand strangely still on a red carpet, radiating wealth and glamour, wearing dresses worth more than a one-bed in Catford, dripping in jewels that demand their own security team, and presumably breathing in with all the tenacity of a synchronised swim team.

So what happens when a woman shows up who *isn't* wearing a bespoke couture gown; a woman whose hair *doesn't* look like it's spent the last three weeks being coiffed; a woman, God damn it, in a pair of trousers?

Enter Jenny Beavan, one of the industry's finest costume designers, who arrived at the Oscars and went on to win an award for her work on *Mad Max: Fury Road*. But in a tale as old as DiCaprio's previous Oscar-shunning, Beavan's work was completely displaced by the fact she showed up in a fake leather M&S jacket, black trousers and had the look of someone who enjoyed clothes for the very fact she could move in them.

Oh, the horror! Just look at those guys' faces as she goes to collect her award! A row of men, almost in a synchronised choreography that looks staged, belie total disbelief that the woman in front of them doesn't look like a Disney Princess, is walking with ease and purpose and is defying every convention she is meant to be upholding. Their faces say it all: an incredulous shock that here is woman refusing to play along with the tired, out-of-date notions of how women should look and should behave. So shocked, it would seem, they forget to clap.

Beavan, (also of Stephen Fry Bag-lady-gate), obviously knew exactly what she was doing. Backstage she said, 'I don't do frocks and absolutely don't do heels, I have a bad back. I look ridiculous in a beautiful gown . . . This is Marks & Spencer with Swarovski at the back. I had a bit of a shoe malfunction and the glitter fell off. I just like feeling comfortable and as far as I'm concerned I'm really dressed up.'

So here we are, the world's media obsessing over a woman who went to the Oscars in M&S, in nothing that resembles a wedding dress on an acid trip, and instead of dripping in diamonds, she was dripping in heaps of defiant, unapologetic self-assuredness.

And the winner is . . . Jenny Beavan.

It took me 17 years to fall in love with my black hair. Why?

BIAS TOWARDS 'GOOD HAIR', EXPOSED IN NEW RESEARCH, IS ALL TOO REAL. KUBA SHAND-BAPTISTE EXPLAINS HOW SHE HAD TO LEARN TO LOVE HER HAIR

BY KUBA SHAND-BAPTISTE

It took me around seventeen years to fall in love with my hair. Not quite convinced by my mother's afro-centric affirmations, and swayed by the pervasiveness of anti-blackness – which carries with it unrelenting disdain towards the most identifiably disparate aspects of being black: the darkness of skin, the coarseness of hair – the idea of embracing my coarse, zig-zag kinks seemed entirely unachievable as a child.

It's a feeling that most black people, and women in particular, will have been exposed to at some point in their lives. Whether or not it stems from home, or society's seeming refusal to accommodate one of the most visible parts of African heritage, the notion that your proximity to whiteness dictates your worth is almost unavoidable.

The widespread resurgence of the natural hair movement just under a decade ago has helped to ease these internal and external prejudices in recent years. But, even within the deepest corners of the natural hair community, biases towards looser, softer and longer hair – so-called 'good hair' – persist.

New research – the Perception Institute's 'Good Hair' study – sought to expose exactly that. With 3,475 participants, the US-based research centre explored women's attitudes towards 'textured hair' (natural afro-textured hair) and 'smooth hair' (straighter, less textured hair). 'Black women perceive a level of social stigma against textured hair,' they said in their key findings, 'and this perception is substantiated by white women's devaluation of natural hairstyles.'

Do you harbour biases, when it comes to hair? You can test yourself. Using a word and image association exercise of sorts, the Hair Implicit Association Test (IAT) measures your prejudice. The test has already found that the majority of participants, regardless of race, show implicit bias against black women's textured hair. It also notes that 'one in five black women feel social pressure to straighten their hair for work – twice as many as white women'.

I'm not surprised by the findings. I know all too well how tactless people can be when it comes to hair, in non-black majority environments. 'How many times a week do you wash your hair?' they ask. 'Can I touch it?'

And it's a global problem. Aversion to afro-textured hair spans nations, from the afro hair ban in South Africa's Pretoria High School for Girls to the pervasion of cultural appropriation in the fashion industry – with the likes of Chanel, Marc Jacobs and other big designers using and, on some occasions, taking credit for distinctly black hairstyles, often without the involvement of black models.

The mere mention of cultural appropriation can be enough to prompt a furore – especially among those who don't understand or experience the relentless micro-aggressions lobbed at black women – but it is endlessly important. Pop culture has cherry-picked the most unique aspects of black culture, yet remains markedly less drawn to the very people who shape it. And it speaks volumes about the way society perceives blackness. The marketability of blackness has long been explored, with more recent analyses of the phenomenon manifesting among mainstream singers like Solange Knowles with her single, 'Don't Touch My Hair', from her third album, *A Seat At the Table*, as well as Amandla Stenberg's widely circulated 2015 video, 'Don't Cash Crop On My Cornrows'.

While it is encouraging that black participants in the Good Hair study tended to view textured hair in a more positive light than their white counterparts – 'Black women in the natural hair community have significantly more positive attitudes toward textured hair than other women, including black women in the national sample', according to the survey – generational differences were also shown to have an impact on the way that participants regarded natural hair.

I resolved to embrace my natural roots a few months shy of my eighteenth birthday. I'd watched my older sister begin to flaunt hers as the natural hair movement gained traction in 2009, with the rise of beauty blogs and YouTube tutorials. I never looked back from there. But how would I, now in my twenties, fare with taking the IAT test myself? I was acutely aware that I, too, may have some unexplored biases towards the tresses that I have had to learn to love.

Thankfully, and despite being aware of some of the criticism that IAT exercises have garnered over the years where accuracy is concerned, I was found to have a strong preference for textured hair. That's me. But what about everyone else? In such a regressive political climate, I worry that the cycle of absorbing bias against black hair, and later un-learning, will carry on. I hope I'm wrong.

The very real anxiety of having nothing to wear

EVER OPENED YOUR WARDROBE TO FIND THAT, DESPITE
ALL YOUR CLOTHES, YOU SIMPLY HAVE NOTHING TO WEAR?
IT'S TIME TO OVERCOME OUR WARDROBE ANXIETIES

BY LAUREN BRAVO

The other week, my colleague Caroline and I were having one of those aggressive compliment battles. 'You're so stylish!' she yelled at me across the desk. 'Nooooo, you are mistaken – I am a human dung heap!' I protested. 'SHUT UP,' she fired back. 'You always look so effortlessly put-together.' And the word 'effortlessly' cut through the middle of my 'Aw shucks' shield and hit a nerve. Mate, I thought, if only you knew.

I will never see myself as any kind of fashion hotshot (not while most of my clothes are covered in Doritos dust, anyway), but if I can lay claim to any style kudos at all, it is 100 per cent not effortless. I try really hard at getting dressed, actually. I think endlessly about clothes. I shop like it's a nervous tic. A few days ago, I changed outfit three times just to go to the end of the road, hungover, to buy a sandwich.

Does the 'effortlessly stylish' woman even exist? She's the industry's favourite unicorn – the off-duty model, the chic French fashion editor. But if I, a non-fashion nobody, find it so hard to put clothes on in the morning, then maybe behind every 'well-dressed' woman is a whole lot of sweat and tears. We're meant to pretend the perfect outfit just falls on by accident, rather than showing our workings.

And I do mean workings. Because getting dressed is a lot like an equation.

Firstly, there's wanting to look 'good' in what you're wearing. You want something 'flattering' that fits well and suits your colouring and performs whatever sorcery it is that 'flattering' clothes are expected to do. But, then, there's wanting to look the other kind of 'good' in what you're wearing – the kind that answers to fashion, to trends, to tribal identities and to your own personal idea of what makes a killer outfit. (NB: to complicate things, this part often ignores 'flattering' altogether, or goes deliberately against it).

Then you can factor in a load of agonising sub-criteria, such as: is it appropriate for the location and occasion? How about the weather? And you subconsciously offset each answer against how much you actually care – because sometimes dressing inappropriately for the situation is exactly the thing that's going to make you feel best, like when I wore a hot-pink wiggle dress to my nan's funeral.

Then (oh, you didn't think we were done did you?) comes comfort. Comfort involves so much more than just 'heels vs flats'. Comfort is a continually evolving challenge. My high-waisted, cropped jeans, for example, look great in the morning but, after lunch, the rigid denim tends to get a bit too pinchy at the crotch. This is, obviously, not ideal.

And even when you've worked through that mental flow chart, there are other considerations and curveballs. Was I wearing the same thing last time I saw these people? What coat works with this skirt length? Hang on, is my 'good' bra in the wash? Do I now have to start this entire, godforsaken process again?

'The process begins while I'm still in the shower, when I mentally go through my wardrobe,' says Leila, a content executive. 'Of course, the outfit I decided on never looks how it looked in my head and, five to ten outfit changes later, I'm fully panicking, about to miss my train.'

'It's completely normal to get changed five times before leaving the house . . . isn't it?' frowns Jemma, an old colleague I bumped into on the bus. 'I don't understand people who get their clothes out the night before,' she adds. 'There are so many variables that may change in the morning.'

For most of my life, I assumed it was normal, too – just the occupational hazard of being a clothes obsessive. Or even, for that matter, just being a woman. It isn't hard to recognise that there are a whole heap of pressures on women as we stand in front of the wardrobe each morning; as Caitlin Moran writes in *How To Be A Woman*, 'When a woman says, "I have nothing to wear!", what she really means is, "There's nothing here for who I'm supposed to be today."' But could the daily wardrobe meltdown be a symptom of something internal, too?

Clinical psychologist Dr Jessamy Hibberd tells me it probably does have a basis in anxiety and low self-esteem. Clothes make a handy outlet for displaced stress, she explains, and deliver quick validation when you feel insecure. 'It feels like an outfit is something you can get right, whereas, for most things in life, there's not a perfect answer. The time you spend evaluating what to wear is a kind of avoidance of those other things,' she says. '[You think] "because I got that outfit right, it's going to be the perfect evening."'

So, how can we curb the 'I have nothing to wear' meltdowns? Well, you could adopt your own sort of uniform, which is great if your style lends itself to a capsule collection of grey roll-neck jumpers, but is basic hell for a trend junkie. Better-quality basics might help, though, fewer tricky prints, more 'classic' shapes – the sorts of pieces that make you feel good and also go with everything else in your wardrobe. Dresses or jumpsuits are also a good bet, as you don't have to match a top and bottom, and recently I've had moderate success with loose culottes, instead of the punishing jeans.

But maybe it's less about what we wear and more about how we feel when we wear it. Dr Hibberd recommends noting down three positive comments you've received each day, beyond your outfit, to build confidence and self-esteem. 'The scrutiny you put yourself under is a hundred times more than anybody else gives you, because they're thinking about themselves,' she says. 'If you're seeing friends, think: how much weight does their outfit hold in the experience you have with them? Remind yourself that it's only a small percentage of what makes people impressed by you.'

If I could start getting out of the door on time in the morning, that might be the most impressive thing of all.

I'm going grey – and I'll style it out however I damn well please

FACED WITH A SALT-AND-PEPPER LOOK, SALI HUGHES IS TAKING BACK CONTROL – AND REACHING FOR THE GREY DYE – IN SPITE OF HORRIFIED CRITICS WHO SEEK TO DERAIL HER

BY SALI HUGHES

I'm going grey. It started about five years ago, with a single, bright white hair nestling in my fringe. As I'm not some sitcom archetype, I didn't scream, wail or fall into existential crisis. In fact, it didn't bother me in the slightest. I like being the age I am, it was wholly inevitable and I'm naturally intrigued by any changes in my appearance. I often think grey, silver and white hair extremely chic. But, gradually, a colony of whites sprouted, until the entire area around both temples looked grey while the rest of my hair stubbornly resisted transition. Being a brunette is part of the signature look I've enjoyed my whole life, so I changed my hairstyle to conceal the greys. In recent times, and despite being positively delighted to have reached my forties, I've gradually become even less enamoured with my salt-and-pepper look.

If, as your years advance, your hair naturally falls like some pearlescent satin nightgown, then I positively envy you. Mine does not. It is naturally two-tone at the front, one shade of brown at the back and doesn't look set to expedite to total coverage any time soon. I can't dye it back to its former colour (I'm allergic to the PPD and PTD present in all 100-per-cent grey-covering dark dyes – believe me, I've done seven solid years of intense research on this), so I'm presented with two choices: let nature have its way or bleach my hair white and tint it temporarily with silver, platinum or ice-cream shades of pink, green or lavender. I certainly don't relish the maintenance of the latter, but nor do I particularly like the look of the former on me personally, and so, in the New Year, I plan to don the gown of no return and go permanently grey overnight. My job allows no painful growing-out period hidden under hats, and even if I were a vet, doctor or CEO, I'd honestly have no desire to embark on it. I feel more in control by making a drastic and sudden change, so I can get on with enjoying my new look. My real colour will just have to play catch-up when it's ready.

Despite spending my life defending the very concept of beauty to complete strangers, even I was shocked at the reaction to my plan. Both social acquaintances and women online I'd never met were horrified that I or anyone else would choose not to let nature take its course and apparently felt completely comfortable in telling me point-blank to step away from the bleach. While some women felt I'd look 'too old', many others felt personally offended and let down by my decision, telling me repeatedly that I should 'grow old gracefully', an expression more likely to send me hurtling down a path towards extreme facelifts and a cryogenic chamber. A brief internet search yielded thousands of articles and posts calling for women to stop dyeing their hair at once, as though this was less about a simple choice of hair colour and more about snatching back control from the patriarchy.

This vehement belief that one should 'embrace' whatever nature 'bestowed' (and other words so wistful they border on the emetic, usually spoken by the young and thin) are notably selective, given that they are usually directed at women. Personally, as a woman and feminist, I positively relish defying nature and will continue to do so for as long as it makes me happy and causes no one else any harm. I believe in the pill, in abortion, antibiotics, orthodox medicine, hair dyeing, contact lenses and Botox, and however else you'd like to pro-actively interfere with nature's process for your continued happiness. As long as you question your motives and acknowledge how society may have played its part, then your due diligence is done and feel free to crack the hell on. The implication that to conceal grey, smooth wrinkles and wear make-up signifies a moral weakness and a pitiful ignorance to the ways of the patriarchy is maddeningly patronising and as sexist as the problem it purports to oppose. Especially when that belief becomes critical, insulting or dictatorial, as it so frequently does, including between women who really should be on the same side. I feel no more obliged to go grey than I do to stop painting my nails or shaving my legs. I am as authentically myself with red lipstick and obviously false lashes as I am barefaced in pyjamas with egg yolk down my chin. Anyone with a prescription on how I or any woman 'should' look should perhaps wonder whether it's really the sixty-year-old woman with the Jayne Mansfield hair, or they themselves, who is really letting down their gender.

All we 'should' be doing, as ever, is encouraging women to do with their bodies whatever they damn well please. In the past forty-eight hours, I've seen some women dismiss grey hair as 'grannyish', 'too old' and 'drab', while others criticised their dyed contemporaries as 'fake' and 'helmet heads' in 'denial'. If some women want to save a load of time, expense and chemicals by opting out of the dyeing cycle, and if very many of them feel a sense of liberation, then I enthusiastically applaud their choice. I'm as likely to gawp in admiration at a grey-, white- or silver-haired woman as I am at any other. Likewise, I don't care if your hair is dyed red, blonde, green, purple, fake, real, short, long, curly or straight, either badly or well looked after. None of it affects my life and nor should it inform how I show myself to the world. This common perception that the personal choices of other women are automatically steered by a judgement of different-minded women (see also: the frequently and equally unpleasant discourse of the natural birth versus elective caesarean battlefield) is understandable given the unending anti-women media and market-ing narrative, but to pick a side is wholly unhelpful to everyone. The prescriptive judgement of how women should look and any qualitative value placed on their choices is exactly what we should be fighting against. It wasn't our game to begin with. Let's not play it and, for goodness sake, let's get out of each other's hair.

As a black woman, I've had to unlearn what beauty means to me

TOBI OREDEIN EXPLAINS HOW SHE TURNED AWAY FROM THE MAINSTREAM MEDIA TO GO ON A JOURNEY OF SELF-APPRECIATION

BY TOBI OREDEIN

By the time I hit my mid-twenties, I had realised many things. Firstly, I came to the realisation that if I wanted to own my own house and have a lifestyle that resembled my parents', I would have to work a lot harder and earn a lot more money. Fad diets are a waste of time and having your own version of a 'uniform' for work makes life a lot easier. Yet, the most profound realisation was coming to terms with the fact that a woman who looks like me will never be the standard of beauty.

On top of the dangerous standard of physical perfection all women are held to – the flat stomach, hairstyles without a strand out of place and flawless skin that rivals a baby's derrière – this near-impossible standard of beauty revolves around the white woman's body. While I would never dismiss the immense pressure white women feel when they watch adverts in TV breaks and before their selected YouTube video begins, black women are rarely depicted in such a desirable manner.

As a black woman, I would be lying if I said that my self-esteem never took a hit in my teens and early twenties, when I would watch romcoms and see that the leading lady was often blonde and blue-eyed. And, on that rare occasion when the woman every man desired, and every woman desired to be friends with, was black, she usually was, and still is, of a lighter complexion. As a dark-skinned black woman, there were moments when I would look in the mirror and ask myself, 'Would I ever see a woman who looked like me being hailed as the girl next door? Or, would a woman who bears any resemblance to me ever star in the latest high-end beauty campaign or R&B music video?' The more I turned to media, the more it became clear that the answer was no.

And, while that took a while to digest, I eventually came to the conclusion that I would have to unlearn what it meant to be beautiful and break away from the idea that there is only one notion of attractiveness.

The first step in this new education was learning that I didn't need to spend an extortionate amount of money on my hair to have a weave that was a carbon copy of Jennifer Lopez's wavy curls. That my curls, my tight, midnight black afro curls, were not only good enough, but they would be an integral statement in telling the world that I was ready to unapologetically celebrate my black body in all its glory. While my hair couldn't be further from the hair textures of women who grace our screens and magazines, that no longer mattered. I was no longer playing by the static rules that society has placed on women and how they looked.

Becoming comfortable with my afro was just one part of the equation when it came to unlearning what it truly means to be beautiful.

I also had to erase the idea that the only black women who were worthy of being called beautiful weren't just those with a more golden skin tone. Black women who had a deeper and darker complexion were just as beautiful. My short phase of yearning for lighter skin or to be considered a 'lightie', as the black community says, wasn't healthy. It wasn't healthy because I was holding myself to a criterion of physical perfection that was whiteness. I internalised that the whiter – the lighter – you were, the more beautiful you were. I was striving for an image of beauty that was beyond perfection because it was an impossible principle of beauty to achieve.

Once I came to terms with this and realised that having a complexion that was closer to Kelly Rowland and June Sarpong was something to embrace, I felt liberated. I no longer feared to go on holiday and return home too dark or too black because I had been kissed by the sun. I began to feel at peace and relished lying on beaches abroad, knowing that the sun wasn't just glistening on my skin, it was enhancing my blackness.

I finally learnt that having full lips are my sexiest asset. The physical feature I was often teased about in my younger years was something I should feel grateful for. I realised that my lips were something some women desire so deeply that they pay thousands of pounds for. Yes, on me they aren't appreciated, but I appreciate them and that is all that matters.

The reality is that no woman can fulfil the unrealistic and downright harmful checkboxes of beauty. The girl I was in my school uniform and early university days didn't know that and wouldn't have been prepared to accept that. Now, at twenty-seven, I accept that as a dark-skinned black woman, with an afro, broad nose and full lips, my body is not only acceptable, but the only beauty standard worth accepting when I look in the mirror.

Is it possible to pull off looking French?

EMMA BEDDINGTON HAS SPENT TWENTY YEARS TRYING
TO EMULATE FRENCH *ELLE*. QUESTION IS, CAN A WOMAN
WITH A BRITISH PASSPORT EVER BE TRULY GALLIC?

BY EMMA BEDDINGTON

Ah, the eternal allure of French style. Catherine Deneuve in chaste-sexy Yves Saint Laurent in *Belle de Jour*, Bardot in a gorgeous fitted shirtwaister, Juliette Gréco, face framed by a black turtleneck. French style is confidence in the classics: belted macs, pencil skirts and sharp tailoring. It's having an Hermès silk square and knowing what the hell to do with it. It's elegant, sure, but isn't it a bit boring? Even 'rebellious' Gallic dressing is strictly codified: think Emmanuelle Alt in tight jeans, spike heels and a masculine shirt, long hair carefully tousled. Would a little originality hurt?

This, French-style devotees argue, is precisely where the British go wrong, with our love of quirky prints and 'fun' jewellery – our sense that caring about grooming is a bit naff, really. Classicism and restraint are precisely what give French women their mystique – when clothes don't distract your eye, you're intrigued by the woman within (sounding like a bad Charles Aznavour song is an occupational hazard of writing about French style).

As a lifelong Francophile and failed Frenchwoman, I'm torn. I ache to look French – I can't walk past Agnès b or Comptoir des Cotonniers without wanting everything in the window – but, on my English face and body, understated elegance just doesn't work. A crisp white shirt that would look ravishing on Charlotte Gainsbourg turns me into a middle manager in a provincial accountancy firm with a strict dress code and carrying off this brand of chic seems impossible above a C-cup. Nevertheless, I owe French style a lot – indeed, I wouldn't be where I am today without it.

As a small-town teenager, I discovered a stash of French *Elle* magazines in our school library and they stole my heart. French *Elle* went one better than mere cool – it was chic. The women in its pages – well-read and fearless, as well as devastatingly sexy – seemed impossible to emulate, but I could at least try to dress like them. When I discovered French cinema, my shopping list lengthened; I wanted a Breton top like Jean Seberg in *Breathless* and Jeanne Moreau's fisherman's sweater from *Jules And Jim*. French dressing – Frenchness itself – encapsulated everything I aspired to and, aged eighteen, I signed up for a gap year teaching English in Normandy. On arrival, I bought a Chanel lipstick, acquired a French boyfriend and prepared for my transformation.

It didn't quite work out like that. Provincial 1990s France was a style wasteland, all boxy jackets and garish pastels. The pickings were slim; I bought a belted camel overcoat and discovered Sephora, but inexplicably failed to turn into Inès de la Fressange. Back in the UK, things started to fall apart. University was lonely – I missed France and my boyfriend, and our stormy long-distance relationship was hugely stressful. I developed alopecia, losing all my hair, and became depressed and obsessed with my weight, starving then bingeing in my college bedroom.

But French fashion provided a lifeline. Every day, to the obligatory Serge Gainsbourg soundtrack, I would get up, put on a Bardot-style headband and carefully line my lashless eyes. Then I would pick out a neat black sweater, Capri pants and ballet pumps and feel fit to face the world. I was quietly, violently miserable a lot of the time, but creating that illusion of icy Gallic insouciance allowed me to feel my unhappiness was somehow glamorous and cinematic. Channelling my French heroines, I could believe I was a strong woman with a complex inner life, not just a floundering twentysomething dithering over a fat-free yoghurt.

Life got easier and my devotion to French dressing slipped, gradually. A spell in Paris, where everything I wore was vocally disapproved of by my Chanel-clad neighbours, put paid to my illusions of 'passing' as Parisian, and life as a dog-owning freelancer in a Belgian suburb with that same French boyfriend and our two semi-feral teenage boys has allowed my inner scruffy Englishwoman to get the upper hand.

But the fantasy never quite dies – my reward to myself for finishing my memoir on failing to be French was a pair of black patent Repetto Mary Janes. I hope Inès would approve.

My dad is my beauty icon and here's why

FROM INVESTING IN A GREAT MOISTURISER TO RECOGNISING THE VALUE OF A DECENT HAIRCUT, DAISY BUCHANAN'S DAD HAS TAUGHT HER THAT BEAUTY IS NOT ONLY A WAY OF TAKING CARE OF HERSELF, IT'S ALSO FUN

BY DAISY BUCHANAN

My father is the best-smelling man – no, person – that I have ever encountered during my time on earth. All of the people I love, and am intimate enough with to notice, produce a broad olfactory range. My mum smells divine after she's sprayed some of her favourite Escale à Portofino, and divine in a different way when she's been digging up the garden all afternoon. Similarly, I adore the scent of my husband's skin when he's just showered, but I didn't adore it any less when our boiler broke and he went unwashed for 48 hours. But Dad's basic, standard scent is somewhere between Sicilian lemon grove, and the John Lewis linen department. I'm not sure that he sweats.

His commitment to good grooming is unwavering. Mum never wears make-up, thinks it's obscene to spend more than £20 on a haircut and until recently, thought that Johnson's Baby Lotion was the best all-purpose moisturiser that money could buy. Dad is the one who showed me that I was allowed to care about what I looked like, and more importantly, that I was supposed to enjoy the rituals and processes involved. I think his love of luxury skincare is something that he sees as a hobby. For him, it's no sillier or more significant than a fondness for football. He's my beauty icon – not because I want to look like him, although the resemblance is already there. But because

I want to be as savvy and sensible as he is when it comes to picking and choosing the smartest parts of grooming philosophy and using them suit his purposes.

As a woman and a highly suggestible person, I'm aware of how the beauty industry manipulates me. I'm encouraged to spend money because I'm 'worth' it, I have flaws that urgently need fixing, I should enjoy 'me time' (bleurggggghhhh) by having a 'pampering sesh' (boak) because I need to make myself feel better after seeing the many multi-million dollar ad campaigns that are created to invent imaginary physical problems that women need to address. When I was growing up, my mum's wise response to this was to see it for the nonsense it was, and refuse to participate in it. But to me, beauty and grooming looked glamorous and fun. My dad's cheery, practical approach showed me that I could enjoy the best bits of beauty without getting bogged down by any sense that I had an obligation to look good. No one was going to suffer to be beautiful on his watch.

When I was an awkward teenager, hugely self-conscious about my skin, my body and essentially everything, Dad had a real knack for buying kind and thoughtful gifts that made me feel happy and pretty. After I had a bad reaction to some paint stripper-strength supermarket cleanser, Dad went to Debenhams in his lunch hour and quietly presented me with a Clinique kit. If something caught his eye – whether it was perfume in an unusual bottle, or nail polish in a perfect shade of Pepto Bismol pink, it would be gifted to me or one of my sisters. Once he came home, very excited, with a brand-new foundation. 'I saw the advert, and they were making all sorts of crazy claims about how it used NASA technology for long-lasting coverage. It's probably rubbish, but I thought you'd like to try it and see!' I will never forget the day he came home from a work trip to New York, laden with the entire Benefit range for my sisters and me to try. He told us how he'd bonded with the women in the Manhattan office over the classic, kitschy packaging, and the fun he'd had when he was choosing it all. His enthusiasm was as much of a present as the huge pile of lipstick. It showed me that make-up is meant to be playful, not prescriptive.

Ultimately, Dad's celebratory approach to grooming has taught me that taking care of yourself is a matter of self-respect. Dad doesn't moisturise because he's insecure about his appearance, or use a particular shampoo because he's heard that it has mysterious anti-ageing properties. He makes an effort because he feels able to set a high standard for himself, and he's proud to meet it. This is what he expects from his daughters too. He's never made me feel as though I have to look a certain way, but he's set a great example when it comes to the link between self-care and self-esteem. Thanks to Dad, I know a great haircut won't necessarily change my life, but there is something life changing about realising that I'm entitled to the nicest haircut I can afford, and I don't need to feel guilty about the hours I spend in the chair. Beauty isn't bestowed on us by a particular magical product. It's all about attitude.

It's time we redefined beauty for every woman

TRANSGENDER VISIBILITY IS FLOURISHING IN FASHION AND BEAUTY – BUT WHY ARE TRANSGENDER WOMEN ONLY DEEMED 'SUCCESSFUL' IF THEY FIT A CERTAIN BEAUTY MOULD?

BY JUNO DAWSON

The 31st of March marks Transgender Day of Visibility. We also have Transgender Day of Remembrance in November but, as that's about reflecting on how many of us are murdered brutally, usually victims of male violence, it's nice to have a more positive day to celebrate the contribution of transgender people. People like me.

I'm very lucky in that I can exist – largely free from hassle – in the liberal arts. Fashion and beauty is another field in which transgender people can go beyond visibility and flourish. Supermodel Teddy Quinlivan came out as trans last year and is featured in the most recent issues of *i-D*, *Vogue* Spain and *Vogue* Japan. Last fashion week, she walked for Versace, Louis Vuitton, Chloé and many, many more.

Globally, Munroe Bergdorf, Andreja Pejić, Valentina Sampaio, Laith Ashley, Rain Dove and Isis King all continue to slay photoshoots and catwalks. Hari Nef is in the Gucci Bloom advert. Laverne Cox was the first trans woman on the cover of *Cosmopolitan*. Paris Lees was featured in British *Vogue* and I, I'm pleased to say, landed my very first magazine cover this year – the March issue of lifestyle mag *Happiful*. But even when shooting the cover, as princess-like as I admittedly felt, there was also a sense of slight unease. The unease, if you'll allow me to mentally unpack on you, was twofold.

The first concern was that I (along with any minority model) was being exploited by brands for my 'diversity value'. Sometimes referred to as virtue signalling, this is the practice of hiring diverse models to make the brand look more woke or inclusive. While this is clearly the case (some brands actively use 'look how inclusive we are' to aggressively sell products), I'm alright with this – had a single trans model been 'signalled' at me in my teens, I'd have come out as transgender ten years earlier. Perhaps it's cynical, but I think seeing Teddy, Hari or Laverne is a beacon of hope to so many young people desperate for a sign that what they're feeling is OK.

That said, if brands want us for our 'diversity value', they must also be aware that belonging to a minority group comes with baggage. Often quite angry baggage. Whether you're trans, black, Muslim or disabled, we experience prejudice and discrimination every day. And we're allowed to be angry about that. When L'Oréal hired Munroe Bergdorf as a transgender woman of colour, it should have been on the understanding she would use her platform to express opinions – sometimes challenging ones – about her race and gender. Simple as that.

My second concern was a broader one. If we look back at that list of transgender people working in fashion and beauty, one thing becomes clear: they are all eminently fuckable. It seems only a certain type of trans person is allowed to be visible in the media.

There's a lack of transgender editors, producers or commissioners working in the UK, so I have been granted certain platforms and opportunities by cisgender (not trans) people. Call it aspirational if you will, but we all seem to fit a certain beauty mould. It's enormously misleading to suggest that all transgender women look like Andreja Pejić or Janet Mock. What's worse is that a trans woman is only considered successful if she has managed to not only be a woman, but a supermodel, too. Every day, I thank my genes that I'm five foot eight inches and slim and never lost my hair. Had I been bald, six foot three inches and built like a brick shithouse, I'd have still needed to transition and I'd still have had the right to live free from harassment and mockery. I'd have still deserved to be visible as an author.

Of course, this goes well beyond trans visibility. If you take out the word 'trans' in the above paragraph, you get 'a woman is only considered "successful" if she has managed to not only be a woman, but actually become a supermodel'. What we need to do is redefine the entire archetype of beauty so that all women can stop feeling like we're competing in a fixed race we're designed to lose, the finishing line perpetually being moved by the beauty business.

Those people at the very top of the industry – the CEOs, the editors and designers – have to feature men and women who don't fit the (very slim) mould. Whether it's virtue signalling or not, I think we're starting to see this: Isabella Rossellini being reinstated as the face of Lancôme at sixty-five (by their female CEO – funny that); curvy models in the window of Primark and on billboards for Pretty Little Thing; models in hijabs on catwalks. The inclusion of trans models is undoubtedly part of the same well-intentioned move, but I hope that, to the casual viewer, being young, ultra-feminine, thin and pretty isn't the mark of a 'successful' transition on Transgender Day of Visibility.

The real power of
a good compliment

ACKNOWLEDGING A FRIEND'S EARRINGS OR A STRANGER'S
DRESS MIGHT SEEM LIKE A PASSING COMMENT, BUT IT CAN
ACTUALLY TRANSFORM THE WAY SOMEONE SEES THEMSELVES

BY ANA KINSELLA

In winter, dressing to impress can seem like a relic from some distant past. Cold days call for swaddling oneself in wool and thermals, rather than digging out the party frock. So, when the older woman in the ramen restaurant tapped me on my shoulder, I was more than a little startled.

'Excuse me,' she said as I fumbled with my chopsticks, 'I just wanted to say I love your earrings!' My fingers flew to my ears. I had on a pair of metal discs with cutouts like a woman's face, complete with dramatic fringe falling over one eye. I thanked the stranger. 'They were my mother's!' I gushed in return. 'I took them from her jewellery box recently, as she claims she never wears them.' The woman crouched down a little to my level and looked into my eyes. She wore her striking silver hair in a low bun and had deep, wine-coloured lipstick on. 'They are fantastic,' she pronounced and then gathered herself and left the restaurant.

For the rest of the day, I felt delighted with myself. The woman's intervention was a reminder of the whole point of fashion and buying nice things: to make ourselves feel good, even on bleak days. A compliment from a stranger can be a form of connection, particularly when you live in a big, anonymous city. One of my friends, for example, swears by the magical effects of a 'bright, eye-catching silk dress, patterned with the signs of the zodiac' that she owns and that never fails to elicit a nice remark. 'It's one of those "people-connecting" items, as every time I wear it I get compliments,' she explains. 'I once wore it in New York and three different women stopped me in the street in the space of fifteen minutes. I could feel myself walking taller each time someone called out, "I love your dress!", and ever since then I've complimented strangers more freely.'

That said, in big cities, the line between well-meaning compliments and catcalls can be tenuous. Another friend of mine was living in Washington DC and on her way to an interview at a prestigious law firm when a man waiting for the same bus as her took a step back, looked at her Zara skirt suit and said, 'Damn, honey. You are looking respectable today.' (She later aced her interview.)

Earlier this winter, I began to ask many friends and strangers about the items they own that elicit the most compliments, and found a wide variety of answers: cocktail rings in striking colours, wool coats with extravagant furry collars, heirloom costume jewellery, vibrant suede boots. The common thread, if there was one, was the unusual, the sumptuous, the head-turning aspect of them all. Which makes sense, since nobody ever flagged me down to enquire where I bought my plain black roll-neck, despite its outfit-transforming abilities. But I often wear a glitzy brooch that I inherited from my aunt on the collar of my winter coat – a good way to guarantee a kind word or two, as it sparkles at eye level. It's a neat and sneaky trick, because even if I haven't brushed my hair, or am wearing leggings and a charity-fun-run T-shirt under the coat, the brooch might be enough to have a stranger tell me I look nice.

But it's not exclusively about the endorphin hit of the confidence-boosting compliment. Compliments can lead to useful insights, as well. My friend Harriet, a journalist, has a rainbow-knit jumper (again, originally belonging to her mother) that has become imbued with something like luck over many wears. 'I always wear it to do difficult interviews because – I am serious – people are nicer to me when I have it on,' she explains. 'It has really made me understand the power of clothes.'

And compliments can change how we feel about particular items and about our own identity, too. Kate, an old friend, told me about one dress she owned that made her reassess the way she dressed: 'It was a white floral Cath Kidston shirt dress I owned when I was twenty. I got over the whole floral thing very quickly, but I kept the dress for about three years, as it never failed to garner compliments.

This was at a time when my self-esteem was horribly low, so I valued the compliments over the fact that I didn't feel like myself in the dress at all! But most of the compliments were along the lines of "English rose", and I really hate being called sweet and lovely. So, finally, last year the dress found a new home via eBay.' Kate and her style moved on, but she learnt something about the complex nature of the compliment, 'from just simple mood-boosters, to some kind of weird behaviour-affecting power currency'.

Now, when I get dressed and reach for the elaborate beaded necklace or the darling vintage silk blouse – the pieces I hope will trigger conversation and compliments in the office or the corner shop – I ask myself: is it shallow to wear something just because we know others will love it?

But I think the answer is no. Billions of pounds float through the industry that exists to sell us clothes and make-up, and if we're to participate in all that, shouldn't we do so in a way that makes us feel good? That doesn't have to mean chasing trends and spending money; I think it's about letting the last compliment you received be a reminder to dress in a way that makes you happy, even if you're constricted by office dress codes or winter weather. Find a little something that will bring you joy. And, while you're at it, always tell a stranger when you love her shoes.

ALEXANDRA HEMINSLEY @Hemmo
AMY JONES @jimsyjampots
ANA KINSELLA @anakinsella
ARIFA AKBAR @Arifa_Akbar
BRIDGET MINAMORE @bridgetminamore
BRYONY GORDON @bryony_gordon
CAROLINE O'DONOGHUE @Czaroline
CATHERINE GRAY @cathgraywrites
CATHY RENTZENBRINK @CathyReadsBooks
DAISY BUCHANAN @NotRollergirl
DOLLY ALDERTON @dollyalderton
EMMA BEDDINGTON @BelgianWaffling
GABY HINSLIFF @gabyhinsliff
HARRIET MINTER @HarrietMinter
JAVARIA AKBAR @javaria_akbar
JEAN HANNAH EDELSTEIN @jhedelstein
JENNIFER RIGBY @jriggers
JOHANNA THOMAS-CORR @JohannaTC
JUDE ROGERS @juderogers
JUNO DAWSON @junodawson
KAT LISTER @Madame_George
KUBA SHAND-BAPTISTE @kubared
LAURA BATES @EverydaySexism
LAURA CRAIK @LauraCraik
LAUREN BRAVO @laurenbravo
LAUREN LAVERNE @laurenlaverne
LAURIE FRANKEL @Laurie_Frankel
LILY PESCHARDT @LilyPesch
LIZZIE POOK @LizziePook
LOUISE MCSHARRY @louisemcsharry
LYNN ENRIGHT @lynnenright
MARISA BATE @marisajbate
NATASHA DEVON @_NatashaDevon
POORNA BELL @poornabell
ROBYN WILDER @orbyn
RACHAEL SIGEE @littlewondering
ROISIN AGNEW @Roisin_Agnew
ROWAN HISAYO BUCHANAN @RowanHLB
SALI HUGHES @salihughes
SAM BAKER @SamBaker
SOPHIE HEAWOOD @heawood
STEPHANIE MERRITT @thestephmerritt
TOBI OREDEIN @IamTobiOredein
VIC PARSONS @vicparsons_
VIV GROSKOP @VivGroskop
YOMI ADEGOKE @yomiadegoke
ZOË BEATY @zoe_beaty